NEW PUBLIC MANAGEMENT AND THE REFORM OF EDUCATION

New Public Management and the Reform of Education addresses complex and dynamic changes to public services by focusing on new public management as a major shaper and influencer of educational reforms within, between and across European nation states and policy actors. The contributions to the book are diverse and illustrate the impact of New Public Management (NPM) locally but also the interplay between local and European policy spheres.

The book offers:

- a critical overview of NPM through an analysis of debates, projects and policy actors;
- a detailed examination of NPM within 10 nation states in Europe;
- a robust engagement with the national and European features of NPM as a policy strategy.

The book contributes to debates and analyses within critical policy studies about the impact and resilience of NPM. It demonstrates, through the study of educational reforms, in a range of political systems, with different traditions and purposes, how a more nuanced and complex picture of NPM can be built.

As such the book not only speaks to educational researchers and professionals within Europe but also to policymakers and can inform wider education and policy communities internationally.

Helen M. Gunter is Professor of Education Policy in the Manchester Institute of Education, University of Manchester, UK.

Emiliano Grimaldi is Lecturer in Sociology in the Department of Social Sciences, University of Naples Federico II, Italy.

David Hall is Professor of Education Policy in the Manchester Institute of Education, University of Manchester, UK.

Roberto Serpieri is Professor of Sociology of Education in the Department of Social Sciences, University of Naples Federico II, Italy.

NEW PUBLIC MANAGEMENT AND THE REFORM OF EDUCATION

European lessons for policy and practice

Edited by Helen M. Gunter, Emiliano Grimaldi, David Hall and Roberto Serpieri

LONDON AND NEW YORK

First published 2016
by Routledge
2 Park Square, Milton Park, Abingdon, Oxon OX14 4RN

and by Routledge
711 Third Avenue, New York, NY 10017

Routledge is an imprint of the Taylor & Francis Group, an informa business

© 2016 selection and editorial matter, Helen M. Gunter, Emiliano
Grimaldi, David Hall and Roberto Serpieri; individual chapters, the
contributors.

The right of the editors to be identified as the authors of the
editorial material, and of the authors for their individual chapters,
has been asserted in accordance with sections 77 and 78 of the
Copyright, Designs and Patents Act 1988.

All rights reserved. No part of this book may be reprinted or
reproduced or utilised in any form or by any electronic, mechanical,
or other means, now known or hereafter invented, including
photocopying and recording, or in any information storage or
retrieval system, without permission in writing from the publishers.

Trademark notice: Product or corporate names may be trademarks
or registered trademarks, and are used only for identification and
explanation without intent to infringe.

British Library Cataloguing in Publication Data
A catalogue record for this book is available from the British Library

Library of Congress Cataloging in Publication Data
Names: Gunter, Helen, editor.
Title: New public management and the reform of education / edited
by Helen Gunter, Emiliano Grimaldi, David Hall, Roberto Serpieri.
Description: Abingdon, Oxon ; New York, NY : Routledge, 2016. |
Includes bibliographical references and index.
Identifiers: LCCN 2015049587 (print) | LCCN 2016011358
(ebook) | ISBN 9781138833807 (hardback : alk. paper) | ISBN
9781315735245 (e-book)
Subjects: LCSH: Education and state--European Union countries.
| Educational change--European Union countries. | Public
administration--European Union countries.
Classification: LCC LC93.A2 N48 2016 (print) | LCC LC93.A2
(ebook) | DDC 379.4--dc23
LC record available at http://lccn.loc.gov/2015049587

ISBN: 978-1-138-83380-7 (hbk)
ISBN: 978-1-138-83381-4 (pbk)
ISBN: 978-1-315-73524-5 (ebk)

Typeset in Bembo
by HWA Text and Data Management, London

CONTENTS

List of tables	*viii*
List of contributors	*ix*
Foreword	*xv*
Gary Anderson	

Introduction   1

1   NPM and educational reform in Europe   3
Helen M. Gunter, Emiliano Grimaldi, David Hall and Roberto Serpieri

PART I
The liberal state   19

2   England: Permanent instability in the European educational
NPM 'laboratory'   21
David Hall and Helen M. Gunter

PART II
The social democratic state   37

3   Finland: NPM resistance or towards European neo-welfarism
in education?   39
Michael Uljens, Lili-Ann Wolff and Sara Frontini

vi Contents

4 Governing by new performance expectations in Norwegian
schools 53
Guri Skedsmo and Jorunn Møller

5 Reforming Swedish education through New Public
Management and quasi-markets 66
Nafsika Alexiadou and Lisbeth Lundahl

PART III
The administrative state 81

6 New Public Management in the French educational system:
Between affirmation of the state and decentralised governance 83
Jean-Louis Derouet and Romuald Normand

7 NPM and the reculturing of the Italian education system:
The making of new fields of visibility 96
Emiliano Grimaldi, Paolo Landri and Roberto Serpieri

8 The dissemination and adoption of NPM ideas in Catalan
education: A cultural political economy approach 111
Antoni Verger and Marta Curran

PART IV
The post-communist state 125

9 New Public Management in Czech education: From the
side road to the highway? 127
Arnošt Veselý, Jan Kohoutek and Stanislav Štech

10 Elements of New Public Management in the context of the
Hungarian education system, 1990–2010 141
Anna Imre and Ágnes Fazekas

11 New head teacher roles following the decentralization of
Romanian education 156
Ana-Cristina Popescu

Conclusion

171

12 NPM and the dynamics of education policy and practice
in Europe

173

Helen M. Gunter, Emiliano Grimaldi, David Hall and Roberto Serpieri

References

186

Index

207

TABLES

1.1	Key features of New Public Management (based on Hood 1991; Pollitt and Dan 2011)	6
1.2	Key features of New Public Management in education	12
1.3	A conceptual framework for investigating NPM reform in education	14
2.1	Key features of New Public Management in education in England: the foundation stage	25
2.2	Key features of New Public Management: the reinforcing stage	28
2.3	Key features of New Public Management: the rapid privatising stage	31
4.1	Criteria for selection of schools	56
4.2	Key features of local school governing	58
5.1	Key features of New Public Management in education in Sweden	68
7.1	NPM and the modernising of the Italian education system – three policy problematizations	99
8.1	Political periods and NPM changes in Catalonia	117
9.1	Key features of NPM in the Czech Republic (based on Hood 1991 and Gunter and Fitzgerald 2013a, b)	129
10.1	NPM in Hungary	143
10.2	Two decades of the Hungarian education system and NPM	144

CONTRIBUTORS

Nafsika Alexiadou is Professor of Educational Work in the Department of Applied Educational Science, University of Umeå, Sweden. Her main research interests are in the politics and policies of education in the European Union and their interactions with the national level. Her most recent publication is 'Europeanizing the National Education Space? Adjusting to the Open Method of Coordination (OMC) in the UK' in the *International Journal of Public Administration* (with Bettina Lange, 2015).

Gary Anderson is Professor of Educational Leadership in the Steinhardt School of Culture, Education, and Human Development at New York University, USA. A former high school teacher and principal, he has published on topics such as critical ethnography, action research, school micro-politics, and school reform and leadership. With Kathryn Herr he has co-authored two books on action research: *The Action Research Dissertation: A Guide for Students and Faculty* (2015, Sage) and *Studying Your Own School: An Educator's Guide to Practitioner Action Research* (2007, Corwin Press). He has also written several books on educational leadership, including *Advocacy Leadership: Toward a Post-Reform Agenda* (2009, Routledge).

Marta Curran is a PhD candidate at the Department of Sociology of the Universitat Autònoma de Barcelona, Spain. Since 2011 she has been a member of the *Globalization, Education and Social Policies (GESP)* research centre where she has participated in several competitive research projects. She is currently collaborating in a research project on Early School Leaving in Spain. Her main research areas include education inequalities, related to class and gender. Her doctoral thesis deals with the effect of gender and social class in shaping youth education expectations and the decision to continue or drop out of school. She

x List of contributors

has participated in seminars and scholarly visits at the University of Amsterdam, University of Buenos Aires, Harvard University, and the Centre for International Development at the University of Sussex.

Jean-Louis Derouet is a former student from the Saint Cloud Ecole Normale Supérieure. He has obtained an *agrégation* in history and a PhD in sociology. Today he is a Professor at the École Normale Supérieure of Lyon, France and a member of the CNRS Research Unit Triangle. He has developed research on the diversification of principles of justice in the contemporary world. His current research interests are the new forms of the Educative State; the new organisation of schools and debates about the notion of leadership; and the transition of European education systems to post-comprehensive patterns. He is chair of the Education, Formation, Socialisation Committee of the International Association of French-speaking Sociologists, and editor-in-chief of the French-language journal *Education et Sociétés*.

Ágnes Fazekas is a researcher at the Faculty of Pedagogy and Psychology of University Eötvös Loránd (ELTE) in Budapest, Hungary. Her work focuses mainly on the impact of developmental interventions and policy implementation in public education. She started to work in this area in 2010 at the Doctoral School of Education of ELTE. At present she is the leading researcher of a project designed to describe and analyse the impact mechanisms of curriculum implementation processes related to (EU-funded) development programmes.

Sara Frontini is a PhD candidate at Åbo Akademi University, Finland. Her thesis focuses on vocational education and training in Italy and Finland, observing how the European discourse of VET has been framed in the two countries at the national and local levels. Her main research interests are vocational education and training; and comparative education. Her most recent publication is: Frontini and Psifidou 'Education and Training Governance through Learning Outcomes: Possibilities and Constraints in Italy' in *Revista de Pedagogia* (2015).

Emiliano Grimaldi is Lecturer in Sociology at the Department of Social Sciences, University of Naples Federico II, Italy. His work focuses on education policy analysis and is influenced by critical theory. He has published books and several articles in international journals on educational governance reforms, inclusive education, educational professions, privatisation in the field of education, and evaluation.

Helen M. Gunter is Professor of Educational Policy and Sarah Fielden Professor of Education in The Manchester Institute of Education, University of Manchester, UK, and is a Fellow of the Academy of Social Sciences. She co-

List of contributors **xi**

edits the *Journal of Educational Administration and History*. Her work focuses on the politics of education policy and knowledge production in the field of school leadership. Her most recent books are: *Leadership and the Reform of Education* (Policy Press 2012); *Educational Leadership and Hannah Arendt* (Routledge 2014); and *An Intellectual History of School Leadership Practice and Research* (Bloomsbury Press 2016).

David Hall is Professor of Education Policy and Head of the Manchester Institute of Education at the University of Manchester, UK. His most recent research has focused upon public sector reform and its re-contextualisation within educational institutions and by educational practitioners. David's research has been funded by organisations including the Economic and Social Research Council; the Department for Education; and the EU; and it has been published in a range of international journals and books.

Anna Imre is a researcher at the Research Centre of the Institute of Education and Development, Budapest, Hungary. Her research interest at present focuses on educational policies related to student and learning issues, and their implementation and impact on schools and students. Her research experiences involve: inequalities within education systems; student pathways; student engagement; school leadership; teacher work; and collaborations for learning in schools and school contexts. She has worked in the OECD INES programme and the EU Early School Leaving Thematic Working Group.

Jan Kohoutek is Research Associate of the Department of Public and Social Policy at the Faculty of Social Sciences, Charles University in Prague, the Czech Republic. Holding a PhD in public policy, he specializes in quality of education policies and, more broadly, in issues of policy work, policy design and implementation. On these topics he has published in peer-reviewed international journals including the *European Journal of Education* and *Higher Education Quarterly*.

Paolo Landri is a Senior Researcher at the Institute of Research on Population and Social Policies at the National Research Council (CNR-IRPPS), Italy. His main research interests concern educational organisations; and professional learning and educational policies. He edited, with Tara Fenwick, a special issue on 'Materialities, Textures and Pedagogies: Socio-Material Assemblages in Education' in *Pedagogy, Culture and Society* (2012), and, with Eszter Neumann, a special issue on 'Mobile Sociologies of Education' in the *European Educational Research Journal* (2014).

Lisbeth Lundahl is Professor of Educational Work at the department of Applied Educational Science at Umeå University, Sweden. Her research interests include education politics, youth politics and young people's school-to-work transitions.

One of her latest publications is 'Guarded Transitions? Youth Trajectories and School-to-Work Transition Policies in Sweden' in the *International Journal of Adolescence and Youth* (with Olofsson, 2014).

Jorunn Møller is Professor at the Department of Teacher Education and School Research, University of Oslo. Her main research interests are in the areas of educational leadership and governance; reform policies; and school accountability. Her most recent publication is: 'Researching Norwegian Principals' in Ärlestig, H., *et al., A Decade of Research on School Principals: Cases from 24 countries* (Springer, 2016).

Romuald Normand is Fulbright Fellow and full-time Professor of Sociology at the University of Strasbourg (Faculty of Social Sciences, Research Unit SAGE: Societies, Actors and Government of Europe). He is convenor of the network Sociologies of European Education (European Association of Educational Research) and is also a member of the editorial board of the *British Journal of Sociology of Education*. His research interests are in European policies/politics in education; lifelong learning and knowledge-based economy; accountability and new public management; and higher education. His latest publication is an edited collection with Lawn: *Shaping of European Education: Interdisciplinary Approaches* (Routledge 2015).

Ana-Cristina Popescu has a PhD from the University of Manchester, UK, and is currently working as a Freelance Education Consultant and Interpreter for Romanian and Moldovan speakers in the UK. Her main research interests are in educational policy and leadership, with a particular focus on the ways in which professionals are being affected by the implementation of new policies. Her most recent publications are: 'The Decentralisation of the School System in Post-Communist Romania' in *Journal of Educational Administration and History* (2010), and 'Romanian Women in Headship: Interplaying Identities' in *Voices: Post-graduate perspectives on Inter-disciplinarity* edited by Vincent and Botero-Garcia (2011).

Roberto Serpieri is Professor of Education Policy and Sociology of Education at the Department of Social Sciences, University of Naples Federico II, Italy. His fields of interest and research are: governmentality studies and educational leadership, with a recent focus on neoliberal educational policies about the evaluation of head teachers, teachers and schools. He is a member of several editorial boards of international journals and has published books and articles in the fields of sociology of education and sociology of organisations.

Guri Skedsmo is Associate Professor in the Department of Teacher Education and School Research at the University of Oslo; and Senior Researcher at the Institute for the Management and Economics of Education at the University of Teacher Education, Zug. Her main research interests are in the areas of educational governance and leadership, and school development and change.

Stanislav Štech is Professor of Educational Psychology at the Faculty of Education, Charles University in Prague, Czech Republic. Between 2003 and 2015, he also held the position of vice-rector of Charles University and currently holds the position of Deputy Minister at the Ministry of Education, Youth and Sports of the Czech Republic. Publishing widely in domestic and international journals on various aspects of pedagogy and educational psychology, he is the author of three books (the most recent: *Introduction to School Psychology*, 2013) and of more than 120 publications, including research reports and reviews. He is also active internationally as a Visiting Professor at the University of Paris and Komenský University in Bratislava.

Michael Uljens is Professor of Education at The Faculty of Education and Welfare Studies, Åbo Akademi University, Finland. His main research interests are the philosophy of education; curriculum/Didaktik; and educational leadership. He has recently contributed to discursive and non-affirmative education theory: 'Curriculum Work as Educational Leadership – Paradoxes and Theoretical Foundations' in the *Nordic Journal of Studies in Educational Policy* (2015).

Antoni Verger is Associate Professor at the Department of Sociology of the Universitat Autònoma de Barcelona, Spain; a founding member of the Globalisation, Education and Social Policies (GEPS) research centre; and deputy director of the Erasmus+ master programme Education Policies for Global Development (GLOBED). A former post-doctoral fellow at the Amsterdam Institute for Social Science Research (University of Amsterdam), Dr. Verger's research has specialized in the study of the relationship between global governance institutions and education policy, with a focus on the dissemination, enactment and effects of public-private partnerships and quasi-market policies in education. He has coordinated several competitive projects and published extensively on these themes in academic books and journals including *Comparative Education Review, Journal of Education Policy, Current Sociology, Review of International Political Economy, Globalisation, Societies and Education,* and *Comparative Education.*

Arnošt Veselý is Associate Professor of Public and Social Policy at the Faculty of Social Sciences of Charles University in Prague, the Czech Republic. His main research interests are educational policy, social science methodology, and policy analysis. On these topics he has published widely in national and international research journals including *Policy and Society* and the *International Review of Administrative Sciences*. He has been Principal Investigator on a range of Czech and international projects.

xiv List of contributors

Lili-Ann Wolff is Lecturer in Education and Adjunct Professor in Environmental Education at the University of Helsinki, Finland. Her research relates to leadership, sustainability, social innovations and ethics from an interdisciplinary educational perspective. Her most recent article is: 'Hållbar välfärd och utbildning (Sustainable welfare and education)', published in the Nordic Network for Adult Learning's anniversary issue of *Dialog* (September 2015, Nordic Council of Ministers).

FOREWORD

Gary Anderson

Changes in the political economy since the mid-1970s until the present have been variously referred to as neoclassical, neoliberal, late capitalism, fast capitalism, and predatory capitalism. These macroeconomic changes have been accompanied by new forms of governance, new forms of management and, at the level of everyday neoliberalism, new subjectivities (Herr 2015). The chapters in this book take up primarily new forms of management, referred to as new managerialism or New Public Management (NPM). A central tenet of neoliberalism is to privatize and marketize society by transferring market principles to the public sector (Friedman 1962) and NPM is the way this is accomplished at the organisational and institutional levels.

Analyses of NPM are in their infancy in the field of education for several reasons. Educational leadership and policy scholars tend to be isolated from scholars in public administration where it has received more attention. NPM also entered education in many countries through World Bank and OECD reports and private consultancies that too few educational researchers study. In some contexts, it snuck in relatively unnoticed at the level of practice. For instance, in the US educational administrators seemed enamoured of Total Quality Management, discourses of modernizing rigid public bureaucracies, and best sellers like *Who Moved My Cheese?* (Johnson 1998) and *In Search of Excellence* (Peters and Waterman 1982). With the possible exception of England, where these policies arguably began, there has been a dearth of nuanced analyses in education that move beyond fairly monolithic notions of privatization, marketization, or new governance.

By comparing the ways NPM has entered European countries in similar, but also idiosyncratic ways, this collection of studies provides a more nuanced way of understanding the global enactments of NPM, not as a list of characteristics, but as a series of discourses and practices that enter diverse contexts in diverse

xvi Gary Anderson

ways. As these chapters explore in detail, sometimes it remains mostly discourse; sometimes it becomes policy, but has little actual impact; and sometimes it brings about significant recontextualizations and restructurings at the economic, political, and cultural levels.

The challenge in some of these chapters – particularly the post-Communist and Nordic clusters – is to explain not NPM's presence, but its relative absence. Or, paradoxically, as in the case of The Czech Republic, 'NPM ideological premises have been selectively applied for labelling some policy prescriptions that took on un-NPM twists and turns in the reality of the implementation process and that might even have been implemented without NPM policy borrowing taking place' (Veselý *et al.* in this volume).

Although I am not trained as a comparativist, it is tempting to make some observations about how these chapters inform our understanding of how NPM has entered countries on the other side of the Atlantic. In a recent special issue of *Educational Policy Analysis Archives*, we have explored similarities in how NPM is constructing new professional identities in England, Chile and the US, three countries that were early adopters of NPM (Anderson and Cohen 2015; Hall and McGinity 2015; Herr 2015; Montecinos *et al.* 2015; Mungal 2015).

We were more struck by the similarities across these three countries than the differences, in part because NPM has made such deep inroads into their educational systems. There is a tendency in the English-speaking academic world to mainly compare English-speaking countries, which are precisely those countries where NPM has found the most fertile ground. So chapters on non-English speaking European countries provide a fresh perspective on other ways that NPM has been taken up.

The chapters on the Nordic countries, for instance, when compared to the chapter on England, remind me of the comparison between Chile (similar to England) and what are sometimes called 'post-neoliberal' countries like Argentina, Bolivia, Brazil, Uruguay, Venezuela or Ecuador. While the Nordic countries have long standing welfare states that mitigate the effects of NPM, some South American countries are attempting to create fledgling welfare states, often in the wake of failed neoliberal reforms. Most now have significant cash transfer programs to the poor that have narrowed inequalities and increased school attendance (Ponce and Bedi 2010).

Argentina, for instance, is more similar to the Nordic countries, where NPM has been mitigated by a complex mix of social forces and norms, including strong unions, a failed neoliberal government in the 1990s, and traditions of strong public institutions and democratic movements. Keynesian economics and a strong state have returned to Argentina under Kirchnerism, and markets, vouchers and high stakes testing have been largely rejected, although the recently elected neoliberal president, Mauricio Macri, is attempting to reverse this trend (Gorostiaga and Ferreira 2012; Grugel and Riggirozzi 2007).

But there are other factors that threaten public schools and stratify Argentinian society beyond NPM. Because of the power of the Catholic Church, the

Argentinian state – much like Chile and some European countries – subsidizes private schools. This has the effect of marginalizing public schools and further stratifying society, and these subsidies predate NPM in most countries. While attendance at public schools in Argentina is still relatively high compared to Chile, where public (municipal) schools enrol under 30 per cent of all students, public schools are increasingly stigmatized (Montecinos *et al.* 2015).

While privatization is a key element of NPM, public schools do not guarantee social equity either. In the US, roughly ninety percent of students attend public schools but social stratification takes place within the public school sector because schools are financed largely through local property taxes. This creates high quality schools for many suburban parents and low quality schools in urban centres.

It is worth noting that in the US proposals for fiscal equity have been relatively unsuccessful, while privatization and charter schools have been promoted with an equity discourse almost exclusively in low-income urban areas, largely in communities of colour. This not only leaves basic inequalities in the financing of schools in place but is also a strategy to reduce the influence of teachers' unions. In many large US cities, neighbourhoods are being gentrified and public schools are being 'taken over' by an influx of new professional couples and families (Lipman 2011). Increasingly, charter schools are being used as spaces for 'gentrifiers' to escape the local population (Cashin 2014). My point is that while many NPM policies contribute to further stratifying societies by class and race, we also need to better understand the ways that different societies engage in social reproduction. It is more often exacerbated through NPM policies but it can likely also take place without them.

Another key insight that runs through this book is the notion that NPM reforms tend to be layered onto previous public bureaucracies and institutional practices; they do not replace them. For instance, we have some examples, particularly in South America, in which post-neoliberal governments are recontexualizing previous reforms. This more commonly occurs at the municipal level, where more studies of NPM might provide further insights.

In New York City, Michael Bloomberg and his school chancellor Joel Klein succeeded in a twelve-year effort to replace the school district with a marketplace of networks and private vendors (and providing principals with the 'autonomy' to purchase these products), eliminate venues for community input, weaken the teachers union, and close public schools and replace them with charter schools. Nevertheless, many of these reforms have turned out to have shallow roots and the current mayor, Bill DiBlasio, is in the process of reasserting a public system by restoring some pre-Bloomberg district practices and adding others, like universal pre-school and community schools. In the case of mayor Bloomberg, it is hard to imagine a more concerted effort—backed by corporate and venture philanthropy – to implement an NPM agenda in an urban school district. Yet, while it is still early in DiBlasio's administration, many of Bloomberg's reforms are being reversed by a new mayor.

It is also important to remember that extreme NPM practices in education, like excessive testing, evaluating teachers by test scores, closing and privatizing schools, and attacking teachers unions, often create powerful social backlashes. In the US, this has included the Chicago teachers' strike of 2012 and the current one in Seattle, a large opt-out-of-testing movement by parents and students, student walkouts, and petitions sent to state departments of education and signed by thousands of teachers, principals, superintendents (Hagopian 2014; Nuñez *et al.* 2015; Weiner 2012). This backlash is even more evident in Chile where student, and more recently teacher, movements have been active since 2009.

Because NPM policies are being promoted by both political parties in most countries, and because they are typically preceded by a language of 'crisis', we also need to better understand the alliances of diverse groups that support these policies and why they are attractive to such a broad base (Apple 2001). We also need to better understand why, in some of the post-Communist and Nordic countries, public schools were not viewed as in crisis, other than in those countries, like the Czech Republic, where funding was viewed as inadequate. In some countries, like the US, the language of a crisis of public schooling is often racial, and the element of race and immigration in Europe may be increasingly part of the moral panic driving NPM practices (Scott 2011).

Even in countries where public schools are constructed as in crisis, there is a growing body of quantitative and qualitative research that suggests that, once socio-economic status is statistically controlled for, public schools actually are more effective than private and charter schools (Kirp 2013; Lubienski and Lubienski 2014). Lessons from diverse experiences with NPM in Europe and, I would argue, in South America and Asia as well can take our analyses of NPM to a more nuanced level. These lessons can also suggest which elements are most problematic under which circumstance and also strategies that might be used to appropriate or resist them effectively. This book is a fascinating tour through Europe and how NPM enters each landscape differently. It is also a vital toolkit for those who wish to influence educational policy.

Introduction

1

NPM AND EDUCATIONAL REFORM IN EUROPE

Helen M. Gunter, Emiliano Grimaldi, David Hall and Roberto Serpieri

Introduction

Public services education within European countries is facing radical change through processes of modernisation. This is more than restructuring with new types of work and cultures, not least because the idea of public education is being challenged and in some countries dismantled through the promotion of a privatisation agenda. New Public Management (NPM) with 'new public managers' who undertake 'new public managing' has been influential in this process, where the main features are: 'the switch in emphasis from policy formulation to management and institutional design; from process controls to output controls; from integration to differentiation; from "statism" to subsidiarity' (Hood 1990: 205). This has and continues to impact, not least through the corporatisation of the purposes and rationales for educational provision, the relocation of the 'ownership' of schools outside of democratic institutions, and changes to the composition and professional practices of the workforce. The implications of this are evident in the emergence of varied types of post-welfare models of public education within Europe, influenced by the juxtapostion of traditions and interventions nested within neoliberal and neoconservative forms of 'private' provision.

The book presents a critical engagement with NPM as an illustrative site of modernising processes in education, with particular attention to how this is taking place within and across ten countries in Europe. The origins of this book lie within the formation and development of the LE@Ds (Leading Education and Democratic Schools) network of social science researchers in the Czech Republic, England, France, Hungary, Italy, Norway, and Spain. A series of seminars combined with conference symposia (See Gunter and Fitzgerald 2013a, b) have produced the intellectual work that we report here, and we are

4 Gunter, Grimaldi, Hall and Serpieri

delighted to have been joined by researchers reporting from Finland, Romania, and Sweden.

The focus of the essays is necessarily on the national state conditions in which NPM has entered education policy processes and so we examine the relationship between NPM as 'travelling' policy prescriptions and the realities of the debates, nuances and variations as it has developed over time and within 'embedded' contexts (Ozga and Jones 2006). Importantly, this enables diverse state models ('Liberal', 'Social-Democratic', 'Napoleonic', and 'post-Communist') to be recognised as sites where we show how legacies generate alternatives as well as mediate the processes of imagining, reading, interpreting and shaping. We locate this within 'bigger picture' analyses (Ozga 1990) through giving recognition to supranational European and international bodies (e.g. EU, OECD, World Bank) and how formal and informal sites for policymaking outside of the nation state are influential.

In this opening chapter we outline our conceptualisation of NPM and why this is an important and enduring focus for analysing system changes to the nation state and public services within and across Europe. We provide an analytical framework for presenting ten European countries as sites for examining NPM and we frame our contribution as *European Lessons for Policy and Practice* through examining how and why the field of critical education policy studies can gain new insights about NPM within the organisation, the locality, nation, and beyond. In doing so we examine the challenges brought by criticisms of methodological nationalism (Seddon 2014) and claims regarding the necessity for normative cosmopolitan visions (Beck 2006). At the same time we argue for a renewed centrality of the nation state as an analytical focus, refusing any reductionist account of a shift from government to governance, for example via the hollowing out of the state thesis, and proposing a more nuanced conceptualization of the state as a social relation (Jessop 2002). This enables our analysis to capture the complexities of the overlapping and interplay between government (i.e. the practices of management by state institutions and public administration), governance (i.e. the practices of social regulation involving a variety of interdependent social, political and administrative actors within and beyond the state – see Rhodes 1997), and governmental practices (i.e. the wider power relations governing conduct in apparently non-political sites – see Lemke 2009). Such a contribution focuses on the intellectual resources within and used by the field, so we consider not only the pre-eminence of sociology but also the importance of political studies in shaping and enabling thinking for and about policies and practices.

New Public Management

Public management is presented in the research literatures as having features of what is regarded as 'old' and 'new'. Essentially, services that have been politicised through the identification and meeting of common needs, public

NPM and educational reform in Europe **5**

funding, political strategy and agenda setting, have been enabled through organisational structures and cultures that are now characterised as 'old' forms of public management, often called public administration. This Weberian form of bureaucracy is legal-rational and based on hierarchy, specialisms, and the deployment of impersonal rules and routines, where it: 'appeared to be the ideal organisational type for the performance of complex yet repetitive tasks, while providing the center with effective control over each of the parts' (Bevir 2008: 37). The 'good' administration of such services is an enduring feature of 'good' government (Du Gay 2005), but increasingly there have been depoliticisation strategies through the retreat of the state and the outsourcing of services to agencies and/or the privatisation of such services, the entry of the private sector as new providers in a marketised system, and the disappearance of issues from the public domain (Flinders and Wood 2014).

Influential arguments have been made in globally influential texts that have set out to challenge the bureaucratic state as inefficient and anachronistic through critiques of shared values, and links to the public domain, and through the characterisation and identification of the problems with common services, particularly in regard to the accountability and responsibility of professional elites (Bobbitt 2002; Chubb and Moe 1990; Osborne and Gaebler 1993). This is core to the modernisation agenda, whereby 'new' structures and cultures of the organisation and the workforce are required to be 'contractual, competitive and calculative' (Clarke *et al.* 2000: 9). Working relationships need to be 'contractual' in the sense of transparent exchanges, not least on targets and performance; 'competitive' through the efficiency and effectiveness of service delivery that drives down costs and so attracts investors; and 'calculative' in regard to how choice decisions by consumers are incentivised by data about the product and the workforce who design and deliver. Hence there has been a shift in terminology from administration to management, and more recently to leadership and entrepreneurialism. Such changes tend to be presented as an imperative, and indeed as inevitable in the logic of change (Hood 1995), and is 'modern' and 'new' in the sense that there are clear differences from the one-size-fits-all of bureaucratic rule bound systems where the workforce do or do not deliver on the basis of repeating administrative procedures disconnected from outcomes that they may not be directly accountable for.

These new forms of public management are visible in target setting and data collection and analysis with performance reviews, through to the outsourcing of services to agencies and the private sector. Public management reforms are replete with a language of delivery and outcomes, of 'can do' and 'no excuses' ways of thinking and talking. The development and articulation of 'newer' forms of public management in regard to specific reform strategies is presented in Table 1.1.

Table 1.1 outlines the main features of NPM whereby those who occupy roles within public service organisations have taken on and developed manager identities, or managers have been appointed to take on new management work.

6 Gunter, Grimaldi, Hall and Serpieri

TABLE 1.1 Key features of New Public Management (based on Hood 1991; Pollitt and Dan 2011)

Factors	Ideas	Tools and practices
Managers	Deliverers who solve problems, collect and use data to monitor, evaluate and support decisions	Trained and accredited in management processes Competition and delivery dispositions through embodied behaviours and language Output orientation and control Appointed to 'units' as the delivery arm for public services
Managing	Use of explicit standards, measurements, and output controls	Data collection, analysis and judgements about performance of individuals, groups and organisations Taking action through planning and performance to respond to and be proactive about service efficiency and effectiveness Hire and fire staff based on business plan, income streams, and market developments
Management	Delivery based on a right to manage through contracts, line management and accountability processes	Restructuring from complex multi-functional bureaucracy to specialised, small and lean 'units' Explicit standards and measurements of performance with the setting of targets, data collection and analysis Performance reviews determining pay and contract renewal Frugality with resources and investment based on performance Removal from post for underperformance
Managerialism	New forms of power relationships based on hierarchy and performance	Use of data, incentivisation through pay, competitive tendering, and value for money assessments

Therefore doctors, teachers, social workers, prison governors, local and regional officers and national policymakers have had to become managers, and have now to work with accredited managers appointed to undertake human resources, budget, contract, purchasing, and marketing management:

> managers are those who 'understand' markets; who can extract the untapped potential from the 'human resources'; who are sensitized to the 'needs of the customer'; who can deliver 'results' and who can be relied on to 'do the right thing'. The unlocking of trade union organization, bureau-

professionalism and local political representation requires 'management' to provide an alternative mode of power. If 'markets' and 'customers' have been the ideological cutting edge of these changes, then 'management' has been the eagerly sought principle of articulation for a new organizational regime for the welfare state.

(Newman and Clarke 1994: 25)

Managers have credentials (often with MBAs), expertise and attitudes that represent a break with the past, and as such they exemplify the modern because they are no longer associated with bureaucracy and bureaucratic professionals: they have had to reject it and take on new identities, or they are symbolic of the rejection through being appointed to new roles that are deemed necessary in order to run a public service as a business. As Apple (2001: 30) states:

> ...we might say that managerial discourse provides 'subject positions' through which people can imagine themselves and their institutions in different ways. Thus, one of the key characteristics of managerial discourse is in the positions it offers to managers. They are not passive but active agents – mobilizers of change, dynamic entrepreneurs, shapers of their own destinies. No longer are the orgnizations they inhabit ploddingly bureaucratic and subject to old-fashioned statism. Instead, they and the people who run them are dynamic, effecient, productive, 'lean and mean'.

If discourses create the conditions in which problem solving takes place, managing is the enactment of the active practices that deliver, where templates structure what can be done, said and recognised, and hence there are statements about standards and quality. Managing is a technology based on targets, data, audits and judgements, where the binaries of reward and punishment, contract award and termination, and cuts and investment are located. Consequently the normal organisational process of management or getting things done is reworked in terms of its status – the processes matter more than the substantive service that is being managed, and in terms of its purposes – it is hollow until it is filled with values and beliefs by those who practice. Hence the management of health is more about management than health, and purposes of health care are reworked to enable it to be better managed.

Efficient and effective management intervenes and reworks the purposes of inclusive shared services (e.g. pedagogy in schools, operations in hospitals, care homes for the elderly) that produce and sustain a skilled workforce but also democratic and creative citizens. NPM has broken welfare settlements by discounting and declaring unmodern the professional values, knowledges and concerns of those who have made public services work. There is no new settlement, 'just wave after wave of managerialization', and so this is 'radical, unfinished and destabilizing' (Clarke *et al.* 1994: 5). Hence managerialism is not bad management (that may or may not continue to be a feature of organisational

8 Gunter, Grimaldi, Hall and Serpieri

life) but is a fundamental reworking of power relationships. The old hierarchies of bureaucracy have been reworked to generate status based on performance rather than expertise, where 'line management' ensures accountability based on delivery data. The Taylorist separation of the design of work from the instrumentalisation of work and the production of outcomes remains strong, and interplays with new waves of responsibilisation for quality and performance located in influential emotional approaches to the connections between customers, worker and work within Peters and Waterman's (1982) prescription for efficient and effective companies. At a basic level, a doctor is value for money based on patient survival rates, ill people actively choose the hospital because of this data, and income streams are maximised through new products (e.g. drugs, equipment) that enhance the overall customer experience. While professionals may have lost control of the purposes and design of their public service, they have been incentivised through the promise of sorting out failure by the removal of underperforming colleagues, local officials and bureaucrats, and new opportunities for promotion, types of work and remuneration that have so far been denied: 'there is a sense in which managerialism has opened up the possibility that "everyone can be a winner"' (Clarke *et al.* 1994: 239).

The key features of NPM outlined in Table 1.1 are ideological regarding the change in the role of the state from provider to commissioner or even to reposition as regulator through outsourcing and privatising, and practical in terms of the reworking of professional conduct, including ways of thinking and talking, and the tools used to support this. Hence Bevir (2008: 143) identifies two main though 'slightly conflicting, schools of thought' as 'public choice economics and business managerialism', where the former is about competitive exchange relationships, while the latter is about the transfering of techniques from business to public services. In articulating this we are aware of how NPM can be usefully regarded as an umbrella term for changes to structures, cultures, and behaviours of those working in public services, there may not be clarity (there is no rule book or blueprint), and where Hood (1991: 3–4) characterises NPM as 'as a shorthand name for the set of broadly similar administrative doctrines which dominated the bureaucratic reform agenda in many of the OECD group of countries from the late 1970s'. As Ridley (1996) identifies, there was a global and globalising movement of ideas carried and popularised through supranational organisations such as the OECD and the World Bank, and consultancies, that spread the language and tools as simple and effective solutions to the problems of government.

The origins of NPM lie within a complexity of reforms, where the intersectionality of economic, political and social have played out differently within nation states. However, in summary the key trends that have been identified are: first, *political*: located in the ideologies and beliefs of particular politicians and parties such as Reagan in the US and Thatcher in the UK; second, *economic*: with crises in capital accumulation generating challenges to public services funded from taxation, universal and free at the point of access;

third, *social*: where cultural and educational changes led to demands for better services (Ridley 1996). It seems that the process of codification that could be communicated and put into practice happened through a combination of particular champions (e.g. Thatcher and Reagan) who 'seem to be united more by what they are against than by what they are for' (Hood 1995: 106), and where 'gradually, partly through doctrine and partly through trial and error, this general attitude crystalized into a more specific set of recipes for public sector reform' (Pollitt and Dan 2011: 4). An important point to consider is that while the gloss of language, deportment, dress and attitude of and to managers suggests a major rupture with the 'old' public management, there is a need to recognise that change has not been linear or coherent, and there have been multiple layers and overlayering of changes, at different rates and in different services.

Localised issues matter, not least that the nation states that are regarded as NPM leaders tend to have been Anglophone with a strong embedding in the UK and USA as laboratories for change with exemplars of major successes and role models. Whether NPM ideas and practices do impact is related to matters of the constitution, public servant identity and legal remits, and the culture and practice of how things get done. As Ridley (1996: 23) states, the focus should not be on the abstracted ideas or who is for or against, but the 'country-specific situations which permit the translation of reform proposals into law and the application of law into practice'. Hence in some countries aspects of NPM are adopted at a time of economic boom, whereas in other countries the discourse of solution provision may be appropriate but there can be resistance. Ridley (1996) identifies an irony that NPM requires a strong hierarchical form of government in order to enable implementation and delivery, but:

> if new rules are not obeyed and new procedures not used, if the holders of posts with new job descriptions carry on as before, reforms remain on paper and nothing really changes. In societies where public administration shows high levels of particularlism, fragmentation, clientelism and some corruption, sometimes described as a low degree of institutionalisation, laws and orders from above are too easily ignored.
>
> (Ridley 1996: 26)

The study of unfoldings and trajectories of NPM within this dynamic and complex context of the nation state is challenging, not least because clarity is usually achieved through codification and backward tracking of policy to ideas and people (Gray 2010). It seems that those located within the unfolding processes recognised the changes but were slow to talk about 'newness', even if issues of marketisation, privatisation, competition, accountability, and so on, were obviously discussed (see Kooiman and Eliassen 1987a; Lane 1987). Importantly, NPM was conceptualised into existence from the 1980s, where Hood's (1991) work has been crucial to the identification, description and explanations of changes within and for public administration. Decades on from

10 Gunter, Grimaldi, Hall and Serpieri

this analysis, ongoing research has been concerned to examine evidence about and paradoxes in the realities of how NPM has or has not been adopted. There have been studies about the maturity of NPM where Hood and Peters (2004) examine how and why early adopters have experienced change, not least through varied successes in reforms and outcomes with paradoxes emerging about the unintended consequences of much reform and a failure to learn.

While Anglophone countries have been early adopters, latecomers such as Italy (Bellè and Ongaro 2014) and eastern and central European countries (Dan and Pollitt 2014) have also adopted NPM features. NPM adoption has not been linear, in particular there have been differently timed engagements and what has been used or not within particular nation states has varied. This means that there is a need to consider constitutional and political matters (see Ridley 1996). Pollitt and Dan (2011) have undertaken a meta-analysis of the research evidence regarding this matter and conclude that there are indeed paradoxes emerging in regard to the varied selection and implementation in different political systems and contexts. And, importantly, they identify some generalizations that can be made: first, that local conditions are necessary for performance related pay to work, where traditions of patronage and corruption can impact; second, the use of targets can only improve performance where incentives and penalities are accepted, otherwise negativity can develop; third, contracting out may not lead to savings; fourth, the political system may enable or inhibit reforms, where majority governments (e.g. UK) can reform more easily than coalition ones (e.g. Netherlands); and fifth, while strong leadership is seen as important, it is the actual reforms and the legitimacy of the reforms that matter (Pollitt and Dan 2011: 46–47).

Such in-depth forensic analysis of the impact of NPM within Europe raises a range of questions and issues for researchers. There are at least two we need to consider here: first, the need to consider that all reforms may not be NPM (Pollitt and Dan 2011: 10, cite 'joined-up government' and 'collaborative networking' as two examples) and so it is important to ensure that what is and is not NPM is vital to commentary and theorising; second, that reforms do not enter an empty space but are seeking to challenge, break and change in ways that may not be transformational, inspite of the rhetorical claims that they should be and are, and this can be because the previous system is not in the past but worked and continues to work well (Hood 1995).

Such arguments can be evident in considerations about the 'post-NPM' world. New and changing relationships generated for and by digitisation have impacted on the relationships and expectations between civil society and government, and this has led Dunleavy et al. (2006) to declare NPM as dead. Whether this is or is not the case, the key point is the endurance of government not only in relation to major threats (banking crisis, terrorism, deadly diseases) but also the need for 'reintegration' regarding the importance of centralised regulation. Consequently, researchers are concerned to locate NPM reforms and outcomes within wider analyses, such as the role of the state (Jessop

1994), where NPM is not only a matter of technical 'tools', but the state, the market and the 'social' imbued with another newness: a diverse and diffuse regime (Newman 2001). Such regimes have been studied through a focus on exchange relationships between policy actors within and outside of government as networks of governance, with a range of projects about the relationship between public institutions and civil society (e.g. Ball and Junemann 2012; Gunter 2012; Kooiman and Eliassen 1987b; Weggemans 1987). For example, Christensen and Lægreid (2007) are aware of the necessity 'to focus on the co-evolution and inter-dependence of reform experience and practice', in order to understand reform as a 'complex process, going through different stages and packaged in different ways in different countries, with each country following its own reform trajectory within a broader framework' (ibid. 3–4). And so it is possible to recognise: a) how forms of *re-regulation* appear after the spreading of markets and quasi-markets and the ideology of competition; b) a step back towards *coordination* was seen as urgent in order to counterbalance the excesses of fragmentation in inter-organisational relations; c) that the *centre* has benefited from a sort of 'revenge' against subsidiarity, particularly in response to the effect of too much autonomy. What is emerging is a need to examine the borders within relationships between the state and civil society, where the continuities within and necessity for 'bureaucracy' is recognised. Furthermore, there is a need to consider the image of the strong and coherent state as integral to the state, while recognising public institutions as sites of struggle and contradiction. So there is a need 'to support the notion of a kind of layering … or sedimentation process … going on that implies that new reforms complement or supplement old reforms rather than replacing them. Old and new institutions co-exist and co-evolve even if they are founded on partly inconsistent principles' (Christensen and Lægreid 2011a: 419). Hence public actors are predominant even if constrained by policy features, historical institutional contexts and environmental pressures, and while the state endures there are complexities within the continuities and ruptures, where the influence of different states within Europe remains crucial to any analysis. We now turn to what this means for NPM and public services education.

NPM and education

NPM has been an important reform process in public services education. With a focus on schools and building on the analysis summarised in Table 1.1, we present the key features of this reform process in regard to education in Table 1.2.

What Table 1.2 illuminates is an overview of NPM features in educational services wordwide. The composition of the workforce is changing in regard to a shift away from trained and accredited teachers to teachers who may or may not be qualified but whose job is to deliver. In addition, there are changes to employment rights that demonstrate a move away from agreed and national terms and conditions of service. Hence professional identities are being

TABLE 1.2 Key features of New Public Management in education

Factors	Ideas	Tools and practices
Managers	Interventions into professional codes of practice and knowledge in order to change identities regarding role and work as managers and leaders	Training and accreditation as managers and leaders, using business models Change from role titles (e.g. head teacher, principal, deputy) to chief executive, senior leader, managing director Entry into workforce by non-education or professionally qualified personnel to take up leadership and management roles
Managing	Interventions to shift from pedagogy and the curriculum towards output technologies and delivery	The generation, analysis and use of data from outputs to make judgements about performance (including grading lessons, using inspection grades and examination results) Using self-evaluation and strategic management processes to plan delivery and evidence policy implementation Implementation of performance management/pay processes Removal of workforce (including the head) who are identified as underperforming. Promotion and increase in pay of of workforce (including the head) who are identified as meeting or exceeding targets A focus on income generation through marketing and bidding, and the modification of the curriculum and pedagogy in order to meet consumer and/ or funder requirements
Management	Destruction of a 'system' of schools co-ordinated locally through the creation of 'autonomous' and 'independent' schools Interventions into school organisational and cultural structures regarding output efficiency and effectiveness	Site-based management where schools are businesses and compete in the market place, hire and fire staff, and are funded on pupil numbers Entry into the market by new providers who take over state schools or set up new schools (Academies, Charters, Free) Establishment of inspections, examination data (national and international e.g. PISA) that produce judgements about, and can enable benchmarking comparisions of, individual, team and school performance The publication of data and league tables combined with vouchers facilitates consumer choice of school and provider

Factors	Ideas	Tools and practices
Managerialism	Separation out of an elite cadre of senior leaders and managers from the school workforce (teachers, human resources, finance, site management)	Bottom-up accountability of the school workforce to the senior leadership team for outcome measures and data Dependence on judgements made by senior leadership team for income generation and contract renewal Promoting delivery and outcomes above inclusion and equity

redesigned in regard to purposes, knowledges and skills, from pedagogy and collegial leadership towards human resource and organisational efficiencies. Professionalism is increasingly about business thinking and practices, with the training of established teachers into new identities and the appointment of school business managers, premises managers, human resource managers to strategically and tactically manage education as a product. Managing is less about the process of curriculum design and pedagogy, and is about the collection, analysis and judgements of competence and success based on outcome data.

The elevation of management from every day processes of getting things done to forms of site-based management of the school as a business (Caldwell and Spinks 1988) means that processes are focused on marketised competition. This has enabled two main trends; first, the regulation of schools that remain within the system through the use of private sector management processes, particularly the technologies of redefining professionalism, teaching and learning, and the wider purposes of education through targets, audit and standardisation; second, the creation of 'independent' schools outside of local democratic control such as 'free schools' in Sweden and England, with 'for profit' services that all can access through consumer choice and vouchers. Managerialism is located in this high stakes environment in which the diversity of school types are being created, where new power relations between those trained, accredited and rewarded as leaders secure the local delivery of reforms. Teachers are evaluated as 'value for money' because data is produced to evidence that student outcomes meet national and international standards, parents choose schools on the basis of this added value, and income streams are maximised through new products (e.g. new curriculum, testing, reporting) that enhance the student experience. Traditional collegial professional relationships, debates and judgements are therefore reworked into hierarchies based on the line management of performance.

A huge industry has developed regarding the reworking and incentivising of the profession to take on NPM identities and practices. Illustrative of this is the emphasis on performance in regard to audit through data, inspection and performance appraisal systems, and how this is linked to the educational professional taking on board new labels such as leader, leading and leadership

14 Gunter, Grimaldi, Hall and Serpieri

(Gunter 2012). While there are global patterns in such developments, not least the circulation of ideas, languages, people and strategies in the production and promotion of solutions for busy professionals (Thomson *et al.* 2014), there are localised differences in regard to whether and how this is recognised and responded to through embedded enactments (Ball *et al.* 2012; Derouet and Normand 2011; Grimaldi and Serpieri 2013; Hall *et al.* 2015; Hangartner and Svaton 2013; Møller and Skedsmo 2013). Consequently, our co-authors not only have to give attention to globalising travelling NPM but also how it plays out within local contexts as constitutional and institutional places characterised as nation states. We therefore present a framework in Table 1.3 through which a critically descriptive analysis can be undertaken in each nation state.

As Pollitt *et al.* (2007: 5) have noted, NPM reforms are crafted and shaped in specific institutional contexts and historical, political and administrative variations play a significant role in selecting, translating and mediating global discourses and technologies in distinctive ways. Therefore the framework in Table 1.3 means we can consider the processes that have been entered into by NPM, but in doing so we are interested in the antecedence to NPM reforms, and how such legacies have been layered and have been sustained or changed, and broader outputs and outcomes of the significance and reach of the effects of change.

This is a complex matter and we have approached this by selecting cases that are clustered in order to represent diverse *administrative traditions* within Europe,

TABLE 1.3 A conceptual framework for investigating NPM reforms in education

	Key questions and analytical foci
Legacies	The main legacies (institutionalised features) influencing and inflecting the embedding of NPM policy recipes in the national space: • state traditions and institutional legacies • institutionalised purposes of education • dominant narratives and political rationalities in the field of education
Processes	Discourses and problematizations opening the space for NPM reforms of education systems
	Technologies, means, mechanisms, procedures, instruments, techniques and professional identities entering the field of education through NPM discourses and policies
	Policy networks and networks of expertise through which all these discourses, technologies and subjectivities flow into the context(s) in focus
Effects	Changes taking place due to NPM in terms of epistemic and technological change, as well as the formation of professional identities
	Effects that are observable in terms of tensions, surprises and paradoxes

and to show how their institutionalised features mediate the processes of recontextualisation of NPM discourses, practices, technologies and identities:

- *Liberal:* England is widely acknowledged as a NPM laboratory. The administrative tradition and some institutionalised governance configurations embody relevant discursive and structural selectivities that created a fertile terrain for the enactment of NPM. A long tradition of unitary, centralised and coordinated state government structures with an uncodified constitution provides favourable conditions for speedy, deep and pervasive reframing of public management and, specifically, the bureau-professional traits of public education (Clarke and Newman 1997). Such a process was also rooted in a *public interest* administrative tradition (Pollitt and Bouckaert 2011: 62) that accords to the state a minimal role within society and to the law a secondary position, giving prominence to pragmatism and flexibility in the pursuit of the public (general, national) interest.
- *Social-Democratic:* Norway, Finland and Sweden, our second cluster, are presented in the literatures as countries where historical legacies and the welfarist 'Nordic' tradition have mediated NPM, making blunt its sharper corners, less ruthless its introduction and more complex its recontextualisation (Pollitt and Bouckaert 2011: 73). In forming this cluster, we recognise, with Pollitt and Bouckaert (2011), that these countries differ in a variety of ways. However, we maintain that they share some general dispositions that, as for the case of England, we frame here in terms of discursive and structural selectivities. In stark contrast with the Liberal tradition, Scandinavian countries partake 'an étatist, organicist inheritance similar to the Germanic tradition with a strong state-welfare orientation' (Painter and Peters 2010: 23) and a related strong 'sense of the weight, centrality and continuity of the state' (ibid.). This is coupled with a disposition towards consensual, and mainly meso-corporatist styles of governance that responds to a conception of the relationship of state and society that is democratic and communitarian. If we look at the state structure, there is a significant variability among the three countries, with Norway having a more unitary (but still decentralised) structure and Sweden and Finland having stronger local governments. However, all three share a great tradition of (and emphasis on) citizen participation and legitimation as a crucial pillar of modernisation (Pollitt 2007b: 24), being the role of societal actors in public policymaking assumed as 'natural'.
- *Napoleonic:* our third cluster comprises France, Italy and Spain (the case of the autonomous region of Catalonia is specifically addressed) and has its distinctive trait in the influence that the 'Napoleonic' state tradition has had in shaping government and public administration (Ongaro 2009). State and government trajectories as well as public administrations of these three countries significantly differ in a variety of respects. However, it is possible to identify some commonalities that have created a less favourable institutional

terrain for the recontextualisation of NPM ideas, policies and technologies in the public sector and, specifically, in the field of education. Despite their turbulent recent past (i.e. the fascist regimes) and their Mediterranean specificities (Ferrera 2005), Italy and Spain share with France an organic conception of the state (a liberal constitutional democratic *Rechtsstaat*). The State is viewed as the central integrating force within society and has a 'legal personality and operative value system' (Pollitt 2007b: 20), which is devoted to nation-building. At the same time, a clear separation between the public and the private spheres is assumed, being the role of societal actors in public policy making depicted almost as an 'intrusion'.

- *Post-Communist:* our fourth cluster includes Romania, Hungary and Czech Republic as former communist countries and it is the most difficult to frame and present (also due to an evident literature gap). We share with Meyer-Sahling (2009: 512) that it is 'problematic to reduce the legacy of the past to a "one-size-fits-all legacy" that is largely equivalent to an ideal communist-type administration', and to have a deep understanding of the multiple and heterogeneous selectivities operating in these countries, it is necessary to focus not only on the heritage of the communist period but also on what came first and survived to the communist period, and also the modes of transition to capitalist democracy. What they all share are 'several fundamental ruptures [that] had major consequences for the organization and functioning of public administration' (Meyer-Sahling 2009: 521), though the mode of transition has to be taken into account, from a paced transition (as in the case of Hungary) to an imposed transition controlled by the former Communist Party (as in the case of Romania) or to a transition that followed the collapse of the Communist regime (as in the case of Czech Republic; ibid. 520).

Political studies scholars have long debated the possibility of clustering countries on a permanent basis, identifying common traits concerning public administration (Ongaro 2009: 247). Such clustering can be a meaningful analytical strategy, but we do not present our use of administrative traditions 'as some kind of unchanging bedrock' (Pollitt and Bouckaert 2011: 48). Rather, in adopting Peters' (2008: 118) definition of administrative tradition as 'a historically based set of values, structures and relationships with other institutions that defines the nature of appropriate public administration within society', we are seeking to analytically address national traditions as 'living systems of thought and practice' (Ongaro 2009: 9), that are institutional assemblages always subject to transformation dependent on recursive strategic actions (Grimaldi 2012). Adding to this complexity, we understand NPM as a globally widespread but 'loose collection of diverse doctrines, principles and measures which are partly in opposition to one another' (Bevir *et al.* 2003: 2), and 'a non-unified, multiple and complex field of play which realises a dispersion of relationships, subjectivities, values, objects, operations and concepts' (Ball 1998: 126). As such,

NPM is currently being packaged in different ways, reworked and redeveloped, and enacted 'to different degrees, at different paces, and with differing emphases on the various elements' of such a dispersion in different countries and sectors (Christensen and Lægreid 2007: 8). Consequently, our core argument is that nation states still play a central role in undertaking distinctive policymaking as well as undertaking processes of packaging, re-working and enactment. A conceptual clarification is needed here, however. Accepting Chernilo's (2006) invitation to challenge the nation state as the accepted and stable unit of analysis, we endorse a non essentialist conceptualisation, as 'a relatively unified ensemble of socially embedded, socially regularized and strategically selective institutions, organizations, social forces and activities organized around (or at least involved in) making collectively binding decisions for an imagined political community' (Jessop 2002: 40). This means, in our view, that we must look at the state as a 'dynamic and contingent form of societal power relations' (Lemke 2009: 48), including both government institutions and networks of governance or governmental practices, where governing takes place across political and non political sites and different scales. Within such networks of governmental practices, the state is a primary instrument and site of strategic action, insofar state institutions have the power to establish boundaries (i.e. state/non state; inside/outside) and act as the prime sites for the elaboration, rationalization and centralization of power relations.

Such an approach to states and reforms confronts the current trend within sociologically informed education policy analysis that is concerned to both deploy 'geographical' thinking tools of place and space to challenge the link between territory and research (Seddon 2014), and to create a European education policy research field (Lawn and Grek 2012), through rejecting 'methodological nationalism' and 'statism' (Dale 2006; Dale and Robertson 2009). Central to our contribution is to give recognition made through this sociological conceptual and empirical research, but we also move beyond this by examining how and why political studies enables vital insights into the endurance of the nation state as more than a mediator of supranational ideas, practices, and policy actor agendas.

PART I
The liberal state

2

ENGLAND

Permanent instability in the European educational NPM 'laboratory'

David Hall and Helen M. Gunter

Introduction

This chapter seeks to make a contribution to debates about New Public Management (NPM) and educational reform and modernisation in England. It does so in two main ways as part of a wider theorisation of how and why these changes came about and through characterisation of the principal features and dimensions of NPM within education in this context. First, building upon previous work on continuities and discontinuities in education policy between New Labour and Conservative administrations (Bache 2003; Ball 1999; Hatcher 2008; Power and Whitty 1999; Whitty 2009) and analyses of the Coalition government's educational reform programme (Husbands 2015; Wright 2012) this chapter offers a distinct contribution to extant debates about educational reform in England. This is achieved through the identification and analysis of a cross-party political convergences on education policy stretching from the 1970s to the present day. This notion of political convergences in education is analysed via a conceptualisation of their evolution within NPM located in three separate stages of development through successive changes of government from the Conservative, Thatcher-led (1979–1990) and Major (1990–1997) administrations, the New Labour Blair- (1997–2007) and Brown- (2007–2010) led governments through to the Cameron-led Conservative/Liberal Democratic Coalition of 2010–2015. Each of these stages is viewed as representing a significant point in the evolution of NPM in education in this context and even though the nature of these convergences are identified as having shifted over time alongside changes in the emphasis of policies through changes of government, it is argued here that NPM related policy convergences have dominated for in excess of thirty years. Our foregrounding of cross political party convergences in education is not intended to distract from the appearance of divergences between these groups over the period of time in question, but to reveal the political basis for the rapid and deep penetration of NPM and post-NPM policies in education in England. It is asserted that these convergences, rather than offering a secure basis for educational institutions and those who work and study within them, has instead resulted in a permanent instability. The second contribution of this chapter is the conceptualisation of England as a global laboratory for educational change. This conceptualisation locates the development of NPM in an English educational context within theoretical work examining the colonial and post-colonial dimensions of international and global educational change (Rizvi and Lingard 2010). As part of this, the English educational laboratory is identified as having started with a neocolonial and outward looking perspective upon educational reform and as having ended with a largely inward focused set of concerns as the contradictions of neoliberal change have become increasingly apparent in this context.

It is asserted in this chapter that NPM continues to retain potency in enabling a critical examination of education policy in England even though the term post-NPM (Christensen and Lægreid 2011c; Dunleavy *et al.* 2006; Hall *et al.* 2015) probably now better characterises this contemporary context.

The research underpinning this chapter has been undertaken by the authors and colleagues in the Critical Education Policy and Leadership research grouping in the Manchester Institute of Education (Courtney 2016; Gunter and Forrester 2008; Hall *et al.* 2011; McGinity 2015; Woods 2014) and has focused upon contemporary developments in English education policy and leadership.

NPM in education in England

The current provision of education in England, following over thirty years of NPM reforms, can be characterised as one of complexity, even chaos. Layering and over-layering of reforms have created a situation in which there are at least seventy types of schools (Courtney 2016), with the 'independent' and 'autonomous' school as the model for the effective and efficient delivery of educational services. Hence there has been a shift from the 'common' school within a community towards a restoration project of distinction, branding and competition between schools. This has two main thrusts: first, the introduction of business models to schools through their local management from 1988, where schools could control the budget, funding was based on a formula linked to parental preferences for a place for their child and in which the right of schools to hire and fire teachers was trialled; and second, the provision of schools as businesses outside of local democratic control and accountability; as explained later in this chapter this has been through the establishment of a variety of school types. Alongside and in tension to such decentralisation have been forms of centralisation through the national curriculum and the regulation of standards through high-stakes testing and inspection audits through Ofsted, whereby data design, collection, control and analysis has become integral to judgements of quality and educational purposes (Hall *et al.* 2016). The interplay between autonomy in a market place and regulation regarding standards has been enabled through the three main stages of NPM identified in this chapter, and is explained as follows through key features identified in the Introduction:

- Managers: educational professionals are trained and accredited to deliver reform changes based on national standards that structure identities, practices and careers. Relocation of educational professionals from local systems of democracy to independent schools and/or chains of schools has shifted attention away from notions of educational professionals to business managers and entrepreneurs. An increased emphasis is on such roles as school leaders, who lead and do leadership, whereby the focus is on the exercise of power in order to deliver performance outcomes. Differentiation is through titles (e.g. school principal, executive head teacher, head teacher, senior leader, middle leader, teacher leader), role and job descriptions linked to performance packages and remuneration.
- Managing: the focus is on delivering and auditing national standards through prescriptive curriculum and lesson packages, testing, and performance reviews. This provides the data to demonstrate continued/discontinued public investment, to support marketing to parents regarding the exercising of preferences, and to enable bidding for income streams. The main management tools are: planning, target setting, data collection and analysis. This has focused increasingly on self-evaluation of the student and staff member with judgements about performance through lesson observation and grading, examination results and general conduct.
- Management: the approach is on securing change through people, and so a strong emphasis is on control through processes of economy, efficiency and effectiveness. Organisational values of consultation, participation and team work may feature, where the increasing dominance of performative leadership enables vision and mission to be used to inspire and motivate the workforce and students to secure improvement and acclaim. Values related to 'school owners' feature from private interests such as faith, philanthropy, business, and local consortia, where local democratic participation remains but is increasingly under threat from UK government reform.
- Managerialism: new hierarchies of power are being intensified through 'within school' distinctions between senior, middle and teacher leaders, and 'outside school' controls through owners (faith, business, philanthropy, consortia) and the wider market. Line management relationships have been installed that clearly identify who manages what and how, and through which performance is measured, instrumental accountability operates, and contracts are awarded, extended, terminated.

Having set out the main features of NPM in education in England, we now move on to detailing the development of this phenomenon. From our

24 David Hall and Helen M. Gunter

examination of Tables 1.1 and 1.2 in Chapter 1 of this book and our programme of research, the evidence suggests that there are three main waves or stages of reform that illustrate how the main features of NPM have been built over time.

The foundation stage of educational reform 1979–1997

The key features of this stage are outlined in Table 2.1.

Taken together, various features of the UK policy context in England, most particularly the political ascendancy of the New Right from 1979 when the Thatcher-led Conservative administration took office, older traditions of a liberal state and a disenchantment with state-led interventions following the economic crises of the 1970s (Gamble 1988), combined to offer an extremely promising set of circumstances for the propagation of an intense form of neoliberalism well suited to an aggressive version of NPM.

The foundation stage of installing these changes within schools came about through major reform initiatives by Conservative administrations in the 1980s and 1990s, building upon a new cross party convergence that emerged during a series of educational 'crises' in the 1970s regarding the need for improved educational standards (Whitty 1989). These reforms are viewed here as representing an attempt to interrupt publicly funded schools as public institutions and to break with the practice of insulating such institutions from private interests (Du Gay 2008).

In 1988 a new Education Reform Act offered a remarkably wide-ranging set of reforms that would inscribe themselves upon generations of school children and teachers and unleash a subsequent 'permanent revolution' (Pollitt 2007a) of subsequent educational reforms.

Some of the key provisions arising out of the 1988 Act included the following:

- Centralisation of curriculum and assessment in schools through the creation of a National Curriculum linked mainly to established academic subjects assessed at four intervals (Key Stages) via national tests;
- The marketization of schooling through the creation of educational quasi-markets (LeGrand and Bartlett, 1993);
- The local financial management of schools establishing them as individual business units;
- The legislative underpinning of privately sponsored City Technology Colleges and the creation of Grant Maintained Schools.

The 1988 Act is viewed as a repurposing of education in England whereby the role of teachers as curriculum developers and pedagogues gradually came to be replaced by one in which they became the deliverers and managers of educational standards in schools newly imagined as business units. In this way the purposes of education, including a marginalization of educational processes, were re-worked so that a cadre of teachers reimagined as managers came into

England **25**

TABLE 2.1 Key features of New Public Management in education in England: the foundation stage

Factors	Tools and practices
Managers	Teachers become managers of data in relation to pupil performance A cadre of teachers are reconstituted as educational managers trained to monitor class, departmental and institutional level performance in schools Competition between schools emerges as a new logic of educational activity Teachers are reconstituted as deliverers of a national curriculum
Managing	Standards of attainment in relation to national testing become the benchmarks against which pupil, teacher and institutional performance are judged School league tables based upon attainment data are developed at national and local levels as a means of enabling educational markets School governing bodies reconstituted to comprise a widened membership including members of the local business community
Management	Line management established in schools whereby teacher performance is evaluated in relation to national performance data Head teachers made responsible for school performance and accountable to Ofsted during periodic inspections Ofsted inspects schools and grades schools according to their performance
Managerialism	National test results established as the key indicators of pupil, teacher and school performance. School managers, as head teachers, afforded responsibility for managing schools in line with performance indicators; teacher appraisal introduced

being with a brief to manage educational institutions around specified standards, national testing and a subsequent system of national inspection run by a newly created Office for Standards in Education (Ofsted)[1].

Within the 1988 Act, the emphasis upon choice, markets and competition and attempts to create independent schools within the state system are seen as reflecting the neoliberal preferences and ambitions of reformers whilst the central control of curriculum and assessment designed to counter educational progressivism and promote educational standards are viewed as reflecting the more neoconservative demands of reformers. These tensions between neo-conservative and neo-liberal approaches to educational reform in England are viewed as being directly analogous to wider tensions within the discourse of NPM itself. These are tensions between a 'hard' version of NPM where the discursive emphasis is upon the controlling of public service institutions and their employees in an environment low on trust and with lower levels of autonomy for employees. And a 'softer' version of NPM the emphasis is more upon enabling change to emerge within the public sector through creativity,

26 David Hall and Helen M. Gunter

innovation and entrepreneurship with concomitantly higher levels of trust (Ferlie and Geraghty 2005). These discursive tensions were especially heightened within the context of education, given its elevated position amongst elite policy makers as a strategic imperative vital to the nation's capacity to compete in international markets. This concern initially manifested in the Foundation Stage as a more generalized policy obsession linking educational to economic success but as described later in the chapter they would in the reinforcing stage come to revolve around OECD/PISA scores and the imagined relative international success of England's education system.

Under the 1988 Act all pupils would come to know and be assiduously reminded of their levels of attainment in relation to targets set against national norms (Wiliam *et al.* 2004). Teachers would come to be managed via class-level data and, despite well established relationships between the institutional performance of schools and the relative socio-economic advantage of their pupils (Ozga 2009; Perryman *et al.* 2011), schools would be judged according to raw performance data published in school league tables. This created near ideal conditions for the emergence of a managerialism in which the managerial purposes of this new performance regime might supplant previous educational rationales. Unsurprisingly this new data rich environment of schooling would have dramatic consequences for those directly affected. In this 'hard', low trust and controlled version of NPM teachers would come to experience not only a substantial loss of autonomy but also, it has been argued, forms of terror (Ball 2003). For young people subjected from a very young age[2] to the performance regime arising out of these reforms, the effects of these changes, although already charted in terms of their early consequences (Reay and William 1999), are commonly associated with rapidly increasingly levels of depression, anxiety and self-harm (Green *et al.* 2005; Nuffield Foundation 2013). The 'softer' version of NPM as expressed in the 1988 Education Act can be located within the affordances offered primarily to head teachers to respond to the quasi-market and to take responsibility for the financial management of their schools. The growth of the field of educational marketing and associated advertising and promotional activities that followed on from the 1988 Education Act in England (Chitty 1992) was directly linked to the new importance school attached to recruiting sufficient pupils within a newly marketized environment. This along with the schools' new found freedoms to manage their own finances did provide opportunities for innovation and entrepreneurship for some head teachers and a newly recruited cadre of school business managers (Armstrong 2015; Woods 2014).

Reflecting England's international role as an early adopter of NPM (Hood 1991), the reforms of this Foundation Stage can be viewed as an early attempt at trialling NPM related policies within a particular national educational context. Whilst England was not alone in experimenting with NPM reforms in its education sector, it is widely viewed as having been especially zealous in this regard in relation to other countries both in Europe and more widely. This 'laboratory' dimension of educational reforms within England and the political confidence which inspired such a radical change from a previous civic-welfarist era it is argued here must also be viewed within the context of 'victories' secured by a newly emboldened Thatcher-led administration during the 1980s. These included repeated national electoral successes in 1983 and 1987 that secured a firm, territorialised basis for the sustained application of NPM policies and underpinning this were symbolically important victories at home over the National Union of Mineworkers[3] (Beckett and Hencke 2009) and overseas via a 'victorious' armed conflict in the Falklands/Malvinas[4]. In the postcolonial context of a nation still struggling to come to terms with the loss of Empire (English and Kenny, 2001; Gamble 1981) this new mood of triumphalism in England during the 1980s enabled the reform of public services to be re-imagined by its architects as a new imperial venture (Harvey 2007). In this reimagined future Great Britain would once again seek to assert its position as a world leader, in this case as the role model and global proselytiser cum exporter of reformed public services in the newly rolled back state. Viewed through this lens, NPM is seen as both the nationally configured and focused venture represented earlier in this section and simultaneously as being intimately associated with its roots in wider European projects of imperialism and colonialism (Rizvi 2007). This analysis of NPM in England both foregrounds the colonial fantasies and ambitions associated with educational reform and offers further explanatory purchase to the intensity with which NPM related policies were applied in this context.

So the Foundation Stage of NPM in education, built upon a cross party political convergence that emerged during the 1970s and regarding the need to improve educational standards, offered a robust and promising basis for further reforms by establishing the normality of management in direct tension with professional norms, and the idea of central regulation of professional identities and practices. Nevertheless it was widely anticipated amongst education professionals themselves that the election of a New Labour government in 1997 would signal a significant and marked change of policy direction.

The reinforcing stage of educational reform 1997–2010

Rather than a marked change of policy direction, the entry of New Labour into government from 1997 is better represented as a further intensification of NPM reforms in education. This 'reinforcing' stage of the main outcomes of change is outlined in Table 2.2.

Much of the reform process under New Labour built upon and continued the principal neoliberal tenets of the reforms of the 1980s albeit in a hybridized form commonly referred to as the Third Way. It resulted in the underlying principles of the 1988 Act being not only maintained by New Labour governments during this period but intensified via a range of key policy initiatives in ways that reasserted their dominance. This wider representation of New Labour's education policies is not meant to imply that divergences did not appear during

28 David Hall and Helen M. Gunter

TABLE 2.2 Key features of New Public Management: the reinforcing stage

Factors	Tools and practices
Managers	Teachers' role as managers of data in relation to pupil performance is reinforced through national strategies that seek to restrict pedagogic practices in schools As the performance regime intensifies and national test performance assumes ever greater importance, the managerial role of teachers further increases Competition between schools is reinforced as a new logic of educational activity Teachers internalise Ofsted prescriptions so that practices become strongly shaped by predominant concern of 'how would Ofsted judge this?'
Managing	Standards of attainment in relation to national testing are further reinforced as the benchmarks against which pupil, teacher and institutional performance are judged School league tables become critical to local and national perceptions of school performance Schools forced to close through national-level intervention where performance falls below benchmarked levels Performance management introduced for all teachers
Management	Head teachers sacked and replaced by 'Super Heads' when they fail to deliver improvements in educational standards Ofsted reports and performance data used as the basis for school closures Performance related pay introduced for teachers and head teacherhead teachers Under distributed leadership a new cadre of teachers reconstituted as leaders are encouraged to assume responsibility for locally managing reform processes and outcomes
Managerialism	National test results reinforced as the key indicators of pupil, teacher and school performance through target setting, audits and inspection School managers, as head teachers, afforded enhanced responsibility for managing schools in line with performance indicators and prescribed pedagogic practices

this phase. New Labour's investment in education through, for example, a new school building programme and the raising of teacher salaries, and attempts to integrate public service provision for children and families are prime example of such divergences reflecting different approaches to educational reform and tensions within the modernization process. Nevertheless, it is argued that such divergences were largely subsumed by NPM-related convergences and continuities.

It is important to note that New Labour's approach to reform during the reinforcing stage was increasingly influenced by the global and international. Two particular aspects stand out. First: the travel of policy between different national contexts and the associated influence of elite global networks in education. A particular example of this was the influence of Charter Schools, a US development, upon the formation of the Academies programme. Second: the increasing importance of PISA as a key indicator of the success of education policies within the media and the so-called Westminster village; a trend increasingly evident across European contexts during this era.

The intensity of New Labour's educational interventions was ratcheted up to hitherto unseen levels during the late 1990s and 2000s. This was manifested most clearly in the 'deliverology' (Barber 2007) approach to public service reform that was implemented in education through a data rich school system in which targets for performance improvement in relation to national levels of attainment became a dominant feature of school life at institutional, classroom and individual pupil level. It extended and supported managerialism within schools by enabling those identified as managers, and more latterly – as discussed below – leaders, to focus ever more upon directing individual, teacher and institutional performance in relation to metrics-based data arising out of national tests. Also present in this hybridized regime was a dominant and persistent neoliberal emphasis upon markets, competition and choice within education with school league tables based upon national test performance continuing to provide a central plank for parental choice (Levacic and Woods 2002). Attempts to extend choice and competition between schools occurred through the introduction of Academies as independent state schools with private sponsors outside of local authority control[5]. In addition, the invitation to all secondary schools to become specialist institutions represented an extended and more determined attempt to break up the comprehensive, common school system that had developed since the late 1950s. The Academies Programme, in particular, was far more extensive than its predecessor under the Conservative administrations, the City Technology College, where only fifteen schools were eventually established. In this New Labour version of NPM, teachers became constructed as managed employees in a low trust, low autonomy working environment rather than deliberative public servants seeking to develop educational provision within their schools in accordance with notions of the 'public interest'. Interestingly, this rise of managers and managerialism within English schools under New Labour was accompanied by the simultaneous rise of a discourse of leadership as manifested most markedly by the creation of a National College of School Leadership (NCSL) (Hall *et al.* 2013).

The importance of these reforms within education for New Labour's wider ambitions for the public sector should not be underestimated. One manifestation of this was Sir Michael Barber's appointment as New Labour's Head of the powerful Prime Minister's Delivery Unit during Tony Blair's second term of office following elevation from his former role as Chief Advisor

30 David Hall and Helen M. Gunter

on School Standards to the Secretary of State for Education. Thus one of the key architects of New Labour's educational reforms was placed in a role central to public service reform, its continued roll out to other parts of the public sector in England and subsequently via his active involvement in international educational networks as a global carrier of neo-liberal reform. This prime example exemplifies the manner in which education during the reinforcing stage occupied a position as a national laboratory for reform in the rest of the public sector in the UK alongside its continued role as part of the colonial spread of neoliberalism under the new imperialism (Harvey 2007). The further intensification of NPM in the reinforcing stage also underlines the Arendtian notion of the boomerang effect (Gunter, 2014; Owens, 2009) which refers to those processes whereby the colonisers as well as the colonised are shaped by their encounters so that the effects of colonial endeavours are experienced both domestically and internationally: in this case by teachers, parents and children in England having been the determined and unrelenting focus of a managerial experiment intended, at least in part, to reassert the UK's position in the matrix of global capitalism.

It can be concluded that this reinforcing stage of NPM in education in England acted to intensify, rather than weaken, the centrality of the managerial within the education sector. A key development during this stage is that the initial educational standards based political convergence on educational reform that had held sway since the 1970s expanded during this stage. This expansion was via the explicit embracing of the neo-liberal so that the reinforcing stage represented not only a redoubling of efforts to secure the standards agenda in schools but also the clear cross political party affirmation of marketized and privatized solutions to perceived educational problems: an approach that was to provide the basis for a new fast tracked privatization of education.

The rapid privatising stage of educational reform 2010–2015

The drive to make existing public education more efficiently and effectively managed has also been accompanied by the entry of new providers with NPM-enabling privatization through outsourcing, new school owners, and the continued shift of education from a public to a private matter (Courtney and Gunter 2016; Hall *et al.* 2016). This is outlined in Table 2.3.

This stage of the educational reform process in England was again marked primarily by its similarities and continuity in relation to previous administrations since 1979 with the discourse of standards remaining predominant throughout this stage of reform; thus representing further continuity in this political convergence. Interestingly, the centralizing dimensions of reform took on new forms during this stage, suggesting that the educational laboratory was beginning to become more inward looking. Socially authoritarian ideas about approved knowledge and values reasserted themselves as the Secretary of State

England **31**

TABLE 2.3 Key features of New Public Management: the rapid privatising stage

Factors	Tools and practices
Managers	Teachers/non teachers become the deliverers not of a public service but of tightly centrally controlled private institutions Following quarter of a century of intense reform, debates about the purposes of education become largely irrelevant to school practices Competition between schools increasingly conforms to private sector business practices through practices such as pupil exclusion and expulsion and the creation of surplus school places (via the Free Schools model) Ofsted attempts to secure conformity of provision come into conflict with the imperative to privatise
Managing	Standards of attainment in relation to national testing are further reinforced as the benchmarks against which pupil, teacher and institutional performance are judged School league tables remain critical to local and national perceptions of school performance Performance management, short term contracts and 'hire and fire' practices become standard for teachers and head teachers
Management	A new cadre of Executive Head teachers or Chief Executive Head teachers with large salaries and executive benefits packages emerges with responsibility for a group of schools Schools within local authority control forced to leave local authorities where performance falls below benchmarked levels Schools outside of local authority control not subject to the same processes 'Leadership' expected from all school employees focused upon the achievement of institutional missions largely shaped by national policies
Managerialism	National test results largely unchallenged as the key indicators of pupil, teacher and school performance through target setting, audits and inspection Executive head teachers afforded wider powers for managing groups of schools through performance indicators Private benefits such as individual salaries and value for money assessment in competitive tendering used as the dominant model for decision making

for Education directly intervened, for example, in what books were to be read by children in English Literature and History and, most notably and ironically in the context of increasingly loud calls for independence from Scotland, with attempts to instill British values in pupils attending schools in England (Muir 2014; Richardson 2015). This inward looking turn needs to be viewed within the context of wider trends, including efforts to secure the UK's exit from the

European Union and increased political support for the UK Independence Party, that reflect tensions arising from neoliberalism. As Tom Nairn (2000) argues, it is England rather than other parts of the UK that has been most deformed by imperial globalization and the consequent fear of decline arising from this leads to intermittent bouts of attempts to define and assert Britishness with political and media elites convinced that addressing this enigma will solve the many problems faced by British society (McCormick 2013). Given that the union of nations forming the UK had been largely held together following the loss of the British Empire by the creation of the welfare state (Devine 2006) it is unsurprising that the subsequent dismantling of welfarism under neo-liberalism would lead to significant tensions in this Union. Correspondingly, it is important to note though that this tendency towards inwardness has remained tempered by concerns about education as a strategic national asset for a nation seeking to assert itself in global markets; hence a continuation of the focus upon PISA that emerged strongly during the reinforcing stage and the borrowing and recontextualisation of policies derived from other national systems including the Swedish Friskolor (Free School).

During the period 2010–2014 over half of all secondary schools, nearly 3000, converted to Academy status and were removed from local democratic accountability. Accompanying the development of Academies has been the rise of Executive Head Teachers made responsible for the management of groups of schools reflecting a trend towards further concentrations of managerial power and the increased distancing of school management from children and classrooms towards data, targets, performance and audit. This further, more determined shift to independent, state funded, schools has been directly inspired during this period by attempts to emulate elite and socially privileged independent schools and in the case of Free Schools, by their Swedish forerunners. So this development that initially emerged on a small scale with the creation of City Technology Colleges, has rapidly developed as the default model for schooling in England influenced and shaped by developments in other national contexts as policy travelled across national boundaries creating interplays between the local and the global. In accordance with its neoliberal origins, it is a policy driven by attempts to create choice and diversity within an educational marketplace and by ambitions to eliminate common schools and to replace what remains of the civic and welfarist in education in England with private interests. Interestingly, during the election campaign of 2015 it became clear that the Labour Party had no clear intention to reverse this trend towards educational privatization thus underlining the continued and enduring strength of educational political convergence (although at the time of writing the election in September, 2015 of a new Labour Party Leader, Jeremy Corbyn, presents the possibility of significant disruption to extant convergences). In these circumstances a post-NPM era can be seen as having come into being (Hall *et al.* 2016). Consequently education has become a privately managed, although still largely state funded system with the potential for rapid conversion to private funding and extended private financing.

England **33**

The election of a majority Conservative government in 2015 seems likely to consolidate and accelerate this latest policy turn.

This account of educational reform in England suggests a near complete revolution in which educational modernization within the socio-political climate of this context and the more internationally located paradigm of NPM precedes a wider move from public to private provision to the point where NPM is less readily identifiable in any coherent sense.

Discussion

The analysis of the stages of the development of NPM in England in this chapter from early experimentation with the centralizing of education combined with marketization through to the rapid privatizing of more recent years might suggest a well ordered transition for schools, children and young people to new forms of educational provision. In reality the process of change in the education system in England has been bedeviled by a series of paradoxes, ironies and contradictions that offer a more complex picture of how these reforms have played out.

As noted by Rose (1999) there has been a marked dissonance between the imaginings of states and their associated ideologues and the enactment of these imaginings by various actors and institutions as policy is variously accommodated, resisted and complied with according to a range of contextual features (Hall and McGinity 2015). In education in England it was imagined that successive waves of reform turning the screw of performance management ever deeper into the professional lives of teachers and schools would result in a significantly higher performing education system where the products of the school system would be able to compete with their international counterparts in an increasingly globalised world. Our research evidence suggests strongly that these reforms have indeed led to significant changes in school and classroom practices where institutional and professional efforts have become ever more tightly focused upon the performance demands of testing regimes (Courtney 2016; Hall *et al.* 2011; McGinity 2015) and new forms of knowledge have emerged in educational contexts (Gunter and Forrester 2008; Woods 2014). Yet judging even by the kind of official performance measures such as PISA and TIMMS now so routinely relied upon by Ministers it is not at all clear that even in this narrowest of senses the reform process has 'worked' in England (OECD 2014a). Indeed our research has raised important questions regarding the deleterious effects of these changes upon learners and education professionals in ways that challenge the entire basis of the reform effort (Courtney and Gunter 2016; Hall 2013; McGinity 2015). Similarly in making the shift from an 'inefficient' public service ethos rooted in bureaucratic and administrative processes it was imagined that NPM would inspire a new efficiency in the public sector promising enhanced value for money for citizen consumers. Again in education, one clear outcome from the reform and modernisation process has

34 David Hall and Helen M. Gunter

been the adoption of a series of intensely demanding and bureaucratic processes in schools. Amongst other things, these additional bureaucratic demands have included the recording, tracking and assessment of pupil progress in relation to national targets for achievement, the preparation of documentary evidence prior to Ofsted inspections and the creation of institutional responses to a myriad of initiatives, policy directives and structural reforms. These have combined in ways that have resulted in schools, teachers and pupils experiencing NPM as a 're-disorganisation' (Pollitt 2007a) of their professional and school lives (Hall *et al.* 2011). Ironically, these additional demands have been directly linked to the very reform process that was supposed to have rendered them unnecessary. In this way a breath-taking gulf can now be discerned in education in England between the discursive regime of NPM inspired reforms and the lived realities of teachers, pupils and schools.

This gulf can be located at least in part within contradictions relating to the role of education for neo-liberal reformers that has generated significant instability in relation to NPM and post-NPM reforms in England. As discussed above these contradictions have previously been manifested in terms of tensions between neo-conservative and neo-liberal approaches to educational reform, but they are also manifested in tensions between the marketized and privatizing agendas pursued by neoliberals and the centralizing tendencies in reform efforts that recognize the strategic importance at a national level of education in terms of enabling the development of a suitably skilled and knowledgeable workforce able to sustain national economic competitiveness. These tensions go deeper still if, as has been argued above, it is the high level of state intervention in education in England that has created the very conditions that have subsequently enabled the marketization of education. This raises questions about the tenability and resilience of an educational system located within such a contradictory policy environment and reveals a neoliberal ascendancy in education in England that is less stable than recent decades of convergence based reform might suggest.

Conclusion

The strong and enduring educational convergences in England focused upon the rapid and intense implementation of NPM that has subsequently morphed into rapid privatization has not provided a stable basis for the future development of schooling. Instead, the educational laboratory in England has offered a permanent instability for teachers and young people. Both the volume and nature of the reforms have contributed to this instability as schools, teachers and young people have been required to constantly adapt to a fast changing and turbulent environment; the laboratory has been a very busy site of activity. This has been an environment in which the professional demands upon teachers from educational managers and the performative demands upon children and young people have continued to multiply as the technologies of managerialism and the processes associated with the breaking up of the common school have been applied with ever more intensity. As referred to at the beginning of this chapter in terms of the sheer number of school types generated by these reforms the situation is probably best described as chaotic. Educational change in this context has offered significant space for educational managers, leaders and entrepreneurs who have been increasingly empowered by successive waves of reform. Yet teachers, children and young people have found themselves increasingly strait-jacketed by a pedagogic turn designed to enable those appointed to manage them. These tensions are currently being managed through a process of privatization that offers the promise to political administrations of simultaneously distancing themselves from the seemingly inevitable fallout of rapid educational change whilst maintaining a tight control over the pedagogic activities of teachers, children and young people. As seen earlier in this chapter, from the very beginning of NPM in education, the replacement of the public with the private has been an integral element of the reform process; this is now an aspect of the NPM project that has reached a dominant position in education in England and, notwithstanding dramatic changes in the political landscape, it seems likely to remain the preferred option for elite policy makers for the foreseeable future as they continue to grapple with the instabilities, contradictions and complexities described in this chapter.

Notes

1   Ofsted was created four years later via the 1992 Education (Schools) Act.
2   Key stage 1 testing was targeted at six and seven year olds.
3   Following the national mineworkers strike of 1984–85.
4   There is some dispute regarding the longevity of electoral benefits accruing to the Conservative Party following the Falklands/Malvinas crisis of 1982 (Sanders et al., 1987).
5   Local authorities were made primarily responsible for schools under the terms of 1944 Education Act.

PART II

The social democratic state

3

FINLAND

NPM resistance or towards European neo-welfarism in education?

Michael Uljens, Lili-Ann Wolff and Sara Frontini

Introduction

In the year 2000, Finnish comprehensive education rose unexpectedly and unintendedly to the global agenda. The reason was top achievements in the PISA test. Finland moved from a peripheral position into the core of the global educational dialogue (Frontini 2009; Uljens 2007). This international awareness about the educational level in Finland would have passed without notice both within and beyond the country, had it not been for the neoliberal take on educational evaluation by the Organisation for Economic Co-operation and Development (OECD). However, what became the real puzzlement was the unexpected insight from this measurement practice, namely that an exceptionally high level and coherent school performance level was perfectly achievable within a state driven comprehensive school system governed by a national curriculum common and equal for all, where the national evaluation system applied sampling methods rather than kept track of individual schools' performance level (Uljens 2007). With regard to its educational architecture, the system in Finland was informed and inspired by a traditional Keynesian, post-war social-democratic approach to citizenship and professional education introduced in the mid-1960s. Although this orientation was not stronger than in other Nordic countries, it obviously went deeper, requiring a contextual and historical analysis to be understood. Our claim is that from an NPM perspective, Finland's success became an aporetic occurrence as it provided evidence that orthodox NPM policy was obviously not required for success. According to the logics of NPM, the means by which Finland reached success is more or less incomprehensible. How should the above be explained?

Methodologically, we assume that educational policymaking refers to societal practices that occur in the form of discursive institutionalised processes from

40 Michael Uljens, Lili-Ann Wolff and Sara Frontini

local to transnational levels (Frontini 2009; Schmidt 2008; Uljens and Ylimaki 2015; Wallerstein 1980). The political rationalities expressed in the development processes in education are connected with more general ideological, historical, geopolitical and economic changes, developments and legacies. Therefore we believe that a discursive understanding of the historically developed policy processes where nation states have many roles in their critical mediation allows us to identify those social technologies, positionings, operations and policy networks that Finland as a state has enacted, adopted, resisted and contributed to in relation to NPM. This approach argues that educational, political and sociological research need further theory development beyond the nation state level, with a sense for both new regional states like the EU (Schmidt 2006) and also cosmopolitanism (Clayton 1998; Beck 2004; Kemp 2005), yet connected to the sub-state level.

First, we aim at providing an initial picture of what shape and form NPM has taken in Finland and of what shape and form it has not taken. Second, we will explore this initial picture by identifying a number of policy positions in the past four decades. Third, we conclude by providing a historical interpretation we believe can cast light on why education received such a paramount role and how a relatively unique educational policy tradition established itself in Finland.

New Public Management in education in Finland

As a nation with a many-decades-long tradition of focusing on equity and also excellence, Finland has not been hit by the NPM wind as thoroughly as many other European countries. Given the features of the four Ms in the introduction of this book (i.e. Managers, Managing, Management and Managerialism), interventions into professional codes of practices and knowledge in order to change the identities of managers and leaders have been weak. The universities or the national educational authorities do not promote business models in school leadership education. The role titles in use (e.g. head teacher, principal, deputy) have remained unchanged and are in fact perceived as old-fashioned in other Nordic countries that have been more eager to adopt titles like Chief Executive, Senior Leader, and Managing Director. Educational leadership positions are only accessible for teachers educated with required training in educational leadership. Workforce in schools is not removed as a consequence of a school's performance. Schools in Finland never departed much from teachers' grading of student achievements, but data from systematic outputs are used for self-evaluation and school development. Grading lessons by inspection does not occur. Increase in the pay of the workforce due to results is unknown. New providers who take over state or municipal schools are rare. National authorities have explicitly resisted the publication of league tables. Leadership teams and teacher teams are frequent, especially in bigger schools, but this reflects a distributed and shared way of working and is not connected to bottom-up accountability of the school workforce. Senior leadership teams making judgments for income generation and contract renewal do not reflect contemporary practices, although annual development dialogues with teachers are planned to be introduced soon. The promotion of delivery and outcomes has always been present, but not above inclusion and equity, reflected in the current system with special education for weaker students.

Finland and other Nordic countries

When discussing education in the Scandinavian or Nordic countries, these are often treated as representing the same values and solutions on public service within a welfare tradition. On one level this is still accurate. We thus support Moos' conclusion when he describes how the Nordic tradition differs from the one in UK/US:

> It is reasonable to conclude that the UK/US had societal and political systems more inclined to build on rational choice theories – because of the belief in a liberal, and weak state; on principal-agent theory because of the bigger power distance and GINI and lower trust in people; and on market-thinking because of the stronger belief in civil society and market. The UK/US thus seems better equipped to take in the transnational ideas of New Public Management.
>
> (Moos: in press)

However, there is a big variation among the Nordic countries. It is really remarkable how different paths Finland and Sweden have taken the past twenty years with respect to all dimensions of NPM pointed out in the introduction of this book (see Lundahl *et al.* 2013; Nilsson Lindström and Beach 2015). A closer analysis might reveal similarities between policies, e.g. in Finland and France where the state has had an integrating force within society with a tradition of nation-building founded on public law. Similarly, while the UK has been characterised as the NPM laboratory, from a Nordic perspective this role is Sweden's. This shows how many different solutions are present with respect to NPM (Pollitt and Dan 2011). However, our conclusion is not that NPM has been an alien phenomenon in Finnish education, but that it has had its own profile.

In Finland, the shift towards NPM has been called a movement towards the educational policy of the 'third republic' (Varjo 2007). The first republic refers to the period from the independence of Finland (1917) up to World War II. The second republic started in 1945 and lasted until the mid-1980s. That period focused on educational expansion, solidarity, equal basic education for all, equal opportunities, regional balance and education for civil society. In other words, it was the educational doctrine of the welfare state assuming mutual positive effects between economic growth, welfare and political participation (Siljander 2007). The 'third republic' started when the previous century 'ended' in 1989,

42 Michael Uljens, Lili-Ann Wolff and Sara Frontini

i.e. after the collapse of the Soviet Union and the fall of the Berlin Wall. However, the political mentality in Finland had already started to change toward a more conservative direction in the 1980s. At that time the public sector organisations started to change the Weberian bureaucratic management and make it more flexible, focused on service, efficacy and efficiency, mostly according to a NPM concept (Ahonen 2011). In contrast to the period of the second republic, the educational mentality of the third republic initiated a discourse on excellency, effectivity, productivity, competition, internationalisation, increased individual freedom and responsibility as well as deregulation in all societal areas (e.g. communication, health-care, infrastructure) including the educational sector (education law, curriculum planning and educational administration – Uljens 2007). This direction was clearly manifested in the governmental programme in Finland after the elections in 1990. The project could be called the creation of the educational policy of the global post-industrial knowledge economy and information society. So-called agency theoretical ideas, according to which the role of the state was still to collect taxes but changed from producing services to buying services, expanded. The model included the lowering of taxes as well as the introduction of techniques for 'quality assurance'. The attention also turned towards profiling individual schools and institutions as well as towards increased flexibility. Curriculum making was decentralised, first to the municipal level in the 1980s and to the school level in the 1990s. This was supported by extended freedom of parental choice at the local level. Parents were included in school boards. Salaries related to achievements were later introduced in the public sector – not in schools, though. This mentality supported a kind of commodification of knowledge, marketisation of schooling as well as a much stronger view of national education as a vehicle for international competition.

A more extensive use of national tests for ranking schools was introduced in the 1990s as a means for promoting a development oriented climate. However, the national Board of Education firmly continued the policy to use a sample-based selection of schools participating in the tests which means that only a general picture of the schools' performance level was reached. Still today no follow-up system for each school's performance level exists. The education of gifted students became acknowledged in addition to the strong emphasis on traditional special education. Limiting school dropout was motivated by its societal costs rather than by many other reasonable arguments.

Although Finnish NPM policy measures are less dramatic in international comparison, and therefore could be called 'light NPM', they have long been perceived as worrying in a domestic perspective (Knubb-Manninen *et al.* 2013). Management tendencies are seen in how PISA results are perceived and in the eagerness to be a country with an outstanding education system. Through its success story, Finnish education has even become an important tool for the country to succeed and become the best on the world market. The Ministry of Education and Culture (2015) regards skills as Finland's most vital capital in the international environment. In addition, Finnish educational know-how has gradually become a product for sale on the world educational market. Marketing initiatives have nonetheless been rather weak, especially given the extraordinary possibilities to move in this direction, and the privatisation of schools has been slow in Finland compared with, for example, Sweden. The signs of managing and managerialism are most apparent in higher education, not least in the polytechnics. Finland has certainly not hesitated to adopt a neoliberal governance policy and neoliberal governance practices in higher education and, to some extent, in vocational education.

Principals

However, business managers or MAs in public administration as educational leaders in schools have not become school leaders in Finland: this is not even possible. A person without a master's degree in education cannot be employed as a principal in a school, and leaders of higher education institutions need to have a doctoral degree in an academic subject. The way principals are trained as leaders/managers and the way they act in their roles is different compared to training programmes for business leaders. To the extent that increasing similarities can be observed, this depends more on that business administration education increasingly emphasises pedagogical leadership issues. Instead, a peculiarity concerning mandatory principal qualification in Finland has been that the absolute majority of the principals receive their licence by taking part in two examinations (total fifteen ECTS) organised by the National Board of Education. Only a minority utilises the opportunities offered by Finnish universities. These National Board of Education exams have been administration and governance oriented, focusing on fundamentals of public law, public administration, administration of the school system, personnel administration and economy administration. However, in a report published by the National Board of Education (2015), a renewed agenda is developed for principal mandatory pre-service education. This report puts educational leadership, curriculum work and school development at the centre, following principles for sustainable leadership in a systemic, multi-level perspective. The National Board of Education itself examines principal education as a public rather than a private good. In the last decades, however, many school leaders and superintendents have also regularly participated in in-service courses targeting leaders of all sectors in the municipalities. These courses are NPM and business-inspired and aim at making the leaders adapt the municipality strategies and lead the schools cost-efficiently. Thus, for the last few decades, school leaders have had to walk a thin line between NPM agendas influenced by strong global forces and mostly driven by state policy, and a deeply rooted Nordic welfare and Bildung tradition.

Four governance phases/positions in Finnish education

To show how the NPM approach was introduced and resisted in Finland from the 1960s and onward, we point out three discursive shifts. Figure 3.1 demonstrates these three shifts and four policy positions regarding primary and secondary education. Positions 1 and 2 to the left reflect a social-democratic policy, while positions 3 and 4 to the right reflect a social liberal policy that grew stronger after the elections in 1991 when Finland received a right-wing coalition government.

Position 1: Centralised curriculum and teacher based evaluation

The first position in Figure 3.1 represents the new educational structure introduced with the nine-year comprehensive school system. It was established in the Basic School Law of 1968 and was gradually implemented from 1972 to 1978 (Ahonen 2014). In the 1960s, Finland started to abandon the dual (parallel) education system where students already, after four years in primary school, followed either an academic or a civic route. To make education more equal, a comprehensive nine-year education for all was established, followed by two parallel systems: the academic upper secondary schools (gymnasia) or vocational schools. Finland was the last Nordic country to adapt this model and the Finnish reform was a joint work of social democrats and agrarians (ibid.). Even though

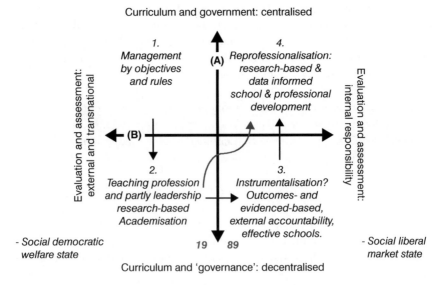

FIGURE 3.1 Four education policy phases during five decades in Finland – de- and re-centralisation of curriculum work related to renewed evaluation policies in education (Uljens and Nyman 2013)

education was still characterised by strict central steering and external control of schools in the 1970s and 1980s with governance through state-set curricula, school inspections and detailed regulations (Jakku-Sihvonen and Heinonen 2001), the aim of equality was set on the agenda (Sahlberg 2012). Consequently, all schools provided health services, served daily meals and supported students with special needs. The educational reform was in line with the ideas of an equal welfare society with similar opportunities for all, since the first nine years of education was basically the same for all children and free of charge. This suited the social-democratic politics well. On the other hand, a strong argument that attracted the agrarians was that unutilised human capital existed in the country's peripheries and had to be exposed (Ahonen 2014).

Position 2: Decentralised curriculum work and enhanced professionalism

During the 1980s and 1990s, which were still golden welfare decades, a decentralisation and deregulation process of, e.g., curriculum work, was obvious in many European countries. This is reflected in the movement from position 1 to 2 (see Figure 3.1). In Finland this decentralisation process increased local responsibility for schooling and was compensated for by an academisation of teacher and principal education. While subject teachers had been educated at the university since the 1860s, the Teacher Education Act 1971 located the education of primary school teachers to the university on a bachelor's level in 1974 by the establishment of separate faculties of education. This education turned into a five year master's degree in 1979. Simultaneously, a systematic development of Finnish schools began. During the 1980s, the teachers' Trade Union of Education in Finland (OAJ) rose as a remarkable power agency to watch over the Finnish educational policy and protect the rights of the teachers (Simola 2015). These developments reflected increasing hope and trust in teaching professionals' ability to carry out an expanded task. In the UK, where Thatcherism initiated a recentralisation of the curriculum and stronger control of teacher education, an opposite orientation could be identified – autonomy was giving way to accountability (Hoyle and Wallace 2005).

Position 3: Finland adopting a NPM light governance model

The neoconservative developments initiated in the 1980s in Finland were strengthened in the wake of the new geopolitical agenda after 1989, which is demonstrated in Figure 3.1 by a movement from position two to three.

Without possibilities to develop our view of the Europeanisation process (cf. Schmidt 2002), we argue that it had a significant effect on the education policy, where many European objectives have become national policy goals. The Finnish approach to European and international matters has been pragmatic and mostly connected to economic, cultural, political and educational motives

46 Michael Uljens, Lili-Ann Wolff and Sara Frontini

(Ollikainen 2000), but also stayed firm at some points. Finland did not 'buy it all'. For example, the internationally widespread use of tests for ranking schools as a means for promoting a competition-oriented climate was refused. Instead, the increase of testing from the 1990s changed from primarily a monitoring approach to a developmental approach. Municipalities and schools were offered the possibility to buy the results for each district for internal use. Some did, most did not. As a consequence, the increased use of evaluation procedures did not lead to competition between schools. The only exception from this rule is the annual national upper secondary exams in which about half of the annual cohort participates. This exam in school subjects has been carried out at the 'Gymnasium' schools since 1874 (Sw. 'studentexamen'). The media in Finland started publishing league tables over these 391 schools in 2002. When the National Board of Education refused to provide the media with the data in electronic form they were sued by the media, and were sentenced by the Supreme Administrative Court in 2007 to share these results, also in electronic form. This should clearly indicate what policy the National Board of Education defended concerning league tables, one of the most visible elements in neoliberal education policy.

Although teachers have been kept from the worst NPM winds, the school framework is not totally free from NPM influences. Even without privatisation, services supplying the daily school activities, such as cleaning and catering, have often been outsourced. According to Kiilakoski and Oravakangas (2010), the expectations on Finnish education overall is oriented towards efficiency and low-cost. In addition, the education system is expected to efficiently fulfil the needs of the labour market, at the same time as the schools are expected to achieve other learning aims. Therefore, good scores in international comparisons are regarded as consequences of good politics and good school practices. Simultaneously, an important goal of the local educational politics is to decrease costs (Kiilakoski and Oravakangas 2010). Further on, according to welfare state logic, the school has to provide safety and a good life for all. This easily makes the whole situation more contradictory the more the municipalities try to save. It becomes paradoxical to both locally and nationally live up to being a traditional welfare state, simultaneously with being a top-achieving but faithful European member.

The Europeanisation process began in Finland even before its official membership in the European Union in 1995. At that time, examples of European influence on Finnish national education policies were related to the reduction of dropouts, the connection between work and school, the highlighting of internationalisation and cooperation, the creation of non-university higher education institutions, and the link between general and vocational education (Malm 1999; Ollikainen 1997). The positive Finnish attitude toward the European Union partly reflects 'a small country's strategy', in which, by being active, it tries to assure its own opportunities as a nation to influence the course of events. This approach is also likely to promote a European consensus and the convergence of national systems (Ahola and Mesikämmen 2003).

Ollikainen (2000) shows how the Europeanisation process went through ideological changes, from a focus on internationalisation and peace until the mid-1980s to emphasising internationalisation and international competitiveness in the 1990s. In particular, the last phase reflects the transformations that also took place on the European level where concepts such as quality, flexibility, efficiency and effectiveness became part of the European discourse in education. This shift has also been examined by Kauko and Varjo (2008), who state that between World War II and its European membership, the Finnish education replicated more of a planning economy where social issues were solved thanks to scientific planning. Successively, from the 1990s onward, education became more like a national enterprise where 'planning, policy making, implementation and evaluation took place within the sovereignty of a nation state, although the general development trend of education policy was aiming explicitly towards more international spheres' (Kauko and Varjo 2008: 225). Within this scenario, quality and internationalisation strategies obtained more importance. On the other hand, during the same period, a severe economic recession hit the country. With the collapse of the Soviet Union at the beginning of the 1990s, important Finnish export markets were gone, which resulted in rising costs for unemployment and cuts in the welfare service; cuts that also affected the schools. Simultaneously, the business world started to influence the Finnish education system (Ahonen 2014), and the municipalities' finances were thus changed according to the NPM doctrine (Varjo *et al.* 2013). These dramatic and unexpected changes reinforced those who wanted to reconstruct Finland according to international market oriented standards (Simola *et al.* 2002). During the 1980s and 1990s the Confederation of Finnish Industries and Employers (CIE) made many attempts to transform the Finnish compulsory education into an international economic competition tool (Simola *et al.* 2013). Finland did not follow these NPM initiatives, however.

Parents and pupils became 'clients' on the educational market in the mid 1990s. A new school law in 1990 allowed free parental school choice and gave the local authorities the right to independently decide, to a certain extent, the financing of schools (Simola *et al.* 2002; Ahonen 2014). Instead of assigned funds, the state paid the municipalities block grants to be used freely according to their own preferences. The result was a decentralised and deregulated mode of governance, and this economic freedom has led to inequity of provisions, according to Varjo *et al.* (2013). Parental free choice, on the other hand, is today accepted by the Ministry (Finland, Ministry of Education and Culture 2012), even if it has caused an increased polarisation steered by the students' socioeconomic background. Accordingly, families with higher economic and cultural capital are those who benefit most from a freer school choice (Silvennoinen *et al.* 2012).

Antikainen (2006) calls this time 'an age of restructuring'. The continuing urbanisation has been steady in the past 30 years. About 100 schools annually have been closed since the 1980s, making in total about 3000 schools, while all new schools are built in the cities. The economic regression is visible in

48 Michael Uljens, Lili-Ann Wolff and Sara Frontini

that nearly 20 per cent of Finnish primary schools running in 2008 were closed in 2013 (Finland, Tilastokeskus 2014). In addition, several stepwise political shifts to the right have changed the educational policy towards a market-based standard – in a more or less hidden process (Simola 2015; Simola *et al.* 2002).

Position 4: Towards increasing transnational policy based dialogical evaluation for pedagogical development

In Figure 3.1, the movement from position 3 to 4 visualises the ongoing recentralisation of curriculum making. This centralisation is visible in an ever-increasing transnational harmonisation of curriculum making. The process has clearly been promoted by transnational evaluation procedures such as PISA. A special feature of the ongoing recentralisation (Europeanisation) is, as noted above, that it moves beyond the level of the single nation state. A parallel process is that regional and municipal decision-making may be weakened with respect to working with curricular aims in the curriculum process.

Quality assurance can be seen as a new form of governance related to the Europeanisation of education (Simola 2011). Quality thinking has emerged from measuring industrial products, but is now an effective tool for evaluating management and processes in educational contexts in Finland. According to the evaluation model published by the National Board of Education in 1995, the Framework for Evaluating Educational Outcomes in Finland, a new municipal auditing committee, was built to assess that the financial as well as operative educational goals were locally reached (Varjo *et al.* 2013). This framework introduced the three Es (economy, efficiency and effectiveness) into the Finnish evaluation rhetoric, but this evaluation model was abandoned after a few years. Subsequently, the Local Governmental Act 1995 stipulating the local assessments was complemented by the Basic Education Act (BEA) 1999 calling for participation in external evaluations. This was a trial aimed at changing from norm steering to control and evaluation of outcomes (Rinne *et al.* 2014). In 2003, the BEA was rewritten and the whole assessment procedure replaced with a network of evaluation experts from the National Board of Education, the universities and other evaluation experts. Since the previous evaluations had hardly any noticeable effect on school praxis, it is understandable that a more efficient system was needed. Therefore, the evaluation that was earlier conducted by the National Board of Education, the Finnish Education Evaluation Council and the Finnish Higher Education Evaluation Council, is, from 2014, handled by an independent governmental Finnish Education Evaluation Centre (FINEEC). The task of the evaluation centre is to evaluate education and the work of education providers from early childhood education to higher education. FINEEC includes an Evaluation Council, a Higher Education Evaluation Committee and units for the evaluation of general education, vocational education and training (VET) and for evaluation of higher education. Additionally, FINEEC supports education providers and higher education institutions with evaluations and quality assurance. The opening of the new centre took place at a time when the learning outcomes in both schools and adult education had decreased, but the question of how to reorganise the national evaluation of education has been on the agenda and intensively discussed for over a decade (Lyytinen 2013). At the opening ceremony in November 2014, the Permanent Secretary at the Ministry of Education and Culture, Anita Lehikoinen, stressed that the strength of the centre is the possibility to study the Finnish education system as a continuum (Karvi 2014). Therefore, according to Lehikoinen, continuous collaboration between the Ministry of Education and Culture, the Board of Education, the municipalities and higher education institutions is necessary. The effect of this new assessment work is still unseen, but will likely result in an increase of interventional school development initiatives. The main point is, however, that the Ministry of Education strengthens its steering of the renewed national centre. Most academic intellectuals in the country opt for developmental and dialogical evaluation (Knubb-Manninen *et al.* 2013), which clearly departs from the so-called 'naming, shaming and blaming' approach supported by PISA. The Finnish quality assessment evaluations have not aimed at control, sanction or allocation of resources and the target has been decision makers and planners, not parents and pupils.

A note on historical legacy

Above we have pointed at the more recent history concerning the dimensions and stages of how NPM policy has been interpreted and put into practice in Finland. A crucial feature of this policy culture has been its orientation towards a consensus that recognises education professionals' interests and that limits short-sighted interests among politicians to use the school as a tool for immediate changes. As such a political culture is not typical in Europe, there is reason to ask how this is possible in Finland. We think that a historical and geopolitical perspective may add to our understanding of why a consensus oriented education policy established itself in Finland.

Like other European nations (e.g. Estonia, Poland), Finland has also tried to find its way between more dominant political powers. A crucial turning point for education in Finland occurred as a result of nothing less than the Napoleonic wars in Europe (Uljens and Nyman 2013). As a result of these wars, Finland was occupied by Russia, but received a semi-independent position as Grand Duchy under the Russian Tsar from 1809 to 1917. Because Finland had formed a unified country with Sweden for more than 500 years the consequences were dramatic by any measure. The separation occurred at the beginning of a new nationalist movement that involved most countries in Europe. For example, Finland and Germany (Prussia) faced a similar fate. Both countries had to be reconstructed from bottom up. According to the Finnish national philosopher J. V. Snellman, the nation was to be rebuilt by the help of Bildung i.e. educating

50 Michael Uljens, Lili-Ann Wolff and Sara Frontini

the people. This solution is reminiscent of Prussia as expressed in Fichte's Talks to the Nation where education was considered the way towards cultivating a new nation from within, not through the expansive occupation of colonies. Fichtean and Hegelian philosophy was received early and had a great impact on Finnish educational theory, especially through J.V. Snellman's works. Schools were crucial cultural institutions for the building of the nation from within. The establishment of the first chair in the science of education at the Imperial Alexander University as early as 1852, one of the first educational professorships in the world, is a good indicator of how importantly education was perceived in Finland.

The nineteenth century was dramatic in many ways and involved a stepwise and firm development towards a strengthening of the Finnish language – the language of the majority (Uljens and Nyman 2013). No other European country experienced a more radical process of nation building with respect to language than Finland. When the nation-state idea in most European countries was about construing a concept of people as 'demos' (political citizens), the concept of people as ethnos (with a shared language) was a given point of departure. This was not the case in Finland with its two languages – Finnish and Swedish. In Finland, this meant the stepwise rise of the Finnish language to parallel that of Swedish, which had established itself as the culturally dominating language during the Swedish period for centuries up to 1809. This political history is necessary for understanding how firmly rooted and highly valued education is in Finland in connecting language and identity.

A second dimension of this legacy is how education and politics were related. We point here to a growing nationalism. Finland as a Grand Duchy was constantly reminded of its semi-independent status. On the one hand, the new status made it possible to establish significant features for a state, such as independent currency (Markka) and a university, but these occurrences were still under surveillance from the Tsar. Our interpretation is that the political interests operating within the Grand Duchy were both focused at controlling and developing but within obvious frames, itself being controlled simultaneously. A successful strategy to support cultural development with the help of schools was therefore, paradoxically, not to control the schools. That is, in order to protect the growth of the culture from within, this semi-independent state protected schools from outer influence (including the demand to teach Russian in Finnish schools). Education truly became a balancing act for this semi-independent nation (see also Uljens and Nyman 2013). It had to trust its teachers.

Conclusion

One assumption in this volume is that nation states still play a role in mediating transnational policies and international developments of various kinds. The Hegelian philosophical and educational tradition in Finland (cf. Snellman) makes it easy to see that 'the state is a primary instrument and site of strategic action'. The way the country has re-worked, adopted, enacted and mediated the global agenda, demonstrates the degrees of freedom that obviously exist for the state. However, the case of Finland shows that beyond functioning as a mediator, a state can act as a contributor in transnational agenda setting. In this respect Finland has moved from a peripheral position to a central one (Frontini 2009). Although it is difficult to estimate the impact that the critical voice of Finland has had in the international debate in developing a counter hegemonic picture, it is beyond question that this has been the case. We hope having shown that there is also reason to believe that more far-reaching cultural and historical legacies guide, or at least influence, solutions made in each country.

Comparing Finland to strong NPM educational doctrines (see Table 1.2 in the Introduction), it is obvious that the progress has been less drastic. The educational management has not seen any fast privatisation; even though many small schools have been closed and merged into larger units to save costs. Likewise, evaluations have not aimed at ranking and competition, but development. In fact, without applying or adapting to an accountability regime, and without any school inspection, standardised curriculum or regulating national student assessments, Finland became a top performing country in the international education arena (cf. Sahlberg 2011). Hitherto, Finnish educational policy has, instead of competition, been based on negotiations and consensus thinking – for better or worse – since consensus also makes people insensible to undesirable changes and, thus, slows down a participative progress. From this perspective, Finland belongs to the countries that have longer and stronger defended a Keynesian welfare national state model but moved towards a Schumpeterian workfare post-national regime (Jessop 2014).

Finland as a state is not at retreat and not in the process of outsourcing services to external agencies. However, there are signs of so-called endogenous privatisation (Ball and Youdell 2008) in, e.g., accepting free parental choice of schools, but in most respects few initiatives have aimed at making schools businesslike, semi-autonomous units including high stake accountability. Exogenous privatisation, to open up schools for commercial interests, sponsorships or privatisation of schools, does not occur.

For decades, Finland has featured a culture of political consensus with broad governments. The Finnish consensus oriented political culture is based on rational argumentation, as developed in the universities and in the administration with highly educated professionals. A consensus oriented and pragmatic polity such as Finland's demonstrates a typical coordinative discourse (Schmidt 2008). This means that broad coalition governments coordinate their interests within the government. Actually, a public for/against debate is much less prominent in Finland, and this demonstrates an inclusive policymaking culture in education. In contrast, communicative discourses prevail in non-consensual politics and are dominated by right and left-wing parties fighting for public opinion. The role education has had in nation building, in addition to a coordinative discourse creating space for professional reflection and decision-making on the part of

52 Michael Uljens, Lili-Ann Wolff and Sara Frontini

the administration and the universities, undeniably builds a strong legacy in Finland.

A strong competitive ethos is obvious, as the Finnish Government is aiming at making Finland into the 'most skilled nation in the world by 2020'. This grandiose rhetoric reflects a new way of talking about educational issues but it does not exclude an interest in social care. Since the number of dropouts has increased and inequality is a growing problem, the focus in the development plan for Finnish education 2011–2016 is to reduce poverty, gender differences, inequality and exclusion, and to improve the situation of disadvantaged groups in education. Other aims are to stabilise the public economy and to endorse sustainable economic growth, as well as to raise employment and competitiveness (Ministry of Education and Culture 2012).

In international comparisons, the Finnish tradition demonstrates a culture of trust in professional autonomy and deliberation rather than a culture of mistrust and control. Globalisation, however, sets a strong pressure on structural changes in small countries such as Finland (Fellman *et al.* 2010). The relation between education, economy and internationalisation is not only related to the need to respond to a global cluster of industries, but, due to the Finnish success in PISA education, has come to be understood as a new export product. To reframe education as a new business, which has to be innovative, anticipate trends, explore new markets and face other educational competitors with the same dynamics as those that regulate the economic world in general, represents a rather dramatic change in the educational ethos of Finland and has only been attractive to a few so far, but the current economic regression might suddenly change the course.

In many countries, the developments in education and social policy have produced unpleasant 'discoveries of cultural surprises' and demonstrated many unintended effects of social interventions in the past two decades (Hood and Peters 2004). It remains to be seen if and how the evolving Finnish model might turn out as an internationally interesting option for how social-democratic and liberal-democratic solutions can be further developed into new forms of European post-neoliberal and pragmatic 'social-liberal neo-welfarism' (Ferrera 2013).

At the final stage of writing this article, the future of Finnish education seems astonishingly cloudy and unpredictable. In 2015, the new three party alliance government between the agrarian Suomen Keskusta (Centre Party), nationalist Perussuomalaiset (Finns Party) and the right-wing Kansallinen Kokoomus (National Coalition Party – NCP) suddenly changed the optimistic educational climate in Finland. The government has suggested large cuts, not least in the education budget (from Kindergarten to higher education). The proposed cuts, entirely in contradiction to the election promises, have led to loud protests and many demonstrations in the biggest cities since the spring of 2015.

4

GOVERNING BY NEW PERFORMANCE EXPECTATIONS IN NORWEGIAN SCHOOLS

Guri Skedsmo and Jorunn Møller

Introduction

The Norwegian education system is part of the Nordic welfare state: for the most part publicly organised and financed and aimed at providing equality and the non-discriminatory right of everyone to achieve their desired level of education. Equity is one of the distinctive features of this model, on which social democracy as a political movement and broader ideology has had a crucial impact, and the system stands out as one of the most equitable worldwide, with small differences among schools (OECD 2012a).

Since the end of the 1980s, the Norwegian educational system has gone through major reforms, influenced largely by new managerial ideas. Strategies to renew the public sector have been promoted as New Public Management (NPM) (Christensen and Lægreid 2011b). During the late 1980s and 1990s, NPM did not directly challenge the established tradition of schooling, since its main consequences were the restructuring of the local school administration at municipal level in terms of deregulation, horizontal specialisation and management by objectives. To date, marketisation as a principle has been less espoused in Norway, probably because the market in school choice for students and parents exists only in the larger cities. The population in Norway is widely dispersed, and decentralised settlement is still a desirable political aim for most political parties. Moreover, the comprehensive educational system remains strongly rooted in traditional ideologies and norms, and procedures for approving private schools are strictly regulated.

However, the development of NPM changed direction and picked up speed when Norway was listed below the average of Organisation for Economic Co-operation and Development (OECD) members by the Programme for International Student Assessment (PISA) in the early 2000s. The need for new

54 Guri Skedsmo and Jorunn Møller

assessment tools to measure and monitor students' performance levels, strong leadership in schools and accountability became key issues in the public debate on education, which centred increasingly on students' achievements in basic skills as the main indicator of educational quality (Møller and Skedsmo 2013; Skedsmo 2009). New assessment policies with an emphasis on performance measurement, expectations about the use of data to improve education, and emerging accountability practices characterise the transition process over the last decade. Yet we have limited knowledge about how managers at the municipal level and principals translate demands and respond to new expectations about performance management in Norwegian schools. This chapter aims to fill that gap.

The present study explores how new modes of school governing are shaped and played out locally, with a particular focus on managerial elements, operative function and underlying logic. Moreover, we investigate how school principals engage with demands for increased performance and accountability, as well as their involvement in shaping and changing these governing structures. The study describes how one municipality has introduced and developed managerial approaches to school governing.

We start by briefly describing some distinguishing features of NPM adopted in Norway. The next sections outline the methodology and data sources, after which a thematic analysis of the data is provided. We conclude the chapter by highlighting tensions and paradoxes in Norwegian educational policy and the persistent dilemmas that are at the core of school leaders' work.

NPM reform in the Norwegian education system

Student performance data as a quality indicator and the means to generate such data were first added to the policy agenda in Norway after the OECD review of Norwegian education in 1988 (OECD 1988–89). The focus on outcomes achieved in relation to formulated goals and targets represents a key element of the NPM framework. Generally, during the 1990s, Norway was reluctant to adopt the new managerialism. After the publication of the first PISA results in 2001, a new discourse emerged, more insistent than anything previously, on educational quality and holding school leaders and teachers to account. In 2005, the parliament decided on a system for assessing national educational quality, called the National Quality Assessment System (NQAS).

According to current national educational policies in Norway, the key to improvement lies in the use of performance data and output controls. Local authorities, school principals and teachers are expected to use this information to improve their practice in ways that enhance student outcomes, particularly national test results (Skedsmo 2009). Reforms in the education sector during the 2000s have been largely shaped by managerialism, but Norway has employed only moderate incentives and sanctions linked to outcomes achieved. Interestingly, the monitoring and controlling aspects are concealed in the national policy rhetoric by a discourse that focuses on learning and development (Skedsmo 2011).

Although professional autonomy was still emphasised in the latest reform, the Knowledge Promotion (K06), trust in the profession itself seems to be replaced by trust in the results. On one hand, it was argued that the managerial approach to education aimed at ensuring a basic standard for all, by levelling out disadvantages; on the other hand, it was a push for de-bureaucratisation and de-centralisation, ostensibly allowing for more differentiation and specialisation (Møller and Skedsmo 2013).

New approaches to school governing have been developed in many municipalities that are responsible for the quality of schools. In policy documents local elected politicians are defined as *school owners*. The national government expects that municipalities use performance data to enhance educational quality.

The key features of NPM, 'the four Ms', as outlined in Chapter 1, can be identified in some of the larger cities in Norway. New titles have been created for managers at the municipal level, who are often trained and accredited as managers using business models. They may or may not have an educational background. Managerial elements include a combination of performance measurement, quality indicators, target setting, accountability and the use of incentives and sanctions. Much faith is put in assessment tools that provide data and information. Results from national tests are used locally for benchmarking, the basis on which schools aim to perform better than the municipal average (Skedsmo 2011). Many Chief Education Officers (CEOs) at municipal level also increasingly use performance-related pay to reward principals who can demonstrate good results in national tests in literacy, numeracy and English.

At the same time, the welfarist legacy, which emphasises education for the public good, remains strong, mediating the reading, interpretation and shaping of international trends. However, conflicting rationales identified as neoliberalism or technical–economic rationality are gaining ground. One of the main tensions is between discourses rooted in socially democratic ideologies, linked to notions of equity, participation and comprehensive education, and discourses of competition and privatisation which underpin NPM. The latter also includes strong leaders and entrepreneurs driving the modernisation project in education, and in many municipalities the logic of contractualism has been successfully institutionalised. The use of new evaluation technologies both by managers at the municipal level and principals to monitor student outcomes can be read as a shift towards what has been termed organisational professionalism, which incorporates standardised work procedures and relies on external regulation and accountability measures (Evetts 2009). It echoes the management discourse promoted by the OECD, where performance orientation is closely connected to output control.

A Norwegian study has identified how teachers are apparently redefining professionalism in this new regime of governing. While holding to classical professional ideals, teachers have become more proactive in terms of creating legitimacy for their work (Mausethagen 2013). Although cautious privatisation[1] is promoted nationally, to date elements linked to a market ideology are evident only in larger cities where competition among schools is possible, and to some degree in upper secondary education. Norway is comparable in size to Britain, but has only five million inhabitants. The population is widely dispersed, and many of the schools are quite small. In small municipalities far from the cities, managerial accountability is expected to happen 'some time' in the future.

Methodology and data sources

This chapter draws mainly on content analysis of selected policy documents that describe the procedures, tools and processes for local school governing in a particular municipality, which happens to be one of the largest cities in Norway. The city was chosen because it has taken a lead in stimulating national debates about testing and achievement scores. We identified and selected three key policy documents for analysis:

- Doc. 1: 'Key Principles for Management by Objectives and Results' describes elements in the school governing system (emphasis on quality management, quality indicators and the online platform where schools can access their results);
- Doc. 2: 'Strategic Chart', based on balanced scorecard, presents prioritised areas, objectives and targets for schools and local administration;
- Doc. 3: 'Guidelines for Comprehensive Risk Management' states the key principles for risk management and preventive measures to identify and reduce risk factors.

The first reading of these documents concentrated on identifying important features in the local school governing system. The second reading focused on the functions of the different tools, accompanying accountabilities, use of incentives or sanctions and inherent logic, with a view to exploring stakeholders' perceptions of the implementation of these concepts and tools. In addition, the Chief Education Officer (CEO) and three principals at three different types of schools were interviewed[2] (see Table 4.1).

TABLE 4.1 Criteria for selection of schools

Criteria/school	School 1	School 2	School 3
Location/SES	Students coming from families with high SES	Mixed group of students – high and low SES	Students coming from families with low SES
School type and number of students	Lower secondary school 420	Primary school 670	Lower secondary school 350
% of minority students	7%	37%	65%

The principal in School 1 is in mid-career, the principal in School 2 is at an early stage in her career and the principal in School 3 is a veteran. The interviews were conducted in locations chosen by the informants. All interviews were audiotaped and transcribed, and the two researchers independently analysed the transcripts to identify emergent themes and characteristics of management approaches. Our presentation of the findings includes some illustrative excerpts from the interviews.

Findings

During the last 20 years, administrative structures with clear definitions of tasks and responsibilities have been established. Each school represents a self-governing unit, and the main type of accountability can be characterised as managerial through hierarchical relationships: the school principals monitor the teachers' work, the principals are monitored by officers at the municipal level and the CEO is accountable to the elected local politicians.

Procedures, tools and processes highlighted in key policy documents

Analysis of the selected policy documents yielded three key features of the local governing system (see Table 4.2).

Hands-on professional management represents an overall management concept for this municipality. It relates to the establishment of schools as self-governing units, with management ensured by different tools. *Performance management* stands out as the main pillar for governing. Objectives and targets are specified in a 'strategic chart', which, together with performance indicators and measures of performance, is the most important tool for monitoring. Performance indicators are divided into three categories: 1) key statistics and facts about the schools and their resources; 2) student outcomes in national tests, local screening tests, the National Student Survey and the local survey of students' learning environments; and 3) self-evaluation of efforts and results in strategic development areas.

The local education authority has developed an extensive plan for testing throughout the school year. The results are used to set targets and initiate efforts to improve, monitor results and hold key actors to account. Students' performance in tests is used to identify those who achieve below the critical limit. The underlying logic is performativity in terms of identifying dysfunctional organisation and management.

The management contract provides a basis for the annual performance appraisal of principals. This reviews the previous year's achievements and sets objectives and targets for the next year, which are negotiated by principals and municipal officers. Salaries may be adjusted accordingly: if targets are achieved or exceeded, the principal can receive an annual salary increase of 3000–4000 euro. Data aggregated from individual schools are publicly accessible, creating

58 Guri Skedsmo and Jorunn Møller

TABLE 4.2 Key features of local school governing

Key features	Tools	Functions	Sanctions/ incentives	Logic
Performance management	Balanced scorecard Measures of performance Management contracts Performance appraisals	Output control Accountability Setting targets	Monitoring Pay-for-performance School reputation	Performativity Contractualism
Risk management	Risk factors Counteractive measures	Process control Accountability	Monitoring	Avoid failure in achieving targets
Financial management	Budget Audit	Output control Accountability	'Put schools under administration', keep the surplus	Budget discipline

reputational risk to schools and their principals. This may have consequences for the enrolment of students. Although most parents at primary level choose a school near their home, they are in principle free to choose any school.

In recent years, *risk management* has become a central feature in school governing. It is defined as an 'analytical tool to ensure that every threat to goal attainment is taken into account and properly managed' (Doc. 3: 12). The analysis involves identifying important factors to achieve targets and assessing possible risks and taking action to mitigate them. School principals are required to develop a plan for each action, with targets, timelines and responsible persons, and are accountable for the implementation and timing of relevant measures to avoid failure to achieve targets.

The third element is *financial management*. Key figures, budgeting and audits are used to control output and hold principals accountable, the underlying logic being to establish budget discipline.

The next sections deal with how the CEO and three principals interpret and translate the policy into practice.

Enactment of policy at the municipal level

The CEO has headed the education sector for over 10 years, consistently promoting a strong focus on classroom practices and student learning: 'My aim all the time was to establish a system with clear expectations and a practice where we can demonstrate effects on student learning'. She describes this as both a self-defined mission and a mandate from city politicians. Leadership has attained a mantra-like status for her, 'leadership, leadership, leadership' is the solution for schools that score low in academic achievement. Accordingly, she has worked in close collaboration with the Norwegian Business School, which offers a master's programme in management that stresses general leadership skills and the principal's role in implementing policies to raise students outcomes (Møller and Ottesen 2011).

The CEO emphasises the need to develop solid structures in the school system and transparent systems for documenting learning outcomes:

> The idea was ... to establish evidence-based practices in schools. ... The principal has a management contract ... this is part of our balanced scorecard system ... They have a strategic chart ... this is part of our governing tools which we follow up on.

She claims that setting high expectations for student achievement, keeping track of principals' and teachers' professional development needs and holding them accountable for results are keys to school improvement. The management contract is a useful monitoring tool. At the same time, she criticises the national educational authorities for 'accepting' low academic scores and weak leadership in many schools, questioning how it is possible to claim that Norway offers equal opportunities for a good education for all within such a low-stakes system, and arguing for the need to act to avoid sliding backwards. Setting high expectations for students is important, particularly so for students from a minority background:

> I do not like to talk about minority language students; I prefer focusing on students who do not speak Norwegian properly. We need to create appropriate help and opportunities for these students because often they do not have support from their parents. There is a risk that they will not fulfil their potential if they do not speak Norwegian fluently.

The CEO is pleased with her accomplishments over the last 10 years, particularly when reflecting on the situation in which she started this job:

> When I started in this municipality, we had creative teaching practices, good teachers and all that ... there is no doubt about that. But there was no direction [knocks on the table for emphasis], there was no structure and there was no focus on results [knocks on the table].

She strongly disagrees with those who argue that teaching in this city has become more bureaucratised during her leadership, because 'we simply need to have control over learning processes'. She also 'models' the type of conversations she expects principals to have with teachers:

> What outcomes did you achieve last year? What is your ambition now? How are you going to work with your students to fulfil their potential? Why did

60 Guri Skedsmo and Jorunn Møller

your students perform less well in language than last year? And so on. It is a matter of what kind of expectations you have. Then, of course, the principal has to create conditions for the teachers to accomplish their goals.

Her deputy directors check on each principal twice a year, asking questions such as: 'What are your ambitions? What went well last year? How do you explain the performance data in your school?' Her style can be characterised as 'hands-on professional management'.

Responses to policy at the school level

The principals in this study have a positive perception of this governing system and the strong focus on students' academic achievements. They all endorse the clear expectations conveyed by the CEO and her emphasis on striving to enhance students' learning and provide them with the best possible foundation for the future. Moreover, they are satisfied with the ways they are monitored at municipal level and emphasise that they maintain a good dialogue about student achievement and maximising their school's potential by taking the context (e.g. demography) and challenges into account. The results of national tests and the municipality's own tests represent the most important quality indicator for principals. Principals use the national test results with a view to initiating strategies for improvement.

The strong performance focus seems to place extra emphasis on the systems and tools used by teachers to monitor and track students' learning. In all three schools, the students are tested at the end of each work period, i.e. after 1–2 weeks. The primary school has implemented a weekly quiz covering the main subject areas students have studied during the week. The results are used to adjust the work plan. If the students appear to have missed out on important areas, they are offered repetition classes.

In the two lower secondary schools, students' learning is tracked through tests administered by the teachers every second week. Additionally, they are assessed on the overall topic across the different subjects. Results from these tests form the basis for grading and recording the progress of individual students.

Principals hold dialogues with teachers, establish routines for collaboration and exchange across teacher teams, and prioritise target areas. In the primary school, the students did not perform well on the national tests in literacy two years ago. The principal met with the fifth grade teachers to target the problem areas and with the fourth grade teachers in order to learn from previous years. She also decided that the teachers should devote fifteen minutes every day to reading with their students, focusing on reading strategies. The next year, the school improved its literacy results and achieved its goal of performing above the average of primary schools in the municipality.

National test data are used to stream students, but the groups are not established permanently, as this would conflict with the Education Act. We identified some differences between schools related to practices for streaming and formulating learning goals. In one of the lower secondary schools, the students' goals are aligned with their achievement levels. In the primary school,[3] the principal states that there is no reason not to have the same learning goals and assessment criteria for all students. The school has invested time in formulating understandable and measurable learning goals and the teachers have worked intensively on differentiated ways of providing feedback to students. The students then differ according to their respective degrees of accomplishing their aims. The school also hopes that teachers will work more effectively on the mandatory written reports that are used as the basis for dialogues between teachers, individual students and their parents.[4]

All three principals realise the need to monitor and support teachers' work in the classroom. In two of the schools, a 'school walkthrough' [*skolevandring*] has been implemented, where the principals conduct brief lesson observations. However, the principals unfortunately cannot do this as often as they would like because of their heavy administrative workload. According to the principals, the teachers in these schools find the observations and subsequent feedback useful and a sign that their work is valued. In the third school, this practice is not yet established.

In one of the schools, the principal regularly meets students who are performing below the critical level, and they sign a contract agreeing on the learning goals for the next six months. When he follows up on these students, he finds the intervention has made a significant difference, because the students take it more seriously than discussions with their teachers.

All the principals have management contracts that state their targets, which are evaluated in two annual performance appraisals with officers at municipal level. One of the principals admits not reaching his targets in the beginning because he was too ambitious. However, he has learned to become more strategic:

> To begin with, it was hard to articulate aims that you could actually achieve. After a while, you become more strategic when you formulate the aims so that it is actually possible to accomplish them.
>
> (Principal in School 3)

National test results are often used as a quality indicator on which the municipality may decide to award principals a salary increase. Additionally, the principals have contracts with their teachers and, in the annual performance appraisals, they assess the teachers' achievements according to the development aims and target areas stated in their contracts.

Although the principals in the three selected schools may agree with the local policies and strong performance orientation, they also reflect on the implications of such a one-sided focus. This came out particularly in the interview with the veteran principal of the school with the most heterogeneous student group. On one hand, he thinks the schools in this municipality have

62 Guri Skedsmo and Jorunn Møller

profoundly improved their practices through their strong performance orientation. On the other hand, he points out some vital aspects of education that seem to receive less attention:

> ... the aspects you focus on get better ... The general part of the curriculum gets less attention; it is saved for public sermons. In our school, we have struggled with social issues among the students and we need to focus on these issues in parallel ... If not ... then the consequences could be very bad for the students involved.
>
> (Principal in School 3)

The principal in the high SES school is also somewhat critical of stressing basic skills to the extent that schools feel obliged to direct all their efforts towards improving students' performance in these skills. She states:

> The students need to develop themselves in a range of areas and I am critical of putting the general part of the curriculum aside to focus only on developing basic skills.
>
> (Principal in School 1)

However, it seems that there is less leeway for discussing such issues at the municipal level. The three principals emphasise that they focus on student learning outcomes and work systematically to foster a conducive learning environment by enhancing collaboration among teachers and establishing effective routines to support practice. By doing so, they try to align high performance expectations with specific school priorities and their own sets of professional norms and values.

Discussion

The present research exemplifies how managerial modes are (or may be) shaped and implemented as part of local school governing in Norway. Our analysis of local policy documents shows how managerialism is integrated into accountability policy, with the aim of setting clear performance targets to hold schools to account for achieved outcomes. The principal's role is framed as that of an organisational manager, expected to respond to external demands and the needs of families or 'consumers'. Performance expectations are closely related to national and municipal test results. By adding risk management, the intention is to ensure that threats to the attainment of goals are taken into account and managed. In certain ways, it implies control of processes leading up to educational outcomes and a kind of rational calculation of possible failure. Financial incentives connected to management contracts are a further motivation to achieve targets.

The document analysis and the interview with the CEO clearly demonstrate how managerial elements have been introduced in local school governing, enabling strong performance orientation through management by objectives and results, transparent structures and processes to monitor school results, and explicit expectations of key actors to improve learning outcomes. Even though the study is small, the interviews with the principals exemplify how their translation of policy is mainly a process of compliance. The principals' understanding of the mission and priorities of education largely chime with that of the CEO. Two of the principals acknowledge some dangers with performativity, as it directs the focus on what can be tested, while other aspects of education receive less attention unless the schools specifically prioritise them. The veteran principal is concerned with social problems among his students, and in his discussions with municipal officers he has to justify the time spent on this issue. Nonetheless, all three principals embrace the strong focus on learning outcomes, realising that their hard, systematic work produces results and highlights how teachers can support students' learning. They also emphasise the importance of analysing data to decide on the actions that will have the most impact on school improvement. The principals' justification of their actions with respect to achieving targets reflects the culture of accountability that exists in the municipality. If the targets are not achieved, the principals must provide explanations; if the results continue to decline, their performance will be scrutinised or they may be advised to find another job.

Compared to the ways in which accountability practices are implemented in relation to high-stakes testing in other countries (e.g. the UK or the USA), low test scores do not lead to closure of schools or dismissal of principals in Norway. Still, accountability policies do influence principals' and teachers' work (Mausethagen 2013). Schools are keen to perform well in the tests because of concerns about their reputation in their municipality (Skedsmo and Mausethagen 2016). The school results are publicly available after some years of restricted availability, and all the schools know how they performed in relation to one another. The use of management contracts and performance appraisals for principals strengthen the basis for the development of performativity. Moreover, accountability is enforced by implementing consequences if the school or the principal fails to meet performance targets.

So far, international research has not verified the effectiveness of high-stakes systems in terms of significantly sustainable impacts (Figlio and Ladd 2010; Fryer 2011). On the contrary, depending on what kind of accountability practices are applied, particularly regarding sanctions, elements such as performance based incentives may lead some teachers to cheat in order to meet their targets. The extent of such occurrences is unknown, but research in major American cities has documented such trends (Meier *et al.* 2004).

The CEO's ideas on the characteristics of teacher effectiveness chime with those suggested by research on overall school effectiveness. It is argued that achieving equality of opportunity is possible when educators are determined that all students can succeed and that this expectation should override the impact of structural disadvantage or a culture that emphasises disadvantage and marginalisation. In a multicultural environment, it is sensible to focus on

64 Guri Skedsmo and Jorunn Møller

basic skills such as literacy and numeracy to give all students the opportunity for social mobility and social access. Access depends on students' proficiency in the Norwegian language and can be aligned to the legacy of a 'common school for all' and of abolishing the class-based society.

The CEO is very clear in what she expects from her schools. At the same time, she advocates a monocultural approach to teaching and learning. Although she expresses concern for students from linguistic and ethnic minority groups, she does not talk about explicit strategies for inclusion but instead focuses on minority students' deficits in speaking Norwegian fluently. It is crucial to enhance basic skills for all students, but inclusion of minority students does not appear to be a strategic priority for her. As Kalantzis and Cope (1999) argued, it would require space and time to develop critical conversations about inclusion in local schools.

In this municipality, individual schools seem free to prioritise such conversations and align the need to promote social competencies with their efforts to drive up performance in basic skills. The emphasis on performativity may encourage principals to be more responsive to external demands. Schools may also experience tensions between improving test scores and the need to equalise learning opportunities and accommodate cultural and socio-economic differences. As a solution, some schools use the national and municipal test data to divide students into groups according to their academic achievement, in an attempt to standardise and make teachers' work more efficient. Standardisation at group level becomes a means to fulfil legal requirements on adapting teaching according to individual needs and abilities. Since the Education Act prohibits streaming in permanent groups in compulsory education, schools have to change the group structure quite frequently.

If student test results are the outcome measure that must be met, schools will be likely to focus on them at all costs. Therefore, as equity is not included as an outcome in economic models of agency theory and public choice, there is a risk of sacrificing equity in the implementation of managerial policies in education.

Conclusion

In this chapter, we have explored how new modes of school governance are shaped and played out. The analysis shows how NPM features are evident in the public provision of education in the municipality studied. The CEO's approach can be characterised as hands-on professional management, and she expects the principals to implement similar strategies. Thus, there are explicit expectations and measures of performance for principals and schools. All these elements show NPM interventions in education and a shift towards organisational professionalism (Evetts 2009), which may replace the reliability of professional ethics with external forms of regulation and accountability. From the interviews with principals it is evident that this new focus brings good results, but at the same time can indicate a narrow focus and a neglect of key features of the legacy of education in Norway, such as citizenship and democracy. Moreover, it can divert from challenges at local school level unless the principals tackle these themselves. Considering these aspects as well as responding to new performance expectations create dilemmas for the principals.

A large emphasis on control of outputs is noticeable, as well as on avoidance of risk. On the one hand, the underlying logic of the managerial elements identified in this local system signifies accountability practices concentrating on performativity. On the other hand, the logic inherent in such elements implies identifying failures in specific practices and systems, which can be traced back to the decisions and performances of individual persons. If the search for failure becomes too dominant, principals may adopt certain strategies in order to avoid negative consequences. Over time, this could imply changes which break with the legacy of professional autonomy and trust in the profession.

Despite variation in the ways the 428 municipalities in Norway have adopted managerial ideas in their local governing system, certain trends may be identified across the country (cf. Karseth, Møller and Aasen 2013). Based on the analysis of documents and the interview data, we argue that the language and local governing practices are changing. Introducing management principles into education has allowed for a reinterpretation of the educational process in terms of an economic transaction. The learner is often described as a consumer, the teacher as the provider and education as a 'commodity' to be delivered (Møller 2007). This new language may erode a broader discussion about education for citizenship over the long term (Biesta 2004).

It may be questioned whether traditional egalitarian values, concepts of equity, are being challenged by these new managerial elements, particularly performativity. However, even though multiple managerial devices have entered educational policy, the narrative of a common public school for all remains as a strong legacy. While equity refers to an appreciation of diversity that values the students' different abilities and competencies, measurement and standardisation imply identifying and aiming to bridge achievement gaps. Such an approach may indicate a belief in minimising or suppressing individual differences. Whether Norway will maintain its legacy of valuing the common school for all as a tenet of equal educational opportunity remains an open question.

Notes

1 According to the Education Act, it is not permitted to make profits from private schools, and companies that have tried to bypass the law have lost their license and can no longer be in charge of schools.
2 These interviews were conducted in 2011 as part of Guri Skedsmo's postdoc project and the Vifee-project which she led together with Therese N. Hopfenbeck.
3 In primary schools, there is no grading, but parents meet the teachers and discuss their children's progress. These schools also provide written reports on the students' progress.
4 The Education Act states that all students in Norway are entitled to have two annual assessment dialogues with their teachers, in which the parents also participate.

5

REFORMING SWEDISH EDUCATION THROUGH NEW PUBLIC MANAGEMENT AND QUASI-MARKETS

Nafsika Alexiadou and Lisbeth Lundahl

Introduction

Considered for a long time a prominent example of a social democratic welfare state, Sweden until the mid-1980s organized schooling on a highly centralized and, in detail, regulated model with an aim of prioritizing equality and justice in education. In one of Europe's most swift and radical shifts in policy orientation, Swedish education reforms in the early 1990s introduced strong elements of privatization and marketization in schools. In the early 2000s, the rapidly growing number of pupils in private (non-fee paying, tax funded) 'free schools', and the restructuring of the free-school sector constitute the most striking aspects of the reforms. However, this obscures the fact that even a majority of the public schools have been subsumed under the market logic. Privatization and marketization were preceded by a decentralization process starting in the 1970s and at that time primarily marked by ideas of strengthening the democratic influence of local political bodies and citizens. Soon however, ideas and technologies of New Public Management (NPM), for example government by objectives and results, and the extended autonomy and responsibilities of municipalities and schools, got impetus. NPM of education in Sweden shares many of the generic features of NPM in other systems in Europe. But, viewing the Swedish case through the lens of re-contextualization and mediation (Gunter and Fitzgerald 2013a, b), these radical changes have been enacted against widely shared principles of equality and inclusiveness amongst teachers and large parts of the population. NPM has evolved into a form of governance where seemingly contradictory elements of steering co-exist. Some of these contradictions are clear from Table 5.1 where we draw out the key features of New Public Management in Swedish education.

This chapter will describe and analyze one of the key dimensions of NPM in Swedish education, the radically new management of the school sector that is now represented by a mix of private and state actors that compete over state resources. We shall account for the peculiarities of a system that still contains older ideals of 'education for all' in a highly marketized system.

Throughout the chapter we use the terms 'marketization' and 'privatization', to describe public sector reforms that have changed the relationships between the state, the market and citizens. The terms do not denote the historical origins or eventual outcomes in the balance of power between the public and the private – these need to be described and analyzed in the specificity of the national contexts and historical circumstances that gave rise to them (Alexiadou 2013). We draw on Montin (2006) who defines markets in social services as a situation where 'several producers compete over public tasks and/or when internal steering systems are developed with the market and industry as models' (Montin 2006: 7). In the Swedish case, the direction of marketization points to the creation of a mixed economy of schooling, a quasi-market where public and private providers funded and controlled by the state compete over state funding for education, and where there has been a significant transfer of 'service production' from the government to the private sector (Starr 1988: 14). Discussions on privatization need to take into account both the locus of responsibility for the provision of education, and the type of education delivered in the mixed economy of education markets (Ball and Youdell 2008; Lundqvist 1988). The background and specific characteristics of these processes in Sweden are described throughout the chapter.

In the Swedish case, New Public Management refers to the reforms of public administration of education services (how the sector is governed and incentivized), but also to overlapping reforms of privatization. Thus, it is examined within a broader context of welfare state reforms, and analyzed as an ideological mechanism to bring more fundamental shifts in a) the balance between state and non-state activity in social services, and b) the values and goals of the welfare state. Drawing on Lundahl (2002) our analysis of policies will be based on a review of: a) the contextual issues around the reforms, to include the historical, economic and political structures that have framed education policies; b) the policy process itself, that describes the definitions of particular system educational goals, forms of governance, and distribution of funding; and c) issues of implementation and outcomes where we present the consequences of the policies and the links between policy outcomes and policy outputs.

'Modernization' of the social democratic welfare-state (1950s–1990)

Continuously in office between 1932 and 1976 and normally with 45 to 50 per cent of the vote, the Swedish Social Democratic Labour Party (Svenska Arbetarepartiet, SAP) held a uniquely strong position in international comparisons during this period of time. As a part of the construction of the modern Swedish welfare state, the education reforms in the 1940s to the 1970s

TABLE 5.1 Key features of New Public Management in education in Sweden

Factors	Ideas	Tools and practices
Managers	State-run interventions into professional knowledge for managers and school leaders, to some extent connected to marketized ideas around changing identities or roles They draw on a mix of bureaucratically rooted practices of professional development and new responsibilities around managerial tasks	Training is provided to school leaders but not in accordance with business models – emphasis more on legal dimensions of school governance Training is provided by the state (through university courses or similar) to all school managers, both in state and independent schools There has been no change of role titles. School leaders are referred to by the same terms as in the 1990s and 2000s School leaders still mainly recruited from within the education profession but their work is increasingly that of a business leader
Managing	A shift from management by rules to management by objectives Increased focus on outcomes in terms of grades and results on national tests Interventions to increase techniques of school visibility through marketing	The generation and use of performance data has clearly increased Schools enjoy very high autonomy in pedagogy and timetabling – within the parameters set by the national curriculum goals Increasing self-evaluation practices for schools, often with school teachers fully involved Teachers' salaries are individually set and negotiated between the head-teacher and individual teachers. There is no process for removing underperforming teachers/head-teachers other than through legal channels if there is impropriety A great surge of marketing activities, especially for schools in densely populated urban areas

Management	Rise of ideas of individualism, user choice, and the ungovernability of a large central state since the 1990s These were combined with ideas of local service responsiveness and democracy through: decentralization of governance and finances, efficiency and effectiveness through supply and demand mechanisms A complete and radical reform of the comprehensive state schooling system, to an extensively marketized system where independent (private) and state (municipal) schools compete over student recruitment A highly decentralized system, with a variety of school providers, but central regulation through a national curriculum, syllabi, and legislation	This aspect of NPM dominates the Swedish education landscape Tax-funded free/independent schools have been established and compete with each other and with municipal schools since the 1990s New providers in the school market, often in the form of large companies that manage large chains of schools for profit. Increasing use of data and league tables in the marketing of the schools The Schools Inspectorate (Skolinspektionen), a national agency, performs all school inspections, including those of private schools
Managerialism	Within schools, workforce management is a mix of bureaucratic and competitive features. There is still a model of collegial and bureaucratic relations between school teachers, managers, and leaders	The managerial role of the school principal is stronger and expressed more clearly in the 2010 Act of Education than in its predecessor of 1985 The discourses of 'equivalence', equality and inclusion, even though under some pressure, are still core to the management of schools The organization of curriculum development varies locally between municipalities and schools

to a large extent, if not exclusively, reflected the social democratic ideology of justice and integration. The reformation and expansion of Swedish primary and secondary education in the post-war period were thus characterised by striving for equality and uniformity to a high degree. Regardless of their social or geographical origin, children were supposed to go to schools of equal and high standards, and young people should have equal opportunities to attend higher education. The big educational reforms of the nine-year comprehensive school (1962) and upper-secondary school (implemented in 1971), where academic and vocational courses and programs were put under the same organizational umbrella, were framed by strong and detailed State governance. Schools and teaching were regulated and controlled through national curricula and syllabi, by a variety of specially destined State subsidies and a vast number of other regulations concerning resources, organization, staff and daily work. Swedish education policies shared important characteristics with the other Nordic countries: an emphasis on education promoting social justice and cohesion, and on equal standards of education, regardless of a child's socio-economic and geographical background. Above all, this materialized in the 1960s and 1970s with the introduction in all the Nordic countries of nine-year comprehensive education with no or very little streaming (Telhaug *et al.* 2004).

In the early 1970s, a twenty-five-year period of political stability and economic growth came to an end, in Sweden as well as in the rest of the Western world. The oil crisis in 1973 hit Swedish basic industries (e.g. wharves, mining and forest industry) hard, and Sweden saw its first recession since the interwar period. At the same time, the political left-wave that had dominated the second part of the 1960s was still powerful and enforced a certain radicalization of the Social Democratic party (Sejersted 2011). Now the political right and industry mobilized to regain 'the problem formulation initiative' and reinstall faith in private enterprise and the market (Lundahl 1997). This neoliberal offensive was intensified in the 1980s and its fruits were reaped in the 1990s. Not least, the neoliberal discursive shift became visible in the 1980s and 1990s, celebrating concepts such as choice, individual responsibility, competition, competence and entrepreneurship. In the 1970s, the social democratic hegemony was increasingly attacked from right and left: the former criticizing the welfare apparatus for being obsolete and inefficient, a 'colossus with clay feet'; while the latter accused the social democrats for failing to reduce fundamental social differences and injustice, and of top-down governing that stifled local initiatives (Lundahl 2002). Furthermore, the perceived cumbersome nature of the local bureaucracies and the difficulties of maintaining high quality at times of cutting costs resulted in public discontent with the effectiveness of services (cf. Blomqvist 2004).

The attempts of the first conservative-liberal coalition government (1976–1982) since the early 1930s to radically transform the public sector met with little success. More importantly, the Social Democrats from the 1980s actively advocated the introduction of NPM as a means of 'modernization', in stark contrast, for instance, to the Danish Social Democratic party that strongly opposed new managerialism at that time (Green-Pedersen 2002). Back in office in 1982–1991 the Social Democrats, in particular the right-wing of the party, initiated renewal work based on ideas of choice, decentralization and contractual relationships in the public sector. For example, the minister of finance Kjell-Olof Feldt advocated large scale reforms of a public sector that he saw as being too big and outdated. Thus, both political pragmatists from within the Social Democrats, and the political right supported the introduction of alternative financing and management of the public sector, with education as one of the main sites where new ideas were tried. This economic and political context paved the way for the conservative-led coalition 1991–1994 to introduce far-reaching reforms that changed a) the role of the State in providing social and educational services, and, b) the way in which services were provided.

The politics of change in the 1990s

Context

In the 1980s, the neoliberal regimes of Reagan and Thatcher heralded a period of ideological and social challenge to welfare systems across Europe. In the early 1990s Sweden experienced a deep recession which resulted in a scaling back of state expenditure at a time when unemployment and refugee immigration grew, and social inequalities increased. In education, worsening economic conditions in the 1990s resulted in considerable reductions, meaning lowered average teaching costs per child, larger classes and decreased grants for a number of tasks, e.g. special education and language instruction of immigrant children (Lundahl 2002). This coincided with another set of political developments that were symbolically significant in that period: the entry of Sweden into the European Union in 1995 following a referendum. The economic and political integration across Europe was seen to take powers away from the nation state, while the processes of regionalization and decentralization were seen as more democratic, 'channeling power downwards' (Hudson 2007: 267). The call for privatizing education was managerially and ideologically driven by the twin beliefs that the central state was unable to govern the sector, coupled with a rise in discourses around individualism and user choice.

Processes: decentralization, creation of semi-autonomous local actors

The Nordic countries have traditionally combined central regulation of local organization and financing in order to attain political goals of equity and equality and have had relatively high levels of local discretion (right of decision), with local governments designed like a political system in miniature with local parties and policies (Page and Goldsmith 1987). A series of decentralization reforms from the 1970s on further increased the local freedom to decide on resources and methods to accomplish the national goals. The decentralization processes were seen as answers to both problems of management, and to the limited influence of local actors (municipalities, local institutions and citizens) on the provision and quality of services. There were increasing difficulties in centrally managing a school sector that was becoming too large and too complex to regulate the quality of its work in any detail.

Several important decentralization steps were taken around the year 1990. Early that year, employer responsibilities for school personnel were transferred to the municipalities despite the strong opposition of teachers who feared that their new employers would be ignorant of the needs of schools. Decisions in 1989 and 1990 meant a clearer division of responsibilities between the state, the municipalities, and schools and a transition from a management by rules to management by objectives took place, giving the local actors considerable freedom to allocate resources and choosing methods to attain the national goals. The 1993 decision to deliver state subsidies for all local services (e.g. education, care of elderly people, street cleaning and refuse collection) as lump sums to the municipalities meant a radical devolution of resource distribution to the local level (Daun and Siminou 2008). Even the responsibility for evaluation, inspection and development work was decentralized to the municipalities. Municipalities and schools were required to have plans for how to achieve educational national and local goals, and municipalities were to deliver quality reports to the National Agency for Education (NAE) annually. At the turn of the millennium Swedish schools had more autonomy in allocating teaching hours, choosing instructional content and methods, and deciding on class sizes than most other countries (OECD 2002).

Principals become managers

The decentralization process was accompanied by a discourse celebrating professional principals and teachers. At a time when local school budgets were subject to considerable cuts, this 'top-down professionalization' was not wholeheartedly embraced by the teachers. In contrast, one may argue that NPM actually helped the principals creating a distinct professional project of their own, separate from that of the teachers (Jarl *et al.* 2012). The role of the school principals was profoundly transformed as a result of the reforms described above. Previously, their work was regulated by the state in great detail. Now the work became increasingly similar to that of a business leader, involving managerial tasks such as planning, budgeting and evaluation. The principals got a high degree of discretion within the wide national curriculum frames and the economic frames given by the municipality (Lundahl 2002; Jarl *et al.* 2012). In the mid-1990s there was a framework agreement between employers and teacher unions where individual performance-related teacher salaries were introduced – yet another local management tool (Lundström, 2012). This was a reform reluctantly supported by teacher unions, after a long period of stagnation of teacher salaries.

School choice and privatization

The decentralization reforms, although not necessarily a manifestation of privatization or NPM, were the necessary precondition for the introduction of quasi-markets in education that were championed vigorously during the coalition liberal-conservative government of 1991–1994, and little questioned by the subsequent Social Democratic governments (1994–2006). In 1992 and 1993 the Parliament passed two so-called 'freedom of choice' bills introducing a legal right to parents to select school for their children by introducing a voucher system, and generous state subsidies for establishing independent (free) schools (Gov. Bill 1991/92: 95; 1992/93: 230)[1]. The rationale behind the school choice reforms was captured by four political arguments:

1   To give parents and children maximum freedom of school-choice. This argument was related to international conventions. To ensure such liberty, equal financial conditions between all schools were seen as necessary.
2   To make schools and municipalities more sensitive and accountable to parental wishes.
3   'Stimulating competition' between schools would raise the quality of schools and the whole education system.
4   Market solutions were seen to offer a more effective and efficient allocation of resources.

Independent schools were by law open to all students who were free to select the school of their choice (NAE 2010). The state (the National Agency for Education, later the Schools Inspectorate) approved new private providers who applied for a license to operate new schools, after consulting the municipalities concerned.

By the mid-1990s, the highly centralized and standardized education services, as well as the (in practice) monopoly of public providers of schooling were at an end. Choice and market mechanisms had been introduced, and the State had parted with most of its earlier steering tools. However, it was still the responsibility of the state to enforce the legal frameworks that regulate schooling (e.g. adherence to the national curriculum, admission policies etc.) and to set the general goals and aims of education by the Education Act. The national curriculum was decided at the central level, and so were the controls of the outcomes and quality of education by the Swedish National Agency for Education (NAE Skolverket) and later the Swedish Schools Inspectorate (Skolinspektionen).

The period 1991–1998, however, also saw reforms that were driven by egalitarian as well as labor market considerations and aimed to retain the inclusive character of schooling. Early childhood education became more closely connected to primary and secondary school through common organization and the introduction of a national preschool curriculum. In upper secondary education, stronger curricular connections were built between the vocational and academic programs, both giving access to higher education. Adult education reforms offered possibilities to people with limited education skills to improve their employment potential.

Consequences

The reforms of the 1990s came about during a period of steep recession that resulted in budgetary cuts in all welfare services. Extensive decentralization and 'professionalization from above' were therefore often perceived as a way of politicians to avoid difficult decisions by transferring them to the local level. Local fragmentation and differences started to grow – perhaps the most visible consequence of the reforms in the 1990s. Furthermore, the two 'freedom of choice reforms' changed conditions for public schools. Now public and private schools began competing for pupils, and hence funding. Research studies have reported increasing variations over time in pupil performance by socio-economic and gender dimensions, and stronger differentiation between urban and rural schools, as well as between public and private schools having different ethnic and socio-economic intake of pupils (NAE 2010; Bunar 2011). This development started in the 1990s and got impetus in the 2000s. At the same time, the 1990s saw a continuation of the positive trend in access to education across all levels, with small increases in the number of young people continuing to post-compulsory secondary education, even though, given the economic downturn, their transitions to the labour market were harder than in earlier periods.

The 2000s and 2010s: Accelerating privatization and new forms of state governing

Context

Swedish education and education policies at the beginning of the twenty-first century have been shaped and framed by several parallel and partly coinciding general trends that are not new but which have gained further momentum: first, a tangible strengthening of knowledge-capitalism, that is an emphasis on education and research as crucial means to improve economic growth and competitiveness; second, a related transformation of the nation state to actively support such a development ('the competitive state'); third, the increasing impact of international comparative assessment in the field of education, the PISA investigations being the most influential, and fourth, the increasing commercialization of the education sector itself.

Processes: market management

The results of the radical changes of the welfare state of the 1990s manifested themselves more clearly in the next decade. Initially, the free school sector largely consisted of single schools run by, for example, parental and staff cooperatives, faith, and other interest organizations – by and large non-profit institutions. A fast restructuring of the private sector took place from the millennium, in terms of owner concentration and transition to for-profit organizations. By 2010, almost ninety per cent of the free schools were run by public limited companies, with possibilities to extract profits for their owners, i.e. without having to reinvest them in the company. Within a few years, three of the four largest Swedish companies in the upper secondary sector were purchased by foreign venture capital companies, none of them previously engaged in education (Lundahl *et al.* 2013).

Throughout the 1990s and 2000s, private schools faced weaker regulation compared to municipal schools. Even though they had to comply with the same overarching expectations as the municipal schools, they had fewer legal responsibilities to provide costly premises (gym halls, science laboratories, school meal premises), and services (health care, school libraries), nor were they obliged to employ specially qualified career guidance staff, or to provide facilities for disabled students (Erixon Arreman and Holm 2011: 641). As a result of these lower levels of expectation, private schools could make profits from such 'savings'. But the main source of profit for private schools comes from reducing the costs of staff by having lower teacher-student ratios. Even if the new 2011 Education Act means that free schools now have the same regulations as public schools in most respects, their remit to act as businesses and extract profits is still fairly large.

In 2013 a total of 13 per cent of Swedish pupils at compulsory school attended a free school, and that figure was 26 per cent for pupils in upper secondary (post-compulsory) level with large variations between the urban conurbations and the sparsely populated municipalities. In addition, the free school market has rapidly changed since its emergence in the 1990s, when most free schools were small single entities. In the early 2010s, the private school market was dominated by large groups of companies that offer schooling in a 'chain' model. In 2015 the largest company, AcadeMedia, had 450 preschools and schools at different levels, 12,000 employees and 90,000 students across the country. In 2013–14 its annual turnover was 679 million euro, with a profit margin of 7.1 per cent (AcadeMedia, 2014).

Managing by performance and quality control

Since the turn of the millennium, several measures have been taken both to raise schools' performance and efficiency but also to strengthen state control over the highly fragmented school market. The 2010 Education Act meant less generous policies for establishing new free schools, and also that similar legislation for public and independent schools should be applied (Lundahl 2014). In the 2000s, the state gradually took a more active role in assessing quality and results. Initially this was conducted by the Swedish National Agency for Education, but since 2008 this is the responsibility of the new School Inspectorate, which has more 'muscle' and possibility to sanction than their predecessor (Rönnberg 2012).

During the 2000s, grading and national testing increased considerably from an initially modest level. SIRIS, NAE's information system on results and quality, was made available in 2001. It includes quantitative and qualitative information on national test results and final marks in compulsory schools; basic facts about schools; pupils and teachers; and reports from quality investigations and school inspections. It also contains a statistical tool for analyzing relationships between school results and a number of local background factors. Although the intention with SIRIS was not to create league tables, the media use it for this purpose and schools commonly use it for marketing themselves. In 2010, a compulsory principal program was introduced to train school leaders on issues around legislation and other management duties. The 2010 Education Act both clarified the responsibilities of principals and expanded their rights when it comes to designing and developing the school's organization.

School managers

In the early 2000s, the role of the principal changed from being a pedagogical leader to being a manager. In the name of quality assurance, various control techniques were introduced, including the setting of standards, audits, benchmarks and indicators, and international comparisons of performance. The focus of assessment was mainly on students and school performance as measured by student performance, but the individual teachers were also scrutinized, following similar developments across Europe (Normand 2012; Ozga *et al.* 2011). In the 2000s, the rapid growth of the free school market and the sharpened competition over students resulted in marketing of schools, profiles and programs becoming a more and more time consuming and costly aspect of principals' work.

Consequences

Similar to reports from other countries that introduced choice reforms in education, as the decade of the 2000s was progressing, the Swedish schooling system began showing signs of increasing stratification of schools mainly in the big urban areas, *inter alia* reflecting the degree of popularity and perceived status of schools. There is not enough evidence to suggest that this is the outcome of the privatization reforms. There is, however, research that relates the choice reforms and the competitive, marketized school system to increasing segregation of 'types' of schools (Östh *et al.* 2013).

There is little evidence that the new mixed system of public and private schools has produced better education outcomes for children. Sweden was highly ranked in the early PISA studies (2000 and 2003), both in academic results and in terms of equity for boys and girls, and students from different socio-economic backgrounds and origins. The low variance between Swedish schools was seen as an outcome of a system designed along egalitarian policy lines (Fredriksson *et al.* 2009). But the above-average performance of Sweden in the early PISA surveys on literacy and mathematics was not sustained, with student performance in consistent decline between the 2000 and 2012 surveys in the three core subjects (OECD 2013a). This trend, which ranks the country below both the OECD and EU averages, is observed throughout municipal and independent schools and applies to all groups of students (although the performance gap is larger between native-born and foreign-born children).

Sweden in an international context – policy learning and policy convergence

Certain international organizations play an important role in the examination of any national system of education since a) they attempt (and to some extent) define what are the desirable goals of education systems, but also what is problematic; b) they identify instruments for the measurement of problem areas and by doing so reinforce the normative definitions of what is worth pursuing and what is not; c) they propose measures for the reform of schooling (Pereyra *et al.* 2011). In the case of Swedish education reforms, we shall briefly review the policy frameworks provided by the European Union (EU) and the OECD that provide examples of 'processes of gradual global convergence of education discourses' and 'have contributed to new modes of regulation of education policy, with real effects on policy and practice' within the national arena (Alexiadou and Van de Bunt-Kokhuis 2013: 345).

The OECD and the EU

The debates instigated by the publication of international comparative studies have become increasingly politically significant in Sweden. In particular, the PISA studies organized by the OECD have attracted media and policy attention, and have also been used by the Swedish government as the 'international' context that informs their reform programs. The OECD assessment highlighted the problems of human resources (teachers' salaries, teacher shortages), limited learning time in mathematics, and the differences in school infrastructures between Swedish schools in high and low socio-economic areas. The latest OECD report (2014b) also raised issues of Swedish schools' low level of autonomy over curricula and assessment (albeit schools have considerable autonomy over resource allocation and selection of textbooks), the variance between municipal and private schools on issues of autonomy, and a relatively negative disciplinary

78 Nafsika Alexiadou and Lisbeth Lundahl

climate. The OECD interpretation of the Swedish characteristics linked to the declining performance was in line with the assessment of the National Agency for Education, especially around issues of human resources and school variance and their implications for high degrees of differentiation of student attainment.

The PISA studies became 'the catalyst for school policy discussions' both in the work of the National Agency of Education, and with Swedish governments of the late 2000s that focused their attention on the teaching profession and the quality of teacher education (Ringarp and Rothland 2010: 423). In that respect, the PISA studies represent a typical NPM instrument that provided policymakers in Sweden with the political impetus to begin reform, as well as with data to evaluate and to support particular reforms.

A second important international policy framework, even though less 'visible' in political terms in Sweden, is that provided by the European Union. Within the EU itself, the trend of adopting NPM-like techniques for the governance of education had been firmly established in 2000 with the introduction of the Open Method of Coordination (OMC). Since the EU cannot legislate for education, the OMC provides a means of governing education developments through the setting up of 'common agreed objectives' and informal normative pressures on member states to perform as well as others. The Commission fixes guidelines with specific timetables for the achievement of education goals, establishes benchmarks and indicators, translates these into national policies with specific targets, and monitors the progress of education reforms with a particular focus on policy learning (Lange and Alexiadou 2010). In a recent Recommendation, the Council of the EU (2014) drawing on the 2012 PISA survey results, discussed Sweden's National Reform Programme. Furthermore, the Recommendation urges Sweden to put more effort in linking the labour market with schooling, especially for migrant students, and suggested early intervention and support initiatives.

This is typical of a new way of managing education reforms in national systems, in a direction that the Commission together with the Council set through agreed objectives. We do not suggest that NPM ideas have their origins within the EU – they clearly do not – and they pre-date the EU attempt to Europeanize education policy from 2000. But there is an interesting convergence of policy ideas that emanate from national and transnational bodies such as the EU. In recognition that its early monitoring processes have not been effective, the Commission has turned towards more 'strict' instruments of control and is considering further 'peer review' techniques which, even though they have always existed as possibilities within the OMC toolkit, have not yet been used (Alexiadou 2014).

Both the OECD and the EU have identified the low attractiveness of the teaching profession in Sweden as an important obstacle to increasing the quality of education (European Council 2013; OECD 2013a, 2014c). The Swedish government is responding directly to the EU and to PISA recommendations for improving education. In their 2014 report on the National Reform Programme, and through various Ministerial announcements, the government outlined measures for providing weak students with homework help, summer schools, improving declining skills in reading and mathematics, helping students who struggle to complete upper secondary schooling, increasing the numbers of places in tertiary and higher vocational education, and putting in place new investments for the recruitment, development and retention of new teachers (Ministry of Education and Research 2015; Regeringskansliet 2014). In this respect, the NPM governance instruments of benchmarks, indicators and policy learning, as used by the EU and the OECD, interact with the national debates, but also seem to be effective in focusing the political attention of the Swedish government on particular areas of reform. The implementation of these reforms and their political framing is, of course, still firmly within the national government remit.

Some concluding notes: NPM challenged?

Even if the glossy picture of NPM and education marketization has started to crack, not least after the bankruptcy in 2013 of one of the largest school chains in Sweden (JB Ltd) and the poor results in the 2012 PISA study, one can hardly speak of a major retreat from these neoliberal policies. Already the former liberal-conservative government (2006–2014) took some steps with the aim of reducing problems and harm caused by the market arrangements and the extensive decentralization to municipalities and schools. For example, a public investigator was appointed by the Minister of Education to look into the possibility of reinstalling stronger state governing of education but his report, launched in February 2014, has hitherto had little concrete effect. As was mentioned above, certain changes in the Education Act were also made in order to reduce the far-reaching liberties of the free schools. In September 2014 the non-socialist coalition government was replaced by a minority government of the Social Democrats and the Green Party. For several years, a majority of political parties and politicians have argued that profit-making in education is acceptable as long as the state ensures high quality of schooling through proper regulation. In March 2015, however, the new Minister for Education, Gustav Fridolin, appointed a committee with the task of suggesting how to prohibit private profit-making in school companies. Other proposals would indirectly mean stronger state government, if they get support in the Parliament to be realized, e.g. higher investments in order to address the teaching shortages by raising teachers' salaries (a matter normally set by agreements between the social partners) and raising the quality of education in the early years through reducing class sizes, and early intervention strategies. Hence the balance of responsibilities between the central and local state is to be revisited.

Today there seems to be some efforts to strengthen state governing of education and a commitment to more proactive policies towards reducing the differences between advantaged and disadvantaged schools and pupils. There is, however, no discussion about a reversal of the privatization or other NPM processes that seem to be firmly established in public school provision. Furthermore, despite the limitations and often perverse incentives that the parental choice and school competition structures introduce into the system, neither are hitherto being challenged by the policy agenda of the new government.

Note

1 The value of the school voucher for independent schools was initially 85 per cent of the average cost of educating a pupil in a public school, later 75 per cent. From 1996 the value of the school voucher corresponded to the cost per pupil in the public schools, and additional fees were abolished (Green-Pedersen 2002).

PART III
The administrative state

6

NEW PUBLIC MANAGEMENT IN THE FRENCH EDUCATIONAL SYSTEM

Between affirmation of the state and decentralised governance

Jean-Louis Derouet and Romuald Normand

Introduction

The French education administration is proud of its traditions dating back to the Enlightenment and stabilized by the Napoleonic Empire. A lot of educational plans were published during the second part of the 18th century, affirming the following principle: education is the affair of the State; it does not concern families, communities and even less so religious congregations. This led to a great mistrust at the local level which was reinforced by State planning in the 1960s. The latter defined a school catchment area for the registration of pupils according to the location of their home. The same Statist concern inspired the definition of a curriculum focusing on academic disciplines and access to universalism. This French republican tradition is held by key professional bodies such as the Inspection Générale or embodied in the Agrégation (a special selection-based exam to become a high-ranking teacher in French secondary education). It has also penetrated the culture of the teaching profession and the trade-unions' countervailing power. All school modernization projects had to adjust and adapt to this framework: it is the case for French comprehensive schools but also for the implementation of New Public Management (NPM).

The education system is also largely public. A private system, Catholic in its great majority, enrols about 17% of schoolchildren. Since the separation of the Church and the State (1905), this private education is no longer subsidized. However, at the beginning of the Fifth Republic political regime, the Debré Act established a compromise (1959): a private and contracted education is subsidized, but it has to respect State regulations by teaching the same curriculum, by being inspected and in giving the same training for teachers.

From the mid-1970s to the 1980s, the French comprehensive school system (college unique) was implemented by both right-wing and left-wing

84 Jean-Louis Derouet and Romuald Normand

governments. This policy was a promise of democratization for many educators and parents but it did not fulfil their expectations and hopes (Derouet 1992). It led to a crisis of trust in the school system while some intellectuals from both the Left and the Right denounced the 'false democratization' in secondary education which led, for some of them, to the 'defeat of reflection'. It was also challenged by claims for the recognition of ethnic and religious differences affirmed during the last years of the twentieth century (Honneth 2000; Fraser 2013). The mistrust of the French republican tradition towards communities and multiculturalism remains an obstacle in intellectually grasping the issue. In a period in which the European Union is putting stock on the social inclusion of minorities, some parts of French society are tempted by a move back to more traditional definitions of the Republic and secularism. These legacies will be described in the first part of this chapter.

The pessimistic climate regarding the failure of the comprehensive school system facilitated the introduction of some recommendations related to accountability from international organizations (Normand 2011). However, the Left and the Right mainly remain hostile to market ideas in education. They also have doubts about management and managerialism. Traditionally, the Left is attached to the civil service and mistrusts entrepreneurial and managerial discourses. However, there is another Left which is promoting some new ideas about governance, decentralization, local democracy and less State intervention. But it has not led to French policymakers converting to liberalism and free market policies: some of them are only reacting against the bureaucratic State and claim for more efficiency and quality. Overall, the French education system has included some principles of New Public Management in its bureaucratic tradition, but the four Ms as outlined in the Introduction are not a strong feature.

All these issues refer to different values and intertwined national and international political agendas. It is therefore difficult to characterize legacies and changes from the last fifty years. However, it is possible to provide the following analysis regarding the introduction of New Public Management into the French administration: a period of relative openness from the beginning of the 1980s. It was marked by the general law on decentralization, voted in in 1981, and by a new definition of justice imported from British examples (Derouet and Derouet-Besson 2008). This movement is at the root of the Education Priority Areas and school autonomy policies. The first Lisbon conference (2000) amplified the movement by instigating France to take into account the key European recommendations. The first measure linked to this new direction was the Institutional Act related to Finance Laws (Loi Organique relative aux Lois de Finances (LOLF)), unanimously voted in by Parliament in 2001, and which proposed a new organization of public services based on accountability. A second proposed direction is a basic skills framework which replaced the structuration of curriculum in disciplines (2005 Act). This conception is far from the French tradition and its real impact among practitioners can be questioned, but now basis skills are part of the professional and political culture. Comparatively, the past few years have given the impression of a closure of national identity. The traditional conception of the Republic is threatened and the governing socialist party has returned to its fundamental principles: public service, centralization, secularism.

In France, there is no regulation by the market, no business, and no high-stake accountability system. Data are provided by the ministry of education to compare student outcomes but they are used to measure inequality of opportunities and not the performance of teachers and students. The idea of performance is mediated through a bureaucratic apparatus linked to the reform of the State beyond education. The words 'management' and 'managers' do not fit the representation of executives who consider mainly that they are civil servants respecting and applying regulations from the State. The LOLF proposes a general restructuring of public services but it has more impacted on accountancy procedures than on actors and schools. LOLF indicators are guiding the action of principals and inspectors but they have no influence on the conditions of teaching and learning which leave great professional autonomy for teachers. A soft accountability is, however, emerging through the changing missions of the bodies of inspection who develop more audit and self-evaluation procedures, but it remains on an experimental and non-statutory basis. The French education system is entering a post-bureaucratic regime and has implemented its first standards in curriculum, literacy and numeracy. But the idea that schools could make a difference is limited to issues about the school climate considered as a means to fight against violence, dropouts and social exclusion. There are no proposals about linking curriculum, assessment and performance. The French public management is a mix of modernization and conservative values inherited from the legacy of the Republic school system: neutrality of the State, equality of opportunity, common citizenship. It maintains its tradition of centralized standardization and it is blind to the recognition of differences and local particularities. It gives a powerful influence to professional bodies and trade unions at the summit of the State while New Public Management reform remains a top-down, loose process. Even the reform of decentralization and the development of national assessments begun in the 1980–90s has slowed down during the last decade. The NPM in France is characterized by a set of paradoxes which are explained throughout this chapter. It is a singular case in the European landscape of NPM reforms and it must be considered as so. It is also necessary to explain some legacies and narratives which characterize this particular situation.

Legacies, narratives and policies of modernization

The last decades saw an intensive legislative activity. The 1975 School Modernization Act created the comprehensive school system (collège unique). The notion of a 'school development plan' was enshrined by the 1989 Act which remains the backbone of the new education system's regulation. This act is

86 Jean-Louis Derouet and Romuald Normand

an umbrella law which fixes the key principles but gives a certain autonomy at the local level. However, this type of compromise, inspired by progressive education and 'placing the pupil at the centre of the education system', has not really been understood and has even been refused by the great majority of the educative community for whom the transmission of knowledge, teaching (and not learning), has to be the main concern of the school system. In the end, society at large was not only disappointed by the poor performance of the comprehensive schools in reducing inequalities, it was also worried about the effect of extensive schooling: the school system had not brought about the social advancement that was expected. But there has also been disillusionment regarding the achievement of pupils. The first publications of international surveys were not reassuring for the pessimists. The republican link between school and society was broken.

Beyond these uncertainties of French society, the Lisbon Conference (2000) introduced some elements which were implemented into the objectives of the 2005 Act. The Right introduced a basic skills framework inspired by the European key competencies framework and defined by the European Commission for Lifelong Learning. When the Left came to power in 2012, it promulgated an Act for the Refoundation of the school system. This title expresses the feeling of a loss of direction in French society regarding its education and the will to return to the neo-Kantian tradition of the republican school's founders in the beginning of the 1880s. The secularist passion, which had faded with the decline of the Catholic Church, has regained power in the face of Islamic fundamentalism. This legislative activity was supported by the creation of policy tools in charge of its implementation.

The decentralisation and the autonomy of schools

The attempt to decentralize followed a reflection after the 1968 movement about the possibility of schools becoming school management units while the centralized school system, with its million civil servants, was often compared to the Red Army. At the beginning of the 1970s, a significant number of measures were experimented with but the 1975 Act ended this shift and France returned to the tradition of State planning. France put into place the comprehensive school system later than other OECD countries. The notion of school autonomy, which had been conceptualized from a pedagogical perspective, then took a managerial meaning. This new idea of a school development plan was introduced in 1982 as an experiment during the reform of junior schools. In 1984, a decree in the general Decentralization Act gave every secondary school the status of Public Local School with the possibility for the board to define its school development plan. The Left added a social objective: adapting teaching methods to pupils' needs in order to prevent school inequalities. However, a certain managerial vision remains and it was inspired by the ideas of the sociologist Michel Crozier. The title from one of his books summarizes his thoughts: Modern State, Earnest State (1986).

While the notion of a school development plan was extended throughout the entire education system, the 1989 Act became the pillar of the new regulations. It proposed to establish a series of individual and moral contracts between the pupil, the school and his or her family without renouncing the concept of the school catchment area. However, the law introduced some possibilities for limited and framed school choice for families that did not accept the school-based project. It was a recognition of the rights of families without moving towards a market-based system. Another limitation of this autonomy was the 'untouchable' national curriculum. Autonomy was therefore quickly limited to a local and narrow management with no flexible means to achieve national objectives.

The 2005 Act attempted to revive the principle of school autonomy via a cautious liberal conception. The main measure was the creation of a 'pedagogical board': the trade unions refused to allow issues on teaching to be discussed at the administrative board level as a lot of board members have no competency in this field. But the pedagogical board, which only includes teachers, could manage the national curriculum and local teaching conditions. However, its implementation has been long and difficult and has resulted in disappointing effects (Barrère 2014). The 2005 Act also took on board the recommendations of international organisations regarding the diversification of the school curriculum as a means to promote effectiveness and equity. Article 34 of the Act scheduled some possibilities for innovation by allowing schools to have more freedom outside of national regulations. This measure could help some schools create a specific identity but their choice and school development plans, with the notable exception of a few of them, were not really new or creative. According to the same logic, in 2007 the Minister announced more flexibility in the school catchment area policy and its abolition was scheduled in 2010. After a lot of heated debate, certain changes were made to this announcement (Van Zanten and Da Costa 2013). Local authorities, which are mostly against school choice, did not implement these instructions and it has continued to limit the possibilities of those families wishing to work outside of its scope. The Left, back in power, overturned the policy and has reinforced the catchment area policy.

The Development of Assessment

The period is characterized by the implementation of an assessment system. It is the result of a long history. During the 1970s, the former system of administrative statistics evolved towards new missions and objectives, developing an assessment system. In 1986, this administrative service became a ministerial directorate: the Directorate of Assessment and Forward Planning (Direction de l'Evaluation et de la Prospective (DEP)). Its successive heads have shared the same thoughts about in-depth large-scale surveys and the culture of the State's statistics. The DEP had important responsibilities. It reassured those who feared that school autonomy would lead to a loss of control in the steering of the education system: the law enabled the assessment system to prevent 'some possible drifts'. In response to society's concerns about the quality of learning, the DEP also had the responsibility of implementing regular assessments of pupils' skills at different key stages of the education system. All these missions were embedded in a certain conception of the education policy: the aim was to design tools for the State via indicators built from a national perspective which would take into account the diversity of local practices.

On behalf of its forecasting mission, the DEP tendered several calls for educational research. The first one, in the late 1980s, regarded the return on investment in education and subtly introduced the principles of French accountability. The return on investment was not only measured through performance but through the reduction of inequalities of opportunity. The second mission concerned the educational investment of families. This call was in the slipstream of the emergence of a movement of school consumers and new choices for private schools. The latter highlighted the reality and importance of school violence. All the research findings from the selected projects were presented in DEP reports disseminated and summarized by the press and media. After this prosperous period, the DEP's missions were revised and reduced at the end of the 1990s: it had gained too much influence in comparison to other directorates including even the Minister, and had to be reintegrated into the rank and file. The debate was shifting: was it normal that assessment was led by a ministry which designed and implemented education policies? Diverse reflections were inspired by Scandinavian examples where evaluative institutions are placed under the watch of Parliament. French policymakers are not entirely familiar with this concept. Even the word 'agency' is considered by them to be too liberal and they prefer 'high councils' which maintain a strong dependency on the State. A National Council for the Assessment of the School System (Conseil National d'Évaluation du Système Scolaire (CNESCO)) was created in 2014. An academic was appointed President of the Council by the Minister, but all the resources are provided by the Ministry's departments. Moreover, this new council has not abolished the previous ones: the DEP remains active and the Inspectorate is still in charge of assessing teachers and schools.

This situation can be considered as emblematic. The principles of New Public Management have been affirmed and this is not purely rhetorical. It has given place to an important legislative and regulative activity: France has progressively adopted European recommendations. But according to a strange mix, these principles have been included in the French administrative mindset, which has reformulated the key issues. This is why some political scientists name this evolution 'path dependency' or 'hybridization of policies' in a national context (Simola *et al.* 2012). This process limits or even neutralizes the impact of international recommendations from the OECD and the European Commission. From this perspective, it is possible to illustrate the paradoxes of this modernization and to examine how New Public Management has been implemented in different areas, with some examples of policy borrowing from other countries and international organizations.

Beyond legacies and reformism: the paradoxes of French New Public Management in education

If planning, through the action of the Planning Committee, was considered for a long time as a lever to reconcile the objectives of equality of opportunity with economic development, the economic crisis and the failure of comprehensive schools forced the Educative State into a change of policy. At the beginning of the 1980s, as described in the first part of this chapter, guidance remained a major concern for policymakers but assessment appeared as a new tool of governance for the education system. This explains the development of the first national assessments and the creation of the Directorate of Assessment and Forward Planning at the Ministry of National Education.

After the devolution acts, the French New Public Management (NPM) corresponded to an education modernization project but, contrary to other countries, it has strongly resisted the market and privatization (Pollitt 1990; Pollitt and Bouckaert 2011). As described in the first part of this chapter, the republican legacy is an initial explanation: the republican school system was always eager to push back private interests while education was being progressively unified as a public service. So NPM reform is a compromise between tradition and modernization, and one which raises numerous paradoxes while, in the past decade, French education policy has become increasingly permeable to the effects of globalization and Europeanization (Hood 1991; Hood and Peters 2004).

Assessment dealing with a bureaucratic logic

The creation of the Directorate of Assessment and Forward Planning or DEP (Direction de l'Evaluation et de la Prospective) is a good example of this kind of French compromise. While it was inspired by the School Effectiveness Unit created at the UK Department of Education, it was first conceived as a planning instrument to forecast student enrolments after the socialist Minister Jean-Pierre Chevènement had announced the target of '80 per cent of a same generation to achieve the baccalaureate in 2000'. But this was also the result of an international expertise with which France was involved, along with the USA and the OECD, in designing international indicators for education. If the assessment logic has progressively penetrated the French education system, it was not to assess its quality and effectiveness, at least at the beginning. National assessments, as indicators for schools, were tools designed to measure the inequality of student outcomes and were presented as a means to reduce these inequalities and to democratize access to education. The objective of the Ministry was not to promote school choice and the market but to fight against the raw rankings published by the press which impeded a fair assessment of the social characteristics and merit of each school. Today, tests are still formative and not summative: they serve teachers in improving their teaching practices but they are not used for selecting students.

It was only during the 1990s that assessment began to be thought of as a tool for measuring the education system's effectiveness and quality. In the meantime a new paradigm was emerging. Claude Thélot, who played an important role as the Head of the DEP, was the driver of this transformation (Thélot 1993). Assessment espoused the principles of New Public Management (economy, efficiency, effectiveness) while a High Council for the Assessment of Education (Haut Conseil de l'Evaluation de l'Ecole) was created. It quickly became a think tank for experts and policymakers. This High Council published reports which claimed to align the French assessment system with the international surveys led by the OECD, particularly the PISA survey (Henry *et al.* 2001). The High Council has also promoted the idea of a basic skills framework after a widespread national enquiry entitled 'the Great Debate on Schools', based on data and questions prepared by the DEP with the support of a consultancy firm (Normand 2011). France was later joined by the European Standing Group on Indicators and Benchmarks to participate in building the indicators of the Open Method of Coordination. The PISA survey has progressively become a benchmark for policymakers, and Finland an example of successful reform in education.

In France, education is a public service and a State administration (Derouet 1992). It is therefore directly subjected to reforms enacted by the State. As we have seen, assessment has become a major component in the action of the State via the promulgation of the Institutional Act related to Finance Laws in 2001 (Loi d' Organisation des Lois de Finance, or LOLF). This Act institutionalized new regulations for public expenditure through national programs and objectives which have to be assessed (Cytermann 2006). Therefore, each administration and department of the State has to be accountable. But accountability in education remains very administrative and financial and, even if it includes pupils' exam results in its indicators, it does not put any pressure on schools regarding performance, contrary to England (Mahony and Hextall 2000; Gleeson and Husbands 2001). Indeed, no system of information or digital assessment tool has been developed to make teachers more accountable. The LOLF remained very bureaucratic and has mainly served to justify the decision making process for the reduction of budgets and cost-cutting processes with raw instruments even from a managerial point of view. In education, management does not share the same values as managers: they more often use the word 'monitoring' to avoid a managerial vocabulary they often qualify as 'neoliberal' (Barrère 2006). A lot of them do not make clear distinctions between 'control' and 'evaluation', even if audit practices in schools are currently being developed by the inspection bodies (Power 1997).

A limited decentralization in terms of transfer of responsibilities

Decentralization is limited in its extent. Certainly the first acts of decentralization delegated important powers to local authorities in building schools, renovation and equipment. The latter used these new responsibilities to receive significant investment and some prestigious operations for electoral purposes. The aim was to prove that local authorities can do a better job in a context of reduced investment from the State. But, in education, decentralization was stopped in the beginning of the 1980s. It was only in 1995 that a new act transferred the responsibilities of the youth vocational training from State to Regional Authorities. However, this decentralization was partial: the State continues to manage vocational schools and apprenticeships even if the regions are in charge of regulating the provision of vocational training via five-year plans.

Education remains narrowly statist and centralized. The State is in charge of defining the curriculum and the volume of teaching hours; the selection, recruitment and careers of teachers and other staff; initial and further training; controlling and inspecting schools; the guidance and professional inclusion of schoolchildren; the diplomas; certifications; and recognition of qualifications. If devolution was implemented into the education system by giving more autonomy to chancellors (recteurs), they remain very dependent on the decisions taken by the Ministry of Education. In the regions, relations between the State and local authorities can be tense, due to conflicts regarding the sharing of jurisdiction or ideological opposition. Indeed, the primary and secondary education sectors are loosely coupled from a cultural and institutional perspective, and this does not facilitate cooperation and shared governance. Objective-based contracts define relations between the State and Local Authorities, but also between Local Education Authorities (Rectorats) and schools. Some networks of schools are emerging in particular to overcome the big divide between the primary and the secondary education sectors and to develop cooperation around the implementation of the basic skills framework (see the next section).

A source of heated debate is the transfer of civil servants to local authorities. It has been carried out for technical and maintenance staff in schools. Some similar attempts were made for the school guidance councillors. But this failed due to large-scale protests by the professional body of School Guidance Councillors and Psychologists (Conseils d'Orientation Psychologues) which was ideologically opposed to a concept of counselling defended by the local authorities via a strong cooperation with regional businesses and services involved in the assessment of skills or professional integration. Counselling also has powerful influence within the Ministry of Education and acts as a kind of internal lobbyist. Experts and policymakers are currently thinking of the creation of a regional public counselling service, but nothing concrete has yet been proposed by the ministry.

The retention of a cultural tradition despite a basic skills policy

The Basic Skills and Knowledge Framework (Socle Commun de Connaissances et de Compétences) is the masterpiece of the 2005 School Act voted under the Ministry of François Fillon. It gave rise to a whole of set of narratives (we could even say storytelling) which described it as the legacy of successive education plans from the foundation of the republican school system. But this framework is a translation, as we have seen – with some minor changes – of the European key competencies framework designed in 2004 by the European Commission while France has been involved for several years in the implementation of the Lisbon Strategy. It only resumed, after more than two decades, the basic skills travelling policy implemented in the USA and in the UK in the beginning of the 1980s (Ozga and Jones 2006). However, the French Basic Skills Framework is completely disconnected from issues of assessment and learning. It has led to a curriculum war in France through ideological and strongly mediatized battles (Shor 1986). In terms of curriculum, modernizers are opposed to traditionalists. The former, named 'Pedagogues' want to adapt the teaching of school disciplines to student needs and claim a stronger link between contents to be transmitted by teachers and skills to be acquired by pupils. The latter, named 'Republicans' wish to maintain a high level of contents requirement and criticize an instrumental conception of curriculum which distorts the culture transmitted to pupils. That is why the current socialist government has added 'common culture' to the 'basic skills and knowledge' framework, to satisfy the claims of the main teachers' trade union which defends the maintenance of a discipline-based curriculum. However, this divide goes beyond the traditional opposition between the Left and the Right and it maintains strong cleavages in the conception of teaching and teacher training, the balance between centralization and decentralisation, the debate about the national citizenship and communitarianism.

From this perspective, the action of the State is torn between several contradictory requirements. It wants the basic skills framework to be a tool of pedagogical diversification to support the individualized counselling and achievement of pupils. But at the same time it remains attached to an objective of equal teaching conditions for all pupils, and it defends a standardized conception of the curriculum. In addition to this paradox between standardization and diversification there is a strong tension between assessment and curriculum.

Each teacher is considered autonomous in his or her classroom and his or her 'pedagogical freedom' is recognized and reaffirmed in the Code of Education. At the same time, as civil servants, they have to apply official instructions enacted by the Ministry for the implementation of the curriculum. However, they have a discretionary power to assess students generally through marking. The lack of a link between curriculum and assessments stops teachers from taking into account the issue of student skills, while they do not feel concerned by student learning but only by teaching content. It explains why the High Council of Curriculum (Conseil Supérieur des Programmes) has had to adapt the curriculum to the Basic Skills Framework, and recently proposed to implement an assessment without marks to graduate students in accordance with their levels of learning difficulties, as has already been done in other European countries. But, up to now, the High Council's recommendations have not had much impact on policymaking.

School choice without the development of the market

The ideology of the market served the policy of deregulation of catchment areas. The Right, under the Sarkozy government, sought to raise the issue of school choice, while the Left was strongly opposed, defending a social mix in schools. However, contrary to England, this deregulation was linked to a certain number of requirements which limited its extent (Ball 2008a). First, there was the issue of limited places in the best schools. Secondly, the selection and enrolment of pupils had to respect strict criteria (siblings, scholarship, special needs, etc.), restricting the number of cases examined via bureaucratic regulations without listening to the voice of parents and their mobilisation. Head teachers, along with some local managers, were also reluctant to implement this policy. However, as has been observed elsewhere, the result was an increase in social segregation with the challenge of schools losing their best students, and this policy did not compensate the dominance of middle-class and upper-class families in the school choice strategies. Nor did it succeed in developing a market for schools and strengthening competition between schools, as is the case in the UK (Tomlinson 2005; Walford 2006). This policy was abandoned by the Left when it came to power in 2012.

Simultaneously, the very strong attachment to the equality of opportunities has led to the conception and implementation of some systems mixing school choice with principles of meritocratic selection against deprived pupils. That is why some higher education institutions, following the example of Sciences Po Paris, have developed mentoring procedures in schools with difficulties, while preparatory classes to higher education institutions have opened their doors to deserving pupils on behalf of positive discrimination. As some sociological research findings demonstrate, this action has allowed higher education institutions to display a policy of openness to silence criticism of their excessive elitism while maintaining a strong selection in their entrance examinations. The other system invented by the Right was the Internats d'Excellence boarding schools, copying the US Charter Schools. These schools for deprived students propose better support in teaching and learning, while they isolate pupils from their family and social context in order to offer better studying conditions. However, management appears extremely heterogeneous from one school to another, depending on the involvement of local authorities, the mobilisation of teaching teams, the recruitment procedures, and the degree of autonomy of the pedagogical structure, etc. These schools have contributed to claims of imaginary meritocracy, whilst serving as propaganda tools in the media to promote positive discrimination with limited effects in the end.

The failures of the conservative reformism of the Left

After the socialists came to power in 2012, this policy of diversification and school choice was stopped as part of their will to reduce inequality of opportunities and to strengthen the school mix. School autonomy, which the Right wanted to promote by giving more responsibility to head teachers, was also stopped while legitimacy was given to the General Inspection Body. Vincent Peillon, the Minister of National Education, brought together all the high-level managers of districts in Paris and told them that 'management' and 'governance' did not belong in his vocabulary. Instead, a rhetoric on a new foundation for the school system was disseminated, while the principles of the republican school system were reaffirmed, particularly through the implementation of the teaching of 'secular morality' in schools. In fact, the minister has a background in philosophy and he has remained very attached to republican values and principles and has been inspired by the founders of the republican school system, particularly Ferdinand Buisson. Sticking to its republican values, this left-wing government is promoting the Basic Skills Framework as a mean of democratisation and reduction of inequalities of opportunities.

The Commission for the New Foundation of the School System, created by the Minister to implement a new Act, despite its numerous working groups and its media coverage, has not led to substantial reform. The idea to focus the efforts of the education system on the primary education sector has only taken on board some recommendations of international organizations. The development of a national plan for digital technologies corresponds to similar aims without profoundly engaging the Ministry, while the equipment is mainly dependent on local authorities. Furthermore, the reaction of local authorities explains the failure of the reform of school timetables while it was presented as a key programme of the Act. Succumbing to the lobbying of physicians close to the Academy of Sciences, the Minister decided to implement a national plan for the restructuring of timetables in primary schools after it was accepted by the trade-unions. Once the reform had been announced, it did not take long for the trade unions to disavow the Minister while teachers, local authorities and parents expressed their dissatisfaction to a badly prepared, poorly negotiated and underfunded reform. It was the same for the reform of graduate schools in education (IUFM) and for the initial training of teachers. It was very quickly embedded in a bureaucratic maelstrom and a resurgence of conflicts of interest. Meanwhile, the Minister attempted to put the reform of the teaching profession on the political agenda, but he did not have the time to implement it and his followers did not give him enough backing. They preferred to focus their actions on restructuring the national curriculum according to the basic skills framework and to try to promote the school mix by transforming school provision, particularly by diminishing some elitist options like German, Latin or some bilingual courses, which has led to a lot of protests from disciplinary-based interest groups and trade unions.

Conclusion

A lack of restructuring of the teaching profession, a limited autonomy for schools, school choice on the margins, a school market with restricted consequences, a managerial ideology with significant opposition, an unsuccessful decentralization: in these conditions, it is difficult to claim that New Public Management has been implemented in the French education system. It contrasts strongly with the health sector where performance management, quality procedures, flexibility and mobility, contracts and agencies have created a new configuration of public service in hospitals. In education, only administrative and financial accountability has penetrated institutions in the long term without having had many consequences for the work of teachers. Head teachers and inspectors are developing assessment and audits, and entering into contracts, but the bureaucratic structure predominates. However, current reflections among experts and policymakers, from both Left and Right, lead us to think that they are searching for a kind of Third Way between the State and the market. A third step in decentralization, following the creation of new regional entities, leading to a restructuring of how local responsibilities are shared could be the main objective of the next reform in education. Another issue is related to the reform of the status of civil servants, which could have consequences on the National Education public service. However, the confrontation between the Left and the Right regarding this project remains very divisive, and the trade unions are ready to fiercely defend their rights.

7

NPM AND THE RECULTURING OF THE ITALIAN EDUCATION SYSTEM

The making of new fields of visibility

Emiliano Grimaldi, Paolo Landri and Roberto Serpieri

Introduction

In the last two decades, the Italian education system has experienced endless reforms. The starting point of this process of modernization can be traced to the 1997 School Autonomy Reform, which in turn was part of a wider redesign of the whole Italian public administration (Ongaro 2009). Since then, a ceaseless series of laws, regulations, curriculum reforms, policy programmes and experimentations have attempted to change the welfarist configuration of the education system, which has been problematized as ineffective and unable to respond to the contemporary societal and educational challenges. NPM as a discourse and its ideas and tools (Hood 1991; Pollitt and Bouckaert 2011) have played a relevant role in this season of reforms, acting as the inspiring and legitimating frame, and as the vehicles for change in the whole Italian public administration and the governing of the Italian education system.

In this chapter we will present and discuss the key NPM features in the Italian education system, highlighting the main ideas, tools and practices that have promoted the construction of new subjects as managers; new forms of managing and management; and the reframing of power relationship according to a managerialist discourse (see Tables 1.1 and 1.2 in the Introduction). We will then focus on the how and why of these changes, using as analytical starting points three NPM policy problematizations presented in Table 7.1 and discussing their translation and recontextualization in the Italian education system. For each problematization, we will frame our argument presenting the main legacies influencing and inflecting the embedding of NPM policy recipes in the national space and the processes through which this is occurring. The conclusion will provide a discussion of the effects of NPM reforms, intended here as epistemic, technological and ethical changes as well as the production of tensions, surprises and paradoxes.

In the face of a literature that presents Italy as a latecomer and education as a public sector which has remained 'largely untouched by massive NPM reforms' (Ongaro and Valotti 2008: 387), we propose a more dynamic and complex reading of both the transformations at stake in the field of education and the role that NPM discourse and tools have played out, paying attention to processes and nuances of change, compromises, mediations and re-contextualisation(s).

NPM in education in Italy

Four policy trajectories are commonly identified in order to map the entering of NPM in the Italian public administration since the early 1990s:

- a gradual shift in the organization of the public sector towards decentralization, autonomy, differentiation and the introduction of market-type mechanisms in welfare provision;
- the shift in the financial management of public organisations from input-oriented spending responsibility to budgeting systems with limited forms of responsibility for results, coupled with the uneven introduction of accounting systems;
- the introduction of audit and performance measurement technologies, with ex post controls that have (only partly) replaced ex ante controls;
- a profound change in personnel management, which has increasingly been linked to performance, responsibility for results, and incentive schemes (Bellè and Ongaro 2014: 386–87).

Reform results are controversial. Italy is commonly presented in the NPM literature as a latecomer (Kickert 2007), a southern variant of a Napoleonic state where NPM reforms have failed and the legalistic framework has performed a significant capacity to neutralize NPM principles and logics (Painter and Peters 2010). Legalism, public sector resistance to change, clientelism, politicization and familism are selectively called into question as factors that explain the 'implementation gap' (Ongaro and Valotti 2008). Education is depicted as a public sector service which, differently from health for instance, has remained 'largely untouched by massive NPM reforms' (ibid. 387) and has seen only 'some NPM-inspired measures, like forms of corporatization and managerialization' (ibid. 384).

Our understanding of the reform process occurring in the last two decades offers a slightly different picture, where NPM ideas and tools have significantly influenced a restructuring and reculturing of Italian education, with specific reference to the issues of governance, evaluation and workforce regulation.

After school autonomy and decentralization were introduced as a strategy of disaggregation, the path was opened to the introduction of accountability policies that shifted the emphasis on output control, the import of private sector management language techniques and the use of apparently soft forms of competition as levers for efficiency, efficacy and improvement. This has recently resulted in the establishment of a national school evaluation system, which promotes standardisation and performance management as levers for improvement and provides the means to introduce performance management technologies at the level of the workforce.

These changes have had a significant impact on the restructuring and reculturing of the education workforce and the redesign of the functioning of schools as organisations. Below, we briefly report on what changes occurred with reference to the 4Ms (managers, managing, management and managerialism) discussed in the introduction of this book:

- Managers: since the school autonomy reform in 1997, head teachers' roles and professional identities have been changed. Interventions into their compulsory training and accreditation have occurred, using business models to socialize them as managers and leaders. Their title has changed from head teachers to school chief executives. They have been asked to act as entrepreneurs, collecting public and private funding to develop their schools' services provision. An increased emphasis is put on their accountability for results and their capacity to match improvement targets. Head teachers are supported by a staff of appointed professionals (deputy and collaborators) who are partly involved in such a process of reculturing as managers. Differentiation is through titles, role and job descriptions, but this is weakly linked to remuneration. There is no entry into the workforce by non-education personnel to take up leadership and management roles.
- Managing: in recent years a major shift is observable in the education field from pedagogy and curriculum to output technology and results improvement. The establishment of a national evaluation system and the introduction of national testing on student learning have provided both: a) the output data and analysis to make comparable judgements about schools and professionals performance; and b) the knowledge infrastructure to sustain self-evaluation and strategic management processes (e.g. the recent introduction of the Annual Self-evaluation Plan that schools are requested to complete, defining their improvement targets). Schools and professionals are asked to use management tools such as: planning, target setting, data collection and analysis. Marketing and bidding are increasingly becoming an obligatory passage point for schools. Only ritual mechanisms of performance-related pay are introduced for head teachers, although diverse policy experimentations have been realized on this matter. There are no mechanisms to remove an underperforming workforce.
- Management: a paradoxical system of centralized de-centralization is in place where autonomous schools are both asked to act as businesses in quasi-market environments but are still involved in a hierarchical chain of command. Public schools are funded based on pupil numbers and have to compete with a historically well-rooted system of private provision (around

TABLE 7.1 NPM and the modernising of the Italian education system – three policy problematizations

Issue	Policy problems	Policy solutions	Key events
Governance	The centralized and bureau-professional mode of regulation produces rigid, ineffective and self-referential organisations	School autonomy and decentralisation as a strategy of disaggregation The mix of autonomy, accountability, private sector management techniques and competition can act as a stimulus for efficiency, efficacy and improvement	1992–1995 legislation on financial management, public personnel management and public services privatisations Law 59/1997; L. Decree 112/1998; L. Decree 275/1999; 2001 Constitutional reform; School autonomy; decentralisation; school choice; school sizing
Evaluation	The Italian education system is ineffective and low-performing, as the international test results (PISA; TIMSS; IEA) show The Italian education system lacks an objective measure to evaluate its output and quality	Put greater emphasis on output control, through the establishment of a national school evaluation system Standardisation and performance management as levers for improvement	1999 Establishment of INVALSI (National Institute for the Evaluation of the Education System) 2000 The PISA shock 2007 *Quaderno bianco* 2008 INVALSI national tests 2013 Establishment of the National Evaluation System
Professions	Public sector professionals are self-referential and not committed to improvement because of the lack of control and incentives	Put hands on professional management through: a) the reshaping of the professional public ethos according to the values of the private sector; b) the introduction of performance management technologies; and c) the establishment of a system of rewards and sanctions	1999 Head teachers became high-level civil servants 2003–2010 Pilots to evaluate head teachers 2010–2011 Pilot to evaluate teachers 2013 Pilot to evaluate schools

10 per cent of the total amount, mainly Catholic schools). Schools do not hire and fire staff, who are recruited at the national/regional level. Choice policies have been introduced with the deregulation of the catchment areas and the publication (voluntary) of output data to facilitate and orient consumer choice.

- Managerialism: initial steps towards the restructuring of the hierarchies of power within schools are observable, with a developing differentiation between the head teacher as chief executive and a middle staff made up of teachers with management roles. As an effect of the importing of private sector languages and techniques, schools are increasingly asked to adopt line management relationships that clearly identify management responsibilities, performance management and accountability procedures.

The following sections of the chapter will provide further analysis and discussion of these changes. Our argument will develop adopting as analytical starting points the construction of three policy problematizations (Foucault 1977) and the related solutions, which concern the governance of the Education system, the evaluation of its quality and the regulation of its professionals. Briefly summarized in Table 7.1, these policy problematizations represent the entry points of NPM and the core of the modernising process of the Italian education system.

Modernising educational governance through a disaggregation strategy

In the early 1990s a dramatic political crisis combined with economic crisis and the pressures coming from the European Union (expenditure cuts, modernization, more efficiency) to create the institutional conditions for the questioning of the bureaucratic and centralistic configuration of the Italian public administration and services.

From 1992 to 1995, three governments of technicians introduced the first regulations about public organisations' financial management, privatizations and public personnel management, where the influence exerted by NPM ideas and tools became evident. This political season was characterized by protagonist technicians (mainly economists) coming from the Bank of Italy and the progressive intensification of the connections between Italian politicians and the EU, the European Central Bank and OECD circuits of expertise (Martens *et al.* 2007) that were supporting NPM measures as policy strategy to modernize public administrations and welfare systems across Europe (Bertozzi and Graziano 2004).

In the political debate, the need to reform the governance of the Italian public administration became an undisputable assumption. Its Napoleonic traits (legalism, centralism, bureaucracy) were under attack as the causes of ineffectiveness and inefficiency. NPM provided the discursive framework and the tools to 'tailor' a policy solution. The education system was included in the debate as part of the ineffective public administration, although it was partially excluded from early reforms on the basis of the recognition of its peculiar character and configuration (a bureau-professional field, an inherently public service) and because of diverse resistances (unions, bureaucracies and political parties of the Left).

In the late 1990s, however, thanks also to OECD pressures, the reform of the education system's governance became a priority, based on the argument that its centralized and bureau-professional mode of regulation produced rigid, ineffective and self-referential organisations which were not able to interpret and respond to the educational needs of the knowledge economy. A break-up of the bureaucratic and hierarchical system into independent organisations acting in a devolved environment was identified as a disaggregation strategy to modernize the system, to make it more efficient and responsive to societal needs and, finally, to raise its performance. In an orthodox NPM guise, the mix between autonomy, accountability, private sector management techniques, competition (imitative) and a system of incentives was referred to as stimulus for efficiency, efficacy and improvement.

It is within this scenario that the Law 59/1997 introduced school autonomy as an innovation in the organisational design of the education system according to the site-based management model, within a broad trend towards decentralization/devolution of competencies to regional and local governments (see the Legislative Decree 112/98 on devolution and Legislative Decree 127/97 on administrative simplification) (Ongaro 2009: 124).

Before 1997, the Italian education system was highly centralized. Governance relationships and policymaking flowed up and down hierarchies and the national curriculum was centrally defined. Local governments had a limited voice in shaping education policy at the local level. Change was produced through national legislation, input standards and procedures, whereas evaluation and mechanisms of control were formal and mainly focused on the input-side (Landri 2009). A large autonomy was recognized for heads and teachers within their 'professional space' (Serpieri 2009).

The 1997 reform profoundly changed schools' identity and functioning, giving them greater room to manoeuvre in financial, organisational and educational matters (although staff recruitment remains a State competence). Schools became entitled to outline their annual educational school plan (POF), realize individual, distinctive school projects, define local curricular priorities and design, at least in part, their internal organisation (Legislative Decree 275/99). In a proper NPM fashion, autonomous schools were asked to self-govern themselves according to the logics of private sector management (efficiency, effectiveness and entrepreneurialism). Head teachers were to assume a managerial role and were defined as responsible for their results. In the same vein, schools were invited to build partnerships with other public and private actors, in order to pursue their educational mission and interact with local authorities and communities. Additional funding mechanisms were introduced as incentives to sustain these changes (i.e. EU funding bids act as the vehicle for the establishment of public/private partnership as an obligatory institutional arrangement for schools). At the same time, at the level of rhetoric, the democratic potential of school autonomy was greatly emphasized. Partnerships and networks were explicitly identified as potential channels through which to gain additional public or private resources and to enrich educational provision. Finally, great emphasis was given to the issue of accountability, underlining the strict links between autonomy, freedom, external evaluation and responsibility towards stakeholders.

This peculiar form of school autonomy was designed within the framework of a soft decentralization. In fact, the Ministry of Education maintains 'control of the general governance of the system, outlining general principles of education and establishing threshold performance levels besides defining the national curricula and managing financial and professional resources through its regional administrative offices' (Grimaldi and Serpieri, 2014: 125). Regions and local governments are become responsible for territorial planning (e.g. opening, closing and merging schools) and school buildings (Legislative Decree 112/98).

Italian school autonomy is widely considered as one of the most limited in comparison to truly decentralized systems (Eurydice 2007; Viteritti 2009). Experts describe a 'blocked' system that has absorbed the innovative potentials of school autonomy and site-based management. Moreover, NPM literature presents education as an institutional field where forms of managerialization have been introduced 'but to a limited extent, and without a massive recourse to other mechanisms, like market-type mechanisms' (Bellè and Ongaro 2014: 384).

The decade after the 1997 school autonomy reform was characterized by a process of re-centralisation in the field of education. The Berlusconi right-wing governments somehow weakened school autonomy, leaving incomplete its regulation and the transfer of competences (e.g. staff management and financial autonomy), changing the policy agenda (e.g. shifting the attention to curriculum reforms and later on to evaluation) and creating uncertainty around the actual possibility of reinforcing school autonomy through a policy of austerity. Interestingly enough, the neo-centralist agenda was the paradoxical point of convergence for a heterogeneous coalition of interests, which included: a) neoconservatives, who were interested in state control over education; b) Left parties and unions, who were worried about the risks of marketization and polarization of the education system; c) central and local bureaucracies, who wanted to preserve their powers.

We argue here that if we look more carefully at the Italian case, the distinguishing features of this trajectory of the modernization of educational governance can be identified in the presence of several counteracting trends and forces whose interaction produces a peculiar process of re-contextualisation of the NPM disaggregation policy recipe (site-based management + decentralisation + marketization/competition + partnership = more efficiency).

The 1997 reform represents, in fact, an institutional fracture where the conditions were created for the permanent entering of some distinctive NPM features in the Italian education system. Here, we will focus in particular on the opening of spaces for quasi-markets. Neo-centralist policies and the strong opposition coming from the 'welfarist block' (unions, Left parties, teachers' associations and student movements) have partially limited both the explosion of competitive dynamics between schools and local systems, but also, somehow inhibited the exploitation of the democratic and bottom-up potential inherent in a collaborative understanding of school autonomy. Our thesis, however, is that the disaggregation strategy enacted through the autonomy reform has opened some spaces for the development of local quasi-markets in the Italian education system (Benadusi and Consoli 2004; Grimaldi and Serpieri 2010).

This is the combined effect, we argue, of some peculiar traits of the 1997 reform. First, schools' micro-politics have been pushed towards a managerialist model (Benadusi and Consoli 2004), through the discursive pressures upon schools and head teachers to become managerial and entrepreneurial organisations and professionals. These pressures have been reinforced in the last decade by the austerity policies which forced schools to find additional funds in the local markets to enrich their educational provision and become more attractive.

Second, this trend towards the shaping of market-oriented organisations has been sustained by two further legislative changes, which forced schools to cope with the problem of attractiveness. On the one hand, the autonomy reform has deregulated catchment areas, whilst on the other hand, the reform introduced a minimum number of students for a school to be considered autonomous, ordering the closure or the merging of those schools falling below the minimum. These processes of quasi-marketization have also been reinforced in some areas by regional policies that have promoted voucher schemes (e.g. the case of Lombardy).

As a result, in a still hierarchical mode of governing, new devolved arenas opened up where schools have become more and more entrepreneurial and have started to compete for students, attempting to fabricate a 'good reputation'. Increasingly, their success and attractiveness depend on their capacity to raise additional funding. Entrepreneurship, in such a context, means the establishment of relationships with public funders, especially local governments, but means also the opening of new spaces for private-public partnerships.

However, a deep understanding of the actual impact of these processes of change and the pushes towards a hidden quasi-marketization requires a systemic reading of the intertwining of governance changes (school autonomy and decentralization) and the transformations of the mechanisms of control (evaluation and performance management) and the relationship between the state and schools and their professionals.

Towards governing by standards in education

A second policy trajectory where NPM has played a relevant role in transforming the Italian education system is standardisation. A few years after the autonomy reform, Italy was struck by the PISA shock (and TIMSS and IEA), that represented the Italian education system as ineffective and poory performing and put the problem of its quality at the centre of the agenda.

The policy solution was identified, in clear NPM style, as the need to put greater emphasis on output control in contrast to the Napoleonic legacy of input control. A national school evaluation system was established to provide objective measures to evaluate educational output and quality and tools for the enactment of NPM 'how to do' technologies, such as performance management and organisational improvement.

The transformation at stake here can be interpreted as the development of new standards of educational practice which were intended to provoke relevant changes in the infrastructure of educational agency. What occurs is an alignment with the logic of the neoliberal agenda in education and with the global shift towards forms of 'soft governance' where standards, data and performance play an increasing role in governing education (Lawn and Grek 2012). The new quantitative, objective and comparable standards are supposed to make more visible and manageable the ecology of schooling. They are aimed at reducing the unpredictability of educational agency and at countering the risks associated with loose coupling in educational organisation.

Historically, the development of new standards in educational practices in Italy is a long term and bipartisan policy that started well before the recognition of the current financial crises. However, school autonomy represents a shift point. The creation of a devolved environment solicited the activity of standard-setting, which becomes a more and more crucial aspect of the government of schools (Landri 2014) in an envisaged post-bureaucratic scenario. The activity of standard-setting reinforced and changed direction by being reoriented from a national and bureaucratic welfarist discourse to a transnational discourse of competitiveness at the European level. Such an activity expanded by revising some aspects of educational input, and including new aspects, like educational outputs. Here, the revision mainly concerned school size, and the teacher-student ratio, while the novelty involved learning outcomes.

The activity of new standard-setting became more articulated with the publication of the 2007 Quaderno Bianco sulla Scuola (MIUR 2007) [White Paper on the School], a key document in which a new mentality of government was elaborated. This policy text translates the questions about standards in technical and scientific issues and contains a diagnosis of the education system and some proposals to improve it. Its knowledge base draws on data from large-scale survey assessments (PISA, TALIS, etc.), datasets from the national institute of statistics (ISTAT) and from the first round of national standardized tests. It emerged from the mobilization of circuits of expertise ranging from the theory of human capital; the models of school improvement; the input-output model of school organisation; and paved the way for the revision of the teacher-student ratio and for a decisive impulse toward assessment by standardized tests. Here, the values of teacher-student ratio appear as the most relevant cause for higher public spending. Later on, and partly based on this knowledge, in order to face the effects of financial and economic crisis, the Law 133/2008 envisaged: a) an increase of the ratio teacher/students of 1 per cent; b) a revision of the curriculum, by the reduction of the student time at school, and c) a reduction of teaching staff.

The standardization of educational practice expanded, in particular, to include the educational outputs. The Quaderno Bianco supported, in particular ways, the diffusion of the standardized national tests, and the consolidation of INVALSI (National Institute for the Evaluation of the Education System) as the research institute in charge of the evaluation of the education system. They were both intended to counter 'the lack of the culture of evaluation in Italy', and to positively improve schools' capacity to raise the quality of educational outputs. The establishment of INVALSI was also seen as checking a chaotic and fragmented development of school autonomy and its negative effects in terms of equity, guaranteeing at the same time the capacity to meet learning outcomes at the national level.

In 2001, 2002 and 2003 INVALSI realized three pilot surveys on learning outcomes. However, it was only in 2004 (Decree 284) and in a decisive way in 2007, after a complex organisational and institutional redefinition (with the Budget Law 296/2006), that INVALSI became fully operational. This redefinition also led to a mobilization of circuits of knowledge experts in quantification, classification, and measurement in education, and the marginalization of classic pedagogical research. From 2008 onwards, standardized national testing was repeated regularly on Italian and Mathematics: with students of the second and fifth grades of primary school first, then with students of the first and third grades of low secondary schools (in this case, the test results contributed to the final marks), and then with students of the second grade of upper secondary schools. The testing is obligatory and covers the whole school population. Each round of testing raises debates, critiques, and even resistances to testing in some schools. However, the exercise of assessment consolidated over time and generated a growing consensus from teachers and head teachers. Moreover, the attention to standardized testing is only one aspect of a tendency towards the standardization of outputs and more in the general area of educational practice. In 2013, the government decided to proceed with the construction of the National Evaluation System (SNV) (Decision no.72 08/03/2013). The SNV is coordinated by INVALSI, and includes INDIRE (the National Institute for Educational Innovation and Research), and the board of inspectors that are expected to work with school in self-evaluation and the design of school improvement plans. While the construction of the SNV is still in its initial steps, it nonetheless prefigures a

106 Emiliano Grimaldi, Paolo Landri and Roberto Serpieri

shift towards a mentality of school government in which, in a proper NPM guise, there is a clear investment in forms and standards to control the ecology of educational practice. This is an investment which implies the revision of education input and also a notable attention to quantified, measured, and comparable educational outputs. Notably, one of the main innovations introduced through the SNV is the Self-Evaluation Annual Report (RAV), which schools are obliged to complete every year since 2014, providing a self-evaluation of their performance and setting improvement actions and future targets to be matched.

Restructuring and subjectifying educational professions

The Italian route to NPM has produced relevant changes in terms of school governance and evaluation but has also acted upon the bodies (and the souls) of educational professions (i.e. the formation of new managers who manage in a managerialist way). A new 'episteme of public service' (Ball 2008a: 51) has required shifting practices and 'changing modes of teacher [and head teacher] professionalism [ranging from]: traditional, managerial, collaborative and democratic' (Whitty 2008) and the meeting of professional lives with new and conflicting dilemmas and 'ethical issues' (Lunt 2008). NPM policies (and their associated regimes of knowledge and relations of power) have tried to erode traditional modes of professional autonomy and democratic arrangements of collegiality, producing new subjectivations. Here we will discuss those concerning head teachers and teachers.

After the school autonomy reform, the head teacher profession was (re) built up as the key lever of transformation and improvement. As in other restructured education systems, the 'lever' of leadership, with its implied ideas of managerialism and entrepreneurialism (Gunter 2012; Hall 2013) has acted as a main policy dispositif (Grimaldi and Serpieri 2014). At the same time, during the last thirty years, and more strongly in the last decade, the teaching profession has been attacked both by austerity policies and NPM policies denouncing teachers' inefficacy, 'laziness', low competence and commitment.

The hybrid head teacher

In 2000, the Italian Minister of Education, Luigi Berlinguer, clearly explained the rationale underpinning the redesign of the Italian head teacher profile as a necessary complement and support to the 1997 School Autonomy reform:

> The autonomous school needs head teachers who are able to assume responsibilities, plan and implement new projects and activities, organise and stimulate teachers' work, listen to pupils, involve families, manage resources and interact with external actors.
>
> (Berlinguer 2001: 111–112)

The policy solution is to lay hands on professional management through: a) the reshaping of the professional public ethos according to private sector values (improvement, competition, entrepreneurship, responsibility for results); b) the introduction of performance management technologies; and c) the establishment of a system of rewards and sanctions.

Similar to what happened in other education systems, headship becomes a part and a device of a wider devolution of the responsibility for quality and performance 'improvement' towards the school level. Thus, the head as manager has been identified as the lever of change to promote improvement, even if nowadays school financial autonomy and staff management still continue to be heavily constrained by central regulation. School governance, as well, designed during the 1970s on the basis of the principles of professional and democratic participation, has remained until now 'untouched' by the reforms, implying the need for the head teacher to continuously negotiate on internal decision-making. Entrepreneurship, finally, represents a central value that has inspired the attempts to reframe the external role of headship, in so far as head teachers have been identified as key actors in the new devolved educational arenas. First, they are asked to establish relations and a positive climate with local governments and to be accountable to peripheral bureaucracies. Second, head teachers are required to explore and exploit partnerships and collaborations with institutional, cultural, social and economic groups. The new head teacher potentially became an 'entrepreneur' with several imperatives. In order to maintain a sufficient number of pupils, he or she has to make his or her school attractive for students and their parents. The loss of students means fewer teachers and the risk of losing autonomous status. To avoid these risks, the head teacher should seek to enrich their school's educational provision by getting additional funding for extracurricular activities. As a consequence, he or she should dedicate a considerable amount of time to promoting external relations with local authorities and other public and private actors. In such a context, the development of entrepreneurial skills becomes a necessity, while competition and customer oriented ethos turn out to be new hidden values (Whitty 2002; Ball and Youdell 2008).

This story of hybridization is also a story of conflict around the hot issue of professional accountability where resistances and struggles against the NPM discourse become highly visible. For more than ten years, attempts to introduce NPM dispositifs of accountability along with the legal-financial control typical of the bureaucratic setting have failed. The history of headship evaluation in Italy started in 1999, with the first hesitant trial whose evaluation technology was mainly based on self-evaluation and self-definition of the objectives to be pursued (Serpieri 2009). In 2001, management by objectives and the principle of 'contractualism' (Yeatman 1994: 110) were introduced, proving the decrease of trust in the school and its professional groups and, consequently, in the forms of self-evaluation. Consistent with the rules of NPM, a process was outlined where the Ministry negotiated directly with the headteacher the objectives to be pursued. We witness here a shift from the ethos of professional self-regulation to a proper economic logic. Trust decreased and professionals were progressively reframed as utilitarian players, whose agency was limited by centrally-defined measurable and accountable parameters. In the following years, different mechanisms to evaluate headteachers were tested, but failed. As a result, however, it is possible to observe the progressive and paradoxical establishment of the belief that school has to be entrusted to the therapeutic care of an 'heroic' leader, consistent with the general trend that elsewhere we have defined as the "diagnostic turn" (Grimaldi and Serpieri, 2013). Heroic leadership is the magic that can guarantee the effective realization of improvement plans, whereas measurement becomes more and more pressing. The last, even if provisional, act of this story is represented by the introduction in 2012 of a new experimental model to evaluate heads and schools, called VALES, which is still ongoing and distinguishes itself through a shift from the evaluation of solely the head teacher to that of schools and teachers within the wider frame of the establishment of an integrated national evaluation system.

Fewer teachers and making them confess

It is not easy to recognize how NPM has affected the teaching profession in Italy because somehow teachers seem to be immune to managerialist pressures. Head teachers, in fact, have no powers of recruitment, evaluation and firing of teachers (although this is nowadays in the government agenda) and just a small space for manoeuvre for their professional development. As educational leaders they are constrained to count on their 'transformational' or 'democratic' style to favour teachers' commitment and participation.

Anyway, it is clear that in Italy the 'first move' on the teacher profession has implied workforce reduction (since 2000, teachers have decreased from about 820,000 to 720,000). Interestingly, this reduction is justified not only in terms of expenditure cuts, but also within a neoconservative discourse. In primary schools, for example, twenty years since the reform that moved from a single teacher to a team of three teachers per class, the Ministry of Education of the last Berlusconi Government launched a campaign to turn back. The traditional role of the 'unique magister', in fact, was presented as a way to secure an adequate pedagogical model to confront educational fragmentation and professional 'negligence'.

Nonetheless, NPM has also tried to stress the moral climate of teacher evaluation, a 'hot potato' (Barzanò and Grimaldi 2013) in the Italian education system. Although we have here a similar, but less intense, story of failed attempts to introduce evaluation dispositifs, as in the case of head teachers; in policymakers and public opinion there is a growing call for a 'meritocratic' turn in the teaching profession, strongly advocated by a powerful assemblage of non-educational agencies, foundations and experts. This is another case where national test results enable a NPM "confessional" (Fejes and Nicoll, 2015) disposition, that makes Italian teachers 'guilty' and prone to continuous improvement.

Conclusion

We have shown how the entrance of NPM ideas and technologies into the Italian education system cannot be interpreted as a coherent and unitary policy trajectory. Instead, we have presented complex transformations which arise as the performative effects of the assembling of diverse policy discourses, new governing and educational technologies, renewed administrative procedures, together with the formation of new subjectivities.

Rather than focusing on resistances, failures and continuities, we tried to highlight to what extent NPM ideas and technologies are contributing to the slow but relentless establishment of a new regime of government (Dean 2010) in the field of education, i.e. the institutionalisation of relatively organised ways of directing the conduct of the subjects of education (ibid. 268–69) which is based on: a) Human capital theory and economics of education as the dominant forms of rationality in education; b) statistics, comparison and performance management as the new techne and the new organising principles of the fields of visibility in education (Rose 1999); c) endogenous privatisation (Ball and Youdell, 2008) and imitative competition as the main driver towards the reshaping of identities, moralities and agencies in education.

As our analysis has shown, this resulted in a scenario where some key NPM features have become institutionalised in the field of education:

- the restructuring of the education system through the creation of autonomous schools that are asked to do site-based management and cope with the conflicting pressures coming from a paradoxical combination of hierarchical command and quasi-markets (management);
- the recasting of the relationship between the state, schools, professionals and public according to a rational goal and neo-managerialist model (Newman 2001), based on a shift from educational issues to output technology and the tyranny of performance, testing, measurement, externally driven self-evaluation and improvement (managing);
- the enactment of a relentless process of endogenous privatisation of Italian public education, through the ongoing formation of new subjectivities (head teachers, middle staff) as managers and the institutionalization into school organisational life of line management languages, tools and techniques.

The combination of the NPM disaggregation strategy and the swinging between decentralization/deregulation and centralization/central regulation has resulted in a progressive stratification of a heterarchical mode of government in the field of education where vertical and horizontal lines of coordination combine and overlap (Grimaldi 2011). Although hierarchy remains the main mode of coordination, the system is increasingly adopting a plural mode of regulation where, paradoxically, the State continues to exert a strong control over the resources allocation mechanism and the definition of the national

110 Emiliano Grimaldi, Paolo Landri and Roberto Serpieri

curriculum but, at the same time, is framing for itself the role of an evaluative state (Neave 2012) that steers at distance through standardization and output control. In the shadow of the evaluative state, policies of deregulation (e.g. school choice, school sizing and merging, competitive funding) are widening the spaces for local quasi-markets.

As another side to this evaluation turn, together with standardizing dispositifs, some other tools of self-evaluation have been launched. As another consequence of the NPM paradoxes (Hood and Peters, 2004), the decentralization strategy has been counterbalanced by the centralized design of a new evaluation panopticon, inspired by the NPM myths of measurability and transparency. In this scenario, even softer tools such as the self-evaluative ones are constrained in a logic of extraction of 'confessions' (Fejes and Nicoll 2015) through rigid and standardized grids proposed by INVALSI.

An area where the performative effects of NPM ideas and technologies are evident is the reframing of the relationship between the state, professionals and public (understood as stakeholders). We have argued that a new moral environment is pushing head teachers subjectivities towards a 'contractualist' regime (Grimaldi and Serpieri, 2013), where they are increasingly supposed to be accountable for their results. This is not truly the same for Italian teachers, who benefit from a welfarist status still rooted in schools as public services and who, together with unions, are showing a significant capacity to resist the NPM attacks to their professional autonomy.

Nonetheless, the complex transformations we have described witness a process of ongoing reculturing of the Italian education field, where concerns for effectiveness, efficiency and entrepreneurship, management, accountability, evaluation and improvement are increasingly marginalizing, hiding or co-opting the welfarist concerns of equity, social justice and democratic citizenship.

8

THE DISSEMINATION AND ADOPTION OF NPM IDEAS IN CATALAN EDUCATION

A cultural political economy approach

Antoni Verger and Marta Curran

Introduction

Since the 1980s, most countries in the world have experimented with New Public Management (NPM) reforms in a range of policy sectors (Hood and Peters 2004). Education, as one of the sectors of public administration with large budgets and large numbers of personnel in most countries, has been widely affected by NPM-driven reforms. As a consequence, the fragmentation of education systems in smaller units – via policies like school autonomy or parental choice – the professionalization of school management, and the logic of results-based performance have strongly penetrated into the regulation of education systems worldwide (Gunter and Forrester 2009).

To a great extent, it can be considered that NPM has become hegemonic within the global education agenda. Many countries in the world, independently of their level of economic development, cultural idiosyncrasy or the ideology of their governments, are converging around the desirability of adopting an NPM approach to educational reform (Maroy 2009). In the beginning of the eighties, in a context of economic crisis, NPM policies were basically embraced by conservative governments, usually for efficiency reasons, but also as a way to weaken public sector trade unions. However, in the nineties, these policies have also been adopted and regulated by social democratic governments, although apparently for different reasons. It has been documented that in many European countries, social-democratic parties have adopted NPM as an attempt to modernize and recover the legitimacy of the welfare state (Wiborg 2013). Catalonia is not an exception to this international trend, since the NPM reforms of education has been led by a social-democratic government. In the 2000s, a coalition of left wing parties initiated an ambitious reform process that culminated with the Catalan Education Act which put an important emphasis

112 Antoni Verger and Marta Curran

on emblematic NPM measures such as school autonomy, professionalization of school leadership and external evaluation.

Consequently, in relation to the four Ms presented in the Introduction, we identify that the main managerial dimensions in the structuring of the education system have been deeply altered in Catalonia, including management (through the fragmentation of the system in smaller management units under the 'school autonomy' rubric), managers (through the professional training of school principals and the empowerment of this figure at the school level), managing (via the introduction of new forms of standardized evaluation and outcomes-based management logics), and managerialism (by creating new hierarchies and relations of power within the education system at multiple levels). However, as we discuss in this chapter, for a combination of political, institutional and economic reasons, these NPM reforms have been enacted rather unevenly – and even contradictorily – in Catalonia.

The objective of the chapter is to explain how and why NPM policies such as those mentioned above have been adopted and enacted in the Catalan education context. The Catalan case is especially relevant due to the fact that Catalonia has pioneered the introduction of NPM reforms within the Spanish educational system, and has influenced similar reforms later introduced in other regions. The chapter is structured in four main parts. In the first one, we explore the main features of the Spanish politico-administrative system and how these relate to the configuration of this country's educational system. In the second part of the chapter, we go through our analytical approach that is grounded on cultural political economy (cf. Jessop 2010) and focuses on how ideas, material factors and strategic actors interact in the promotion of institutional and administrative transformations, such as those advanced under the NPM paradigm. In the third part of the chapter we develop the case study on the ambitious NPM educational reform that Catalonia has gone through in the last decade. The case study is based on thirteen interviews with key education stakeholders (individuals interviewed include Ministry of Education officials, policy entrepreneurs, teachers' unions and the school principals' lobby) conducted between February 2013 and January 2014, as well as on document analysis of policy briefings, press releases, media kits and legal documents. In the fourth and last part we present our main conclusions.

NPM in the Spanish context

In order to analyse the introduction of NPM ideas in recent educational reforms in Catalonia, we first take a step back and reflect on the complex relationship between managerialist reform ideas and the Spanish politico-administrative system.

As in most southern European countries, the public administration system in Spain is part of the so-called Napoleonic tradition, which is a politico-administrative model that differs considerably from the model that prevails in the Anglo-Saxon context. While the Anglo-Saxon administrative tradition establishes a reduced role for the state in the provision of services, the Napoleonic tradition aims at strengthening the legitimacy of state intervention through the modernization of public administration (Ongaro 2009). The Napoleonic model is mainly characterized by the importance of administrative law as a cultural paradigm, and by an administrative system that can be qualified as 'centralized, hierarchical, uniform, accountable and controlled' (Kickert 2011: 807). Overall, within this model, civil service enjoys social status and significant labour rights, which are underpinned by the influential role of trade unions in public employment policy (Ongaro 2009).

Despite Spain having historically taken part in this state-centred administrative tradition, with the democratic transition and the approval of the 1978 Constitution, the Spanish administrative structure was drastically reformed via the decentralization of the state in seventeen 'Autonomous Communities'. The emerging regional governments were provided with important levels of administrative autonomy in key areas such as education, health and welfare. Catalonia, the Basque Country and Galicia achieved higher levels of competences than other regions due to historic, cultural and political reasons. In fact, the heterogeneity in this process of administrative devolution enabled experimentation and innovation with various managerial models in different territories. Another key moment to understand the process of modernization of the public administration in Spain was the incorporation of the country into the European Union in 1986, since this meant the introduction of changes in formal management systems as a way to evaluate and measure the performance of European policy programs (Gallego 2003).

Overall, the Spanish public administration system has experienced what Verheijen (1998) calls an incremental reform. This type of reform has been characterized by a moderate modification of the traditional governance, and by continuity in the organizational structure of the state, especially in terms of public personnel policies (i.e. high stability in the civil service, promotion systems based on seniority). The level of politicization of the Spanish civil service, together with the legalist and formalist tradition that prevails in public administration, have prevented a stronger penetration of managerial ideas (Kickert 2011). According to García-Sánchez (2007), in the public management reforms that Spain has gone through, some of the core elements of the NPM doctrine such as technical control and accountability have been laid aside. However, as we discuss below, specific public sectors such as education have been more permeable to managerial ideas than others. Furthermore, during the last decade the economic recession has contributed to public sector reform ideas (such as the streamlining of the state structure and mechanisms to improve public employees' productivity) being discussed more determinately than ever in the Spanish context.[1]

NPM in the education sector

The education sector in Spain has moved away from the Napoleonic public administration model for at least two reasons. First, the education system is highly decentralised with the regional governments enjoying important levels of autonomy in education policy matters – although political conflicts and tensions are recurrent among the different scales of governance (Engel 2008). Second, the education system is organized as a public-private partnership in which the private sector plays an important role in the provision of education. In the 1980s, the Catholic Church influenced decisively a reform process that ended up with the consolidation of a dual public education system in which private schools (mainly religious) could apply for public funds on the condition that they follow public sector regulations. This public-private partnership, in its time, allowed for an important education expansion at a low cost. However, there are also important drawbacks in its application, including issues of discrimination in students' enrolment and the collection of uncovered school fees from an important part of the publicly funded private schools (Benito and González, 2007).

One of the milestones in the privatization of education in Spain is found in an ambitious and, paradoxically, progressive education reform that was adopted in 1990. This reform revolutionized the pedagogic methods – by mainstreaming constructivism – and strengthened the comprehensiveness of the education system by expanding compulsory education for two more years. However, despite its education democratization purpose, the reform was not implemented with sufficient resources, which is something that contributed to the deterioration of public schools and to middle class families exiting them to enrol their children in the more selective publicly-funded private sector (Fernández-Polanco 2007).[2]

The extension of access to education, together with the increasing migration flows in the nineties, introduced new sources of pressure and challenges to the system, especially in terms of education quality (Vidal 2009). Since many initiatives had already been implemented in terms of inputs, processes and pedagogy, the reforms to come had to focus on different aspects such as school governance, leadership and management. In fact, recent regulatory changes in Spain and in the different Spanish regions converge on the idea of strengthening school leadership and 'modernizing' the management and organization of schools by following NPM principles. Nonetheless, as we show in this chapter, the Catalan Education Act (2009) represents one of the regulatory frameworks that pioneered and is more clearly committed with the NPM doctrine in the Spanish context, and specifically with the promotion of school autonomy, the professionalization of school leadership and external evaluations.

The cultural political economy of education reform

Cultural political economy (CPE) is an analytical approach that provides us with useful theoretical and conceptual tools to study the adoption of (global) policy models in education, such as NPM, as well as other types of educational reforms. The CPE approach conceives culture, ideas and semiosis as important entry points to analyze processes of institutional change (Jessop 2010; Robertson and Dale 2014). According to this approach, paying closer attention to the mobilization of ideas and to political actors' perceptions is key to understanding the nature and results of policy dynamics. In most situations, policymakers intervene in policy fields where uncertainty prevails and, as a consequence, they need to resort to inferential shortcuts and external inputs to figure out how to position themselves (Weyland 2005). Here is where the role of experts – including external advisers, international organizations, and other types of knowledge brokers – and the mechanisms of persuasion and construction of meaning need to be seen and analyzed as key variables in processes of policy change (Risse 2000). A premise that derives directly from this is that an important dimension of power in policymaking has an ideational nature. Thus, 'soft power', in interaction with the material or political dimensions of power, needs to be seen as a key driver in processes of policy change.

Jessop's (2010) development of CPE is useful to operationalize these ideas in education policy analysis research. According to him, in all institutional transformations, material and semiotic factors interact through the evolutionary mechanisms of variation (which relates to the contingent emergence of new practices), selection (which relates to the subsequent privileging of these practices), and retention (their ongoing realization). This categorization of evolutionary mechanisms is especially valuable from both a heuristic and analytical point of view. The variation, selection and retention categories can contribute to identifying more systematically the sequence of contingencies, events, forms of agency and technologies of power involved in policy adoption, as well as the specific mechanisms – of both a semiotic and non-semiotic nature – that conduct or inhibit policy change. In other words, a careful analysis of each of these categories separately can contribute to building more complex explanations of why certain policies are adopted in particular settings (Verger 2016).

The adoption of NPM in Catalan education

Next, we analyse why and how NPM has penetrated the Catalan education context so decisively according to the evolutionary moments of variation, selection and retention. Nevertheless, we also show that despite NPM policies such as school autonomy, the empowerment of principals and external accountability measures have been widely adopted at the regulatory level, they have been rather deployed in a selective and limited way.

116 Antoni Verger and Marta Curran

Variation: from rejecting to opening the doors to NPM

In Catalonia, the social-democrats have not traditionally been in favour of the NPM approach to education and to other public services. In 2001, the Catalan government, at that time in the hands of the Catalan conservative party, passed a Strategic Education Planning Decree that, among other things, aimed at eliminating the centralized approach to the allocation of teachers. The teachers' unions filed a complaint against the government for this measure and the three left wing parties in the parliament (the social-democrats, the left-republicans and the eco-socialists) became additional plaintives in the complaint. Interestingly, however, these same three parties would start governing in coalition in 2003, two years later, and would initiate an ambitious education reform process grounded in NPM ideas that would introduce policies with a very similar approach to that of the mentioned contested decree.

The left wing coalition governed Catalonia for two legislative periods: 2003–2006 and 2006–2010 (see Table 8.1 for a chronology of the different political periods covered in this case study). In the first period, the ministry of education was in the hands of the Left-Republican party, and NPM measures were not a central part of the education agenda. At the policy level, the government focused on the organization of a major National Conference of Education that ended up drawing up a broadly disseminated National Education Agreement. This agreement, which was subscribed to by the government and most key educational stakeholders, would aim at defining the main guidelines and principles for the education reform that had to come. Among other things, the agreement promoted the idea of school autonomy, but it did so from a non-managerial and rather pedagogically driven approach. In that period, the Catalan government also started piloting a school autonomy program, which aimed at promoting both primary and secondary schools, designing a context-sensitive 'school autonomy plan' to fight against school failure and promote social cohesion. Schools that were part of the programme received a significant grant to develop their plan but in exchange had to adopt external evaluation and self-evaluation mechanisms, as well as to receive training on strategic planning and school leadership from the Catalan Education Ministry. The conception of 'school autonomy' they advanced through this program gave a lot of importance to participation at the school level, and to distributed leadership (Garcia-Alegre and Del Campo-Canals 2012).

In the second period of the left wing coalition, the education reform came with the Ministry of Education in the hands of the Socialist Party (i.e. the social-democrats) and with the approval of the first Catalan Education Act (LEC: its acronym in Catalan). The possibility for Catalonia to have its own educational law came with the approval of a new Statute of Autonomy (2006), which arrived after a long period of tense negotiations between the Catalan and the Spanish governments. The Statute gave Catalonia the capacity to pass its own education legislation, and the left wing government coalition

Catalonia **117**

TABLE 8.1 Political periods and NPM changes in Catalonia

Government ideology	Period	NPM changes in education
Conservative government	1981–2003	Attempts made but resisted by the left
1st left-wing coalition	2003–2006	National Education Agreement Piloting school autonomy (with a more pedagogic focus)
2nd left-wing coalition	2006–2010	'NPM revolution', ambitious legislation in 2009 (new Catalan Education Act)
Conservative government	2010–today	Selective implementation

took advantage of the opening of this window of opportunity to promote an ambitious education reform.

Surprisingly, however, this reform introduced a strong NPM approach into the education system, including a more managerial perspective on school autonomy and the professionalization and empowerment of school principals at the expense of teachers' power. It needs to be acknowledged that NPM ideas were not central in the Socialist Party education discourse at the time the government was formed. In fact, in the Socialist Party electoral program for the 2006 elections, references to NPM measures were absolutely marginal. In terms of education governance proposals, the socialists initially put much more emphasis on the municipal decentralization of the education system.

Overall, education reform in Catalonia needs to be seen as part of a broader political and contested process in the constant redefinition of the relationship between Catalonia and Spain (Engel 2008). Approving a new educational law was a way for the Catalan government to vindicate their competencies in educational affairs. However, other reasons of an educational nature also made the left wing coalition consider reforming the education system. These reasons were related to quality issues, especially evidenced by mediocre results in PISA, but also by early school-leaving rates much higher than the European average. The economic crisis that started showing its teeth in 2007–8 was also one of the triggers of change, since the modernization of the education system was seen by the Catalan government as an effective way to struggle against the economic crisis.

Selection: Perceiving NPM as a suitable policy solution

So far, we have reflected on the reasons and circumstances that predisposed policymakers to consider introducing important changes in education. But why did NPM become the privileged policy option to drive such changes? What are the narratives that crystallized among Catalan policymakers that justify

118 Antoni Verger and Marta Curran

NPM as the most suitable policy solution to existing educational problems? What factors of both a semiotic and non-semiotic nature intervened in the selection of NPM?

Two main arguments were deployed to justify the focus of the reform on school management issues and on the idea of school autonomy in particular. The first argument says that previous education reforms in Spain had already introduced sufficient systemic changes, such as expanding compulsory education, strengthening the comprehensiveness of the system, improving the pedagogical approach, and guaranteeing the necessary resources for the system to work. However, despite these important changes, the performance of the education system continued to be mediocre. The only dimension of the system that was left to be reformed, and that consequently had the potential to reverse this problem, was that of school management and organization (Garcia-Alegre and Del Campo-Canals 2012). The second argument, although compatible with the previous one, says that LEC focuses on school management issues due to the distribution of political competences between Catalonia and Spain. Specifically, the LEC had to focus on improving how schools are managed (and made accountable) because this was one of the few dimensions of the school system in which the Catalan government had more room of manoeuvre at the legislative level (Vidal 2009).

However, the emphasis on 'school level' changes was not only a policy option by process of elimination since, to many, it was also an inherently desirable policy. OECD/PISA has contributed enormously to construct such a preference among local policymakers. In many ways, the PISA report is a key reference for Spanish and Catalan education policymakers and politicians, independently of the party they come from (Bonal and Tarabini 2013). PISA has made them become more aware of the 'education quality' problem the system faces, but also to identify potential policy solutions. Several interviewees stated that the LEC took ideas on school autonomy and school leadership from OECD because PISA – along with other OECD products – relates these policy options to more effective education systems (MoE 1, 27 February 2013; MoE 2, 16 May 2013). In fact, OECD officials advocating for school autonomy were regular speakers at conferences and in courses organized by the Ministry of Education, and one of them even worked as an external advisor to the school autonomy program mentioned above (ExMoE 1, 15 May 2013).

Finally, when it comes to understanding the managerial focus that was imposed on the LEC, we also need to consider the particular preferences of the Catalan Education Minister, Ernest Maragall, and his personal group of advisors, since they did not necessarily fit within the education agenda of the Socialist Party at that time. In fact, in a book Maragall wrote on his experience as Education Minister, he complains of the Socialist Party not having backed his reform ideas sufficiently (Maragall and Colomé 2013). However, for him, a politician with a long and well-established career who comes from a cultural-political elite and upper-class family, following his 'ideals' was more important than party discipline.

When Maragall started his mandate, he did not have a strong background in education, but had strong opinions on public administration – and, specifically, on how the public sector was not working well on many levels, which some attribute to his strong links with ESADE (Stakeholder 1, February 27 2013), a prestigious business school and one of the most active promoters of NPM ideas in the country. He taught economic theory for a brief period in ESADE and is very close to its director, Francisco Longo, who has also specialized in 'school direction and management' and became Maragall's personal advisor in the context of the education reform (ExMoE 3, 27 January 2014).

In his public and private interventions, the minister constantly insisted on the need to make state apparatuses slimmer and more oriented toward results and complained about previous governments' acceptance of the mediocrity that prevails in public schools[3]. He acknowledged that there are many 'committed teachers', but also considered that 'there are others that are simply settled in, too many of them' (Maragall, 2009, p.18). For this reason he insisted on the importance of introducing teachers' incentives and evaluation schemes to improve schools. He also considered one of the fundamental problems in public schools to be the lack of a proper 'owner' in charge and that, to work properly, schools would need to operate more like a private company[4]. According to him, deep changes of both a cultural and organizational nature would be necessary to modernize the Catalan education system (Maragall 2009).

Retention (i): Stakeholders' position and the accommodationist effect of 'school autonomy'

Retention represents a final and necessary step for the realization of the adoption of a new policy. There are many policies that are selected by decision-makers but which end up not being finally retained in their particular settings, usually due to the opposition they face. Retention of new education policies means their institutionalization and inclusion into the regulatory framework but also into the network of educational technologies and practices of a system (Colyvas and Jonsson 2011).

The NPM approach to education reform had the strong support, but also the consent, of key stakeholders. In Catalonia there is an organization of public school principals called Axia that aims at strengthening the role of school principals in the education system and that was a key advocate of managerialism in the context of the LEC debate. In fact, the Minister Maragall valued the contributions of Axia – and other school principals – in the debate quite highly. According to him, school principals were one of the few stakeholders that really understood 'the ambition and authenticity' of his reform agenda (Maragall and Colomé 2013: 118).

The teachers' unions' opposition to the LEC was fierce. In their opinion, the main proposals of the LEC undermined the democratic control of schools and would lead to the 'atomization' and 'privatization' of the system. The intensity of their opposition to the government at that time, and against the figure of Maragall in particular, had no precedent in the democratic period, with the organization of four sectoral strikes in eighteen months. However, the Ministry was not open to the unions' demands – especially those against school autonomy and the hierarchization of school management – because they altered the essence of the reform excessively.

Other education stakeholders did not have such a tense relation with the Ministry over the LEC. For instance, progressive pedagogical movements and family associations did not engage substantially in the NPM debate. In their public reactions to the LEC, they emphasized the pedagogical (and not the managerial) dimension of school autonomy and, consequently, were supportive of those changes that would strengthen it (Biosca 2009).

After an intense parliamentary and extra-parliamentary debate, on 10 July 2009 the LEC was passed. In the final weeks of deliberation, one of the parties in the government coalition, the eco-socialist party, retired its support of the LEC, while the conservative party – in the opposition – voted in favour. The eco-socialists argued that the LEC did not defend public education sufficiently and raised concerns about the potential equity implications of the type of school autonomy that was being promoted.

The final reform passed was a law that focuses on the governance and organization of schools and that is structured around three main pillars: school autonomy, schools' leadership, and evaluation. Each of these pillars was further developed in three corresponding decrees in the months after the act's approval: a) The *school autonomy decree* (Decree 102/2010, 3 August 2010) promotes schools having greater autonomy in three main domains: financial management, school organization and pedagogy. However, the pedagogical component is not so well developed in the articles of the decree; rather, the text focuses on aspects of school management and specifically on the role of the principal; b) The *direction decree* (Decree 155/2010, 2 November 2010) promotes the professionalization of the figure of the principal as the manager of the school, establishing evaluation and promotion mechanisms for principals – including salary incentives – and gives them responsibilities in new domains, such as the hiring of teachers and school fundraising. The decree promotes the competitive selection of school principals on the basis of a *direction project* candidates must elaborate. According to a ministry official, the direction decree aims at challenging the 'horizontal culture that is rooted in the schools, which is very difficult to eliminate' and is 'the most important barrier to modernizing schools' (MoE 6, 13 July 2013); c) Lastly, the *evaluation decree* (Decree 177/2010, 23 November 2010) focuses on the creation of an independent Evaluation Agency with numerous competencies over the evaluation of directors, schools, teachers' performance and students' results.

Interestingly, the last two decrees were approved just before Catalan elections were held on 28 November 2010 (the evaluation decree being passed only five days before the elections). The Education Ministry rushed their passage because the expectations were not for the socialist party to win, which meant that the continuation of the NPM agenda in education would not be guaranteed. As we show next, their concerns were certainly justified.

Retention (ii): The uneven deployment of the NPM reform

The conservatives won the 2010 elections comfortably, and inherited an education law they felt very comfortable with for different reasons: it does not alter the conditions private schools enjoy to get public funding; it does not focus excessively on education equity; and last but not least, in many aspects, it requires the public schools to emulate the managerial practices of the private sector. However, the conservative government is implementing the reform in a very uneven and selective manner, basically implementing those NPM policies whose costs are zero or relatively low and that, at the same time, meet their political preferences. Such preferences would fit under what Apple (2001) calls 'conservative modernization', an ideology that combines, in an apparently contradictory way, the belief in market ideas (such as school choice and the superiority of the private sector) and the state control of schools (via performance indicators, curriculum control, standards-setting, and nationally standardized evaluations).

The Conservative government has argued that it cannot implement the content of the LEC in a strict sense due to the budget constraints that the management of the financial crisis requires. For this reason, they cannot provide well-performing schools, principals and teachers with further economic incentives, as established in the different decrees already explored (MoE 5, 13 July 2013). Based on the same argument, the government has suspended the establishment of the independent external evaluation agency[5], although motives of a non-economic nature are also in play here. The aversion of the conservative education minister, Irene Rigau, to the possibility of creating an evaluation body that she cannot control directly is well known. Instead of creating such an agency, and far from the NPM ideal, the Minister has mandated its body of inspectors to adopt further evaluation responsibilities (ExMoE2, 17 June 2013), which reflects a more hierarchical and bureaucratic approach to school evaluation and control.

At the same time, the conservative government has advanced a range of policies that undermine school autonomy, especially the pedagogic dimension of school autonomy. The school autonomy program has been frozen and its leaders expelled from the Ministry due to its links with the former government (MoE 7, 13 July 2013). The conservative government considers the school educational project, which all schools must carry out under the law, as not central whereas it considers the principal's project as the main tool to define the school strategy and management (MoE 5, 13 July 2013). At the same time, the government has promoted an ambitious programme on 'basic competencies'

122 Antoni Verger and Marta Curran

that establishes what primary and secondary schools should teach, and how, in the areas of Mathematics and Language.[6] This initiative, in fact, contradicts the rhetoric of school autonomy in the pedagogic domain and undermines the capacity of teachers to autonomously determine what should be taught, and how, in their schools.

From the wide NPM agenda regulated under the LEC, the conservative government is basically focusing on professionalizing and strengthening the role of principals as managers. In this respect, they have promoted training programmes and accreditation mechanisms for principals and enacted meritocratic procedures to select principals at the school level, which will reduce the power of the school council in this respect. They have also passed a new decree that allows principals to contribute to the hiring of part of their teaching staff based on the argument that this will contribute to building a more cohesive staff at the school level.

All these changes have been introduced in a context of relative social peace since the strong opposition to NPM policies among teachers' unions has declined in comparison to Maragall's period, as their current focus is on resisting the huge budget cuts that are affecting education and, in particular, teachers' working conditions.

Conclusions

In Catalonia, NPM reforms have translated into the triangulation of three main policy measures: school autonomy, the professionalization of school management, and external evaluation. Catalonia has become an early adopter of NPM reforms within the Spanish context, which has made of this case a sort of Trojan Horse in a highly bureaucratized politico-administrative system. As we have shown, the strategic alignment of a range of factors of both a political and educational nature at the variation, selection and retention stages has contributed to NPM ideas penetrating into this country's education decisively.

At the variation moment, the Statute of Autonomy of Catalonia, approved in 2006, gave the Catalan government the legal possibility of promoting an ambitious educational reform via the approval of a regional educational law for the first time since the beginning of the democracy. At the same time, international assessments, such as PISA, together with a low level of performance against other international education indicators, contributed greatly to introducing a sense of an urgent need for reform among the Catalan government and other educational stakeholders. A broad debate on how to address such situation was initiated. However, in the context of this debate, not all types of policy changes were considered as equally feasible and desirable by Catalan policymakers.

When it comes to understanding the selection of NPM as the main focus of the Catalan educational reform, a range of factors operating at multiple scales need to be considered. Here, the complex relationship between Catalonia and Spain needs to be highlighted again. To some extent, the Catalan government perceived school-level and school organization reforms – such as school autonomy and managerial leadership – as the missing piece in the modernization of the education system but also as the only dimension of the system in which the Catalan government could fully intervene without interferences from the central government, or without entering into contradiction with Spanish legislation. However, internal political dynamics also operated here since the left wing government coalition considered that, by focusing on school management issues and leaving other sensitive issues at the margins (i.e. school segregation, privatization, municipalization and so on), the reform would receive support from the influential Catalan conservative party, which was in the opposition at that time. Furthermore, the policy recommendations and knowledge products coming from the education division of the OECD – despite being translated in a very selective way (see Verger and Curran 2014) – became strategic in the legitimation of the Catalan policymakers' push for NPM measures.

At the selection moment, we have also focused on the impact of the particular policy preferences and charisma of the Catalan Ministry of Education at the time of the reform. Maragall was a very peculiar Minister, with strong convictions about NPM being the best formula to improve public schools, and willing to confront the powerful teachers' unions, and even factions of his own party, to advance his policy preferences. However, beyond an individual crusade, Maragall's ideas and decisions need to be contextualized within the evolution of contemporary social democratic thinking in Europe and, in particular, within the prevailing approach of social democracy to public sector reform. As happened in the UK and in Nordic and central European contexts before, the social-democratic party in Catalonia ended up adopting NPM reforms because they perceived them as an effective way to modernize public education and fix its main problems in a period in which the public sector faces a legitimacy crisis globally and is perceived by many as too hierarchical, ineffective and monolithic.

Interestingly, the Catalan conservatives had tried to introduce and retain similar managerial reforms before, but they did not have the same political capacity and legitimacy as the Left to alter the way the public sector is regulated and organized. In fact, the Catalan social-democrats, together with other left wing groups, fiercely opposed NPM educational policies in the beginning of the new century when the conservatives were ruling the country. However, just a few years later, they took power and ended up promoting an ambitious education reform precisely based on NPM ideas.

The retention of NPM ideas in the Catalan education system has also been facilitated by the accommodationist effect that policy ideas such as 'school autonomy' have (cf. Linder 1999). School autonomy, which is the flagship of NPM reforms in education, is an idea that is ambiguous enough to generate support among a broad range of audiences and ideologies. The social-democrats see it as a way of promoting the public sector and making it more effective. The neoliberals consider it as a way to make the state apparatus slimmer and to introduce market logics into the public sector. The conservatives see it as a way to professionalize and hierarchize the management of schools. And progressive educators consider it as a way of introducing alternative pedagogies, relevant education, and greater cohesiveness among teachers.

In the end, the core of the education reform battle in Catalonia was not about whether NPM ideas, like school autonomy, were right or not – or should be adopted or not – but about the concrete meaning these ideas should have, and about the way they should be regulated accordingly. Somehow, the fact that the unions rejected and opposed the adoption of any NPM-based changes left them outside of this semiotic battle and facilitated the Ministry gaining legitimacy with an important segment of the population. In contrast to the unions, the managerialist advocacy coalition, including the school principals' lobby took advantage of the juncture and contributed to promoting a definition of school autonomy as inseparable from managerialism and the professionalization of school leadership. The conservative party, in power since 2010, has reinforced this particular perspective on NPM as it completely coincides with its 'conservative modernization' approach to education reform.

As a result, today the dominant rationale behind the NPM reform in Catalonia is that school autonomy can only result from the efforts of a strong and professionalized school management. A school should have a strong leader, with a clear vision of where the school should go, and sufficient powers and authority to take it there. According to this rationale, the participatory organizational culture that has prevailed in the Spanish school system since the 1980s is one of the main barriers to the modernization of the education system and should be gradually substituted by more hierarchical forms of management and leadership. In this sense, one of the paradoxes of the NPM reform in Catalonia is that it is not being adopted because the system is too bureaucratic and hierarchical but because it is apparently too democratic and horizontal.

Notes

1 On 26 October 2012, the Spanish Council of Ministers established the Commission for Public Administration Reform (CORA) with a mandate to produce proposals for more austere, useful and effective public administrations.
2 Today, around 30 per cent of Spanish students in compulsory schooling are enrolled under the modality of publicly funded private schools. Only 4% of students are, in fact, enrolled in fully private schools (MECD 2012).
3 See: www.ara.cat/premium/societat/Ernest-Maragall-Nomes-millors-ciutadans_0_908909196.html.
4 See: www.elperiodico.cat/ca/noticias/opinio/ernest-maragall-mira-dels-centres-ningu-vol-ser-director-240106.
5 See Decree 294/2011, 8 March 2011.
6 See http://www.govern.cat/pres_gov/AppJava/govern/grans-reptes/aixecar-catalunya/177430/departament-densenyament-presenta-competencies-basiques-curriculum-primaria-secundaria-canvi-paradigma-metodologic.html .

PART IV

The post-communist state

9

NEW PUBLIC MANAGEMENT IN CZECH EDUCATION

From the side road to the highway?

Arnošt Veselý, Jan Kohoutek and Stanislav Štech

Introduction

Having witnessed the fall of the communist regime in 1989, the Czech Republic is embedded in the tradition of a post-Communist state (Meyer-Sahling 2004). This tradition bears the legacy of centralized party rule, rigid ideological control of curricula and education for the needs of an industrial economy. The post-Communist transformation of the educational system was quite rapid and entailed depoliticisation of curricula, acknowledgment of students' rights, academic freedoms and de-monopolisation of provision by allowing private schools (Cerych 1997). It was followed by changes in funding, decentralisation, curricular organisation, testing and teacher training (Greger and Walterová 2007). These changes have been influenced by domestic and international factors. Whilst the former comprised the political situation, economic development and demographic changes, the latter showed though the introduction of large-scale comparative student assessment (PISA and TIMSS) and Europeanization (mobility programmes, support from the Structural Funds). Involvement in these international activities was underlain by admission of the Czech Republic to major international organisations and structures, namely the OECD (in 1995) and the European Union (in 2004). So far, the foregoing changes have been studied mostly from the transition and transformation perspective, focusing upon the outcomes of the post-Communist transformation process (Greger 2011; Kotásek 2005a, 2005b; Štech 2008). However, these studies leave something to be desired when it comes to exploration of the role and influence of New Public Management (NPM) as a popular, modernising approach to education. In line with the aim of this book, we analyse in our chapter how NPM has played out in Czech education after 1989.

128 Arnošt Veselý, Jan Kohoutek and Stanislav Štech

The chapter is structured as follows. First, we provide a brief overview of the role of NPM in Czech education policy after 1989. Then we discuss in more detail three aspects of Czech education reform that are most closely related to NPM: decentralization, standardized testing and teachers' discretion to manage classrooms professionally. After that we discuss to what extent NPM has been present in terms of ideas, measures and practices. We show that despite the fact that there are several *measures* that are very much in line with NPM, they have not been introduced in relation to NPM *ideas*. We conclude with a discussion of the possible future of NPM in Czech education.

New Public Management in the Czech Republic

The dominant discourse underlying post-1989 educational reforms could be summed up as 'getting rid of the Communist legacy' and a 'return to the West'. This was amplified by various means of west European assistance and consultancy taken up by the Czech authorities. Although such a situation could present a breeding ground for widespread application of NPM, in hindsight, we argue that only isolated policy prescriptions were borrowed from NPM core ideological features building upon management, managers, managing and managerialism outlined in Chapter 1. Despite the (ideational) relegation of managerial powers over schooling to principals and selected regional bureau units, the actual delivery shows the absence of relevant management tools such as explicit performance standards making, among others, removals for underperformance personalized rather than evidence-based. Moreover, taking due account of a plethora of national, oft-changing policy directions makes Czech school principals take on the role of administrators rather than managers in the NPM sense who would have time for managing through proactive planning and service efficiency.

Hence, the actual implementation of these prescriptions to the educational realities of the day seems to owe much to centralized steering and not NPM-inspired managerialism. This is mostly due to prevailing national idiosyncrasies still acknowledging the prominent role of the state (Ministry of Education, Youth and Sports) and vertical organisational hierarchies (cf. Greger and Walterová 2007). Neither was NPM as a self-standing ideological approach fully adopted into the rhetoric of educational policymakers largely because of their minimal awareness of NPM ideology. To sum up, 'hearing about NPM through the grapevine' has been enough for Czech educational policymakers to apply, recently more than ever, *some* NPM-*inspired*, *repackaged* policy prescriptions but not to advocate implementation of NPM as a 'catch-all' policy solution. The Czech approach to NPM in education thus represents a paradoxical case in which NPM ideological premises have been selectively applied for labelling some policy prescriptions that took on un-NPM twists and turns in the reality of the implementation process and that might even have been implemented without NPM policy borrowing taking place.

TABLE 9.1 Key features of NPM in the Czech Republic (based on Hood 1991 and Gunter and Fitzgerald 2013a, b)

Key features	Rhetoric	Policy measures/practices
1. Hands on, professional management in the public sector	The need for school leadership raised in the 2000s but not yet enacted	Principals and officials are not really 'free to manage' because of financial and legal constraints No performance reviews No removals because of underperformance
2. Explicit standards and measurements of performance	National standards and tests widely discussed from 2011 onwards	Standards and standardized testing for 5th and 9th grade trialled in 2004 and 2008; piloted from 2011
3. Greater emphasis on output controls	Inputs and processes stressed rather than outcomes	Inspection and evaluation based predominantly upon congruence with legal norms Control of inputs and processes rather than outputs
4. Shift to disaggregation of units in the public sector	Autonomy as a means of democratization and subsidiarity, not as a means for greater effectiveness	Very strong decentralisation starting in 2001 Limited privatization
5. Shift to greater competition in the public sector	School choice as an expression of individual freedom Competition considered important but not related to NPM	Almost unrestricted school choice in practice
6. Stress on private sector styles of management practice	The private sector as a source of innovation	Rather marginal private sector Accountability overload of principals
7. Stress on greater discipline and parsimony in use of resources	No discussion about underfinancing rather than cutting costs and efficiency	Formula funding (funding goes with students) Competition for students among schools Moderate competition for funds, mostly linked to EU structural funds

130 Arnošt Veselý, Jan Kohoutek and Stanislav Štech

The core features of NPM that apply to education in the Czech Republic are summarized in Table 9.1. In addition to the seven core features, we argue that it is useful to distinguish between three different facets of NPM: *ideas* or *rhetoric* (how we talk and think about education), concrete *realized measures* (public policies actually implemented at the systemic level, such as standardized testing) and everyday life *practice* (how NPM ideas work in practice, including actual implementation of policies). One thing is how and to what extent NPM ideas are present in education debates, while another thing is whether these ideas are actually implemented in concrete public policies. Still another thing is how NPM is internalized in everyday school practices. As we will show, these three aspects might not be necessarily linked to one another.

It should be noted that while Table 9.1 provides a rather sharp picture of the Czech case, the reality is much more complicated and often even contradictory. For instance, school principals have a lot of responsibilities and competencies (including the hiring and firing of teachers). The importance of their independent leadership is ceaselessly stressed. However, as we will show below, in practice this independence and 'freedom to manage' is hugely constrained by political factors and administrative overload. In reality, educational policy is rather inconsistent and non-coherent. It is full of contradictory trends which sometimes lead to almost paradoxical situations.

Therefore, it is necessary to discuss each point in more detail and in a broader context. Given the space limit, in this chapter we focus on three aspects which are most important from the NPM perspective: decentralization, curriculum reform followed by the introduction of standardized testing and changes in the status and preparation of teachers. While decentralization corresponds with feature 4 in Table 9.1, standardized testing is closely linked to feature 2. The changes in the status and preparation of teachers discussed above cut across most of the features. After that we return to Table 9.1 and discuss in more detail the actual role of NPM ideas, measures and practices in Czech education.

Core reform changes from the NPM perspective

Decentralisation and its consequences

The Czech educational system before 1989 was characterized by a highly centralized administration based on the totalitarian principles of Communist ideology. The right to establish, administer, and direct schools was held exclusively by the state and the decisions about the goals and content of teaching took place in the bureaucratic apparatus of the Communist party (Švecová 2000). This was changed abruptly after 1989. The first wave of decentralization took place immediately after the fall of Communism when municipalities and schools were granted a lot of autonomy, especially in personnel issues. The second wave of decentralization started after 2002 following a major reform of overall public administration. Prior to 2001 each of the 76 Czech school districts and Prague had a District Schooling Office (DSO) that was subordinate to the Ministry of Education, Youth and Sports (MEYS). The DSOs supervised schools, employed school principals, provided pedagogical consultations and guidance, and transmitted the educational guidelines and instructions put forth by the MEYS (Herbst *et al.* 2012). In the public administration reform, the competencies of the centre were devolved to the newly established regions as well as to the municipalities. At present each region is the organising body for secondary schools, while municipalities take responsibility for pre-primary and basic schools.

The data from the *OECD-INES Survey on Locus of Decision Making* (OECD 2012c, 2012d) show that the Czech Republic has one of the most decentralized governance systems. Decentralization in the Czech Republic has both its supporters and critics. It was blamed for having caused a decline in PISA performance (Herbst *et al.* 2012). There is, however, also evidence of positive effects in terms of the inclusion of social partners and stakeholders (Vojtěch *et al.* 2011).

First, while the central level has been hollowed out and divested of instruments for influencing educational processes, it is still considered the principal education actor to be held accountable. Because the central level has traditionally been very powerful, many people call first on the central government to render an account for schools' performance. The centre still has the ability to set the framework within which the schools make their choices. Yet, the central government cannot directly influence what is happening inside schools. The MEYS is responsible for the concept and strategy of the development of education, including its content, and the necessary conditions for its realization including overseeing the education system and financing education and labour relations (Eurydice 2010). It is often argued that the Ministry now has the strategic role, but at the same time it has very limited power in realizing the strategy.

This is not a unique phenomenon; it has also been observed in other countries and other policy domains, e.g. in Australian rail policy (cf. Edwards 2009). In the Czech case, however, the incongruence between the power of the centre and its accountability have led to the temptation to repair and close this gap with inadequate and hasty 'solutions', especially by introducing high-stakes testing and making schools directly responsible to the centre (OECD 2012b).

The second problem relates to the accountability of the municipalities and regions. They have become the founders of primary and secondary schools, respectively. According to the current law, municipalities are responsible for establishing and closing down basic schools and ensuring compliance with compulsory school attendance requirements at basic schools established by another municipality or union of municipalities. Similarly, regions are obliged to ensure the conditions for the secondary and tertiary professional education of pupils and students who are disabled or disadvantaged by health conditions. In the current legislation, however, there is no clause that explicitly obliges municipalities or regions to provide *quality* education. Nor are there sanctions

132 Arnošt Veselý, Jan Kohoutek and Stanislav Štech

for regions or municipalities if they fail to provide quality and relevant education. For any failures only the principals are held accountable. The only accountability of regions and municipalities is political. However, given the fact that normally education hardly matters in regional or municipal elections, there is no mechanism that would make regions and municipalities truly accountable for school management.

Last but not least, there is a problem with the accountability overload of school principals. They have extensive responsibilities for a huge number of things, ranging from pedagogical quality via administrative accuracy to maintaining the school's facilities. As in other countries, there has been a vast increase in the quantity of bureaucratic tasks required from school principals.

This leads to an overload of responsibilities. Instead of being felt as autonomy and empowerment, the decentralization change is felt by many school principals as increased accountability (Prášilová 2008). Even worse this might result in contradicting expectations placed on principals, leading to a kind of professional disorientation under which a given actor (principal) is caught in a position where no way of acting is ideal, because different forums assess his or her actions from competing perspectives. Thus, to be able 'to win' in terms of one accountability perspective (such as compliance with rules), means 'to lose' in terms of another accountability perspective (such as exceptional performance).

In this respect, Mikáč (2011) analysed the reasons (i.e. 'accountability consequences') why public school founders in the Czech Republic (usually municipalities or regional councils) dismiss principals. He found that quite often principals were dismissed for very insignificant, usually just formal reasons. The actual motives for the dismissals were often that a newly elected council did not like the principal, either because of personal characteristics or because of differences in personal judgments on the school's performance. For principals it is thus almost impossible to fulfil all the expectations at once (to be a good financial manager, to be a good leader of educational processes, to be in good communication with school founders etc.).

Curriculum reform and national student assessment

One of the most significant education changes after 1989 was curriculum reform. The 2004 Education Act established two levels for determining the content of instruction in the Czech Republic. At the central level, the MEYS determines Framework Education Programmes (FEPs) for each educational area within pre-primary, basic and secondary education. These define the compulsory content, scope and conditions of education and provide a national framework for student learning. In agreement with such a framework, schools further develop School Education Programmes (SEPs), which consist of the operationalisation of FEPs to fit the contexts of individual schools. Schools have considerable room to design their own learning strategies as FEPs are not markedly detailed.

Curriculum reform and decentralization have generated the feeling among many stakeholders that the educational 'loosening' has gone too far. It is not surprising that in a country where instruction has been standardized in detail across the whole state for decades, many teachers, principals, politicians, parents and even education experts have started to be quite insecure about what is supposed to be 'good teaching' and a 'good school'. This has led to an understandable call for specification of standards, guidelines and above all some sort of monitoring of students' outcomes across schools.

Although curriculum reform has never been linked to NPM ideas, the NPM maxim 'tight on goals, but loose on means' describes the debate well. While the autonomy of teachers and schools in deciding about *how* to teach and manage has never really been challenged, the generally accepted argument is that the state is still responsible for ensuring quality in all schools and that fulfilment of this goal cannot be avoided. The demand for some kind of standards and standardized testing was further triggered by a sharp decline in students' performance in international assessment, especially in PISA 2006 and 2009.

The 'PISA shock' in the second half of the 2000s was pivotal for the initiation of standardized testing. However, the very idea of student assessment standardisation had already entered the Czech educational discourse in the mid-1990s through the OECD recommendations for further action. The recommendations centred on forming a comprehensive assessment system that would balance the traditional teachers' role with nationwide testing. The standardized nationwide testing was to be introduced from scratch in two ways. First, by assessing learning achievements in primary schools, taking the form of national standardized testing at the end of primary (fifth grade, ISCED 1) and lower secondary education (ninth grade, ISCED 2); second, by standardizing and differentiating the secondary school leaving examination (OECD 1996). These recommendations were adopted and made part of the 2001 White Paper. This is, however, when things started to go wrong.

The following decade and a half was fraught with erroneous designs and redesigns of both testing schemes resulting in their problematic implementation. Development of the national standardized tests for the fifth and ninth grade was helped by a series of pilot trials voluntarily undertaken by about 1800 schools between 2004 and 2008 (Greger and Kifer 2012). Despite five years of piloting funded from the EU Structural Funds, the test designs turned out to be erroneous and were widely criticized by educational experts as well as parent initiatives. One of the main reasons was the unclear relationship between the assessment aims and the content of the newly created educational standards for the fifth and ninth grade (Veselý 2011). Although this criticism might get some political acceptance, the reason for the unclear future of the standardized testing after two runs in 2011 and 2013 more probably lies in the drying up of targeted funds for this purpose totalling 296 million CZK.

Implementation of the standardized secondary school leaving examination (SSLE) presents a similarly convoluted story. The standardized SSLE was

134 Arnošt Veselý, Jan Kohoutek and Stanislav Štech

referenced in the 2001 White Paper as an exam with two difficulty levels with basic and profiling parts. This was followed by protracted practical realisation due to repeated postponements in the late 2000s. After its implementation in 2011, the whole scheme of the standardized SSLE still suffers from some test design and technical issues, with doubts raised as to its overall value for individual schools as well as the (higher) education sector. In the main, controversies prevail over (not) keeping two difficulty levels of the exam although results of the standardized SSLE have practically no bearing on admission decisions by individual universities (Greger and Kifer 2012).

In short, the last twenty years have seen little progress towards consolidating standardized testing through an integrated assessment framework (Santiago *et al.* 2012). Standardized student assessment thus remains a long-time problematic area in the country's educational policy due to the lack of clarity of purpose, organisational non-transparency and low levels of policymakers' expertise (Straková and Simonová 2013). The situation is not helped by political instability, with fourteen ministers of education changing seats since 2007, and the divisive standpoints of principals, parents and the general public on the matter (Veselý *et al.* 2012). In this light, the latest ministerial plan for introduction of a standardized entrance examination for upper secondary education (ISCED 3) seems to be another ill-conceived and belated try, as such examinations are already administered by a private agency in eight of out fourteen Czech regions (Feřtek 2014).

Professionalism – free to manage?

In the early 1990s, public discourse was dominated by the idea of the freedom to teach, of transforming schools from within and of principals' and teachers' autonomy. This was reflected by the establishment of the civic associations 'NEMES' and 'PAU: Friends of Engaged Teaching/Learning' (Červenka 1993). In response to the previous rigid ideological management of the education sector, 'freedom to teach' was the ethos shared by the majority of stakeholders. A ministerial regulation adopted in 1991 made it possible for teachers to use up to 30 per cent of teaching capacity at their own discretion.

However, this political measure reinforcing the autonomy of teachers and enabling 'free education' seemed to answer to the second part of the NPM maxim 'tight on goals, but loose on means' only. Teaching practice was marked by a measure of unease. The content and the quality of the work of such autonomous teachers were never an issue. With the extension of compulsory schooling to nine years in the mid-1990s, the room for autonomy was fulfilled by means of revising and consolidating the curriculum. The notion held by engaged civic associations that autonomous teachers would spontaneously take advantage of the offer of alternative education schools was fulfilled only in part. The emergent reform educational groups (Montessori, the Waldorf School) and methods (critical thinking, project-based education) were not reflected

Czech Republic **135**

in the new, formally extended capacities of teachers. Educational decision-makers themselves did not offer such inspiration and were half-hearted about the activities of civic associations. Teachers considered curricular freedom as an unacceptable failure of the government to specify a key constant of education. Alternative methods were seen as an amusing distraction in the teaching process (Štech 1995; Chalupová 2002).

Gradually, this situation led to a specific form of the purchaser-provider split. The idea behind this split is that public institutions may remain in control of the provision of public services and benefit from letting private agencies or NGOs supply the services. In the mid-2000s, the curriculum reform mentioned earlier reinforced this split. In procedural terms, it consisted of the elaboration of School Education Programmes (SEP) within Framework Education Programmes (FEPs), set down at the central level. Formally, space was created for the autonomous creativity of teachers and of principals and for their discretionary power. The gist of the reform consisted in a very general (even vague) specification of the framework objectives of education and in allowing for great liberty as to the concrete knowledge content of the curriculum.

Most teachers are sceptical about the elaboration of SEPs (Straková 2010, 2013). The government has made use of European projects and of related NGOs and educational agencies to help teachers with their new 'freedom'. Thus, external actors have become educators of teachers when it comes to methods of achieving educational objectives (key competences). As a result, the formally emphasized autonomy of teachers is paid for with an external, authoritative specification of the methods and objectives of education which are then to be sanctioned by government bodies and institutions. In the context of the mentioned resistance of teachers and principals against this curricular reform, the prominent terms of 'freedom' and 'autonomy' have acquired a negative connotation (cf. Janík 2013).

In the Czech Republic, graduate (initial) education of teachers was formalized as MA university education for more than 60 years. After 1989, however, there were several waves of contestation suggesting that teacher education should be shorter (a BA cycle). At first, this was only rhetorical: in 1992–1994, it was argued that practical educational skills were the decisive professional competence and the theory-practice split was settled in favour of practice. Teaching theory (didactics) and research were undervalued; aspiring teachers should be oriented towards classroom pedagogy and psychology. The said discourse, however, was not guided by a desire to achieve greater efficiency and better education outputs.

The traditional conception of the teaching profession was affected to a much greater degree by the implementation of the Bologna process and the consequent re-structuring of tertiary studies into a BA level followed by a separate MA level (2001–2006). This was a legal measure which reduced the room for student-teachers to develop the required professional prerequisites to make use of the freedom to manage practices (Mareš and Beneš 2013). Nevertheless, it inspired

136 Arnošt Veselý, Jan Kohoutek and Stanislav Štech

recurring attempts to shorten the university education of teachers and to focus it on non-reflected practice.

Today, these arguments have resulted in the adoption of legislation which stipulates that principals (sic!) may recognize long-term practitioners of a higher age who have thus far worked as non-qualified staff or 'recognized experts' as possessing a professional teachers' qualification (Amendment to the Act on Pedagogical Staff 2014). To this may be added that continuing professional development, its close link to career rules and a stable status of the teaching profession have been repeatedly proclaimed in vain at the political level since the 1990s. Professional education (development) has therefore never been related to career advancement (Spilková *et al.* 2014) and improved pay. On the contrary, excessive decentralization after 2001 led to the abolition of the District Educational Centres' network providing in-service teachers with professional training and impacted the central National Institute for Further Education (NIDV) which has subsequently been unable to draft professionally relevant and critical further education content.

NPM in educational ideas, policies and practices

We can now address the questions underpinning our analysis in Table 9.1: how widespread and pervasive has NPM been in Czech education? And to what extent have educational changes been brought by NPM ideology? Let us first discuss the first two facets of NPM – *rhetoric* and actual *policies*. NPM stresses performance and management by outputs. Until recently, performance had never been an issue in the Czech Republic. It is only with the sharp decline in PISA results in the second half of the 2000s that policy makers have started to discuss how to boost the overall results. Until then, very little attention had been paid to *performance* and *outputs,* especially to those that are easily measurable, which attests to the rising significance of PISA data for *managing* Czech education and policymaking strategies. After 1989 the curriculum emphasis upon encyclopaedic knowledge was criticized and so-called key competencies were endorsed instead. One possible explanation is that education was always strongly associated with values which are very hard to measure. This is still clearly visible in the Education Act from 2004 which states seven basic aims including, e.g. the personal development of the human being, environmental protection, ethical and spiritual values for personal and civic life and understanding of and application of democratic principles comprising equality of women and men. This is not to say that reading literacy and numeracy had been unimportant, but until recently the students' performance in terms of achievement in standardized tests had never been a real issue.

A 'shift to disaggregation of units in the public sector' (Hood 1991) is another core NPM feature. As we have seen above, it is one of the most visible changes in Czech education after 1989. Decentralization, however, has never been unambiguous. While the first wave of decentralization has generally been taken positively as a natural and necessary development towards truly democratic governance, the second wave has been questioned more. The abolition of District Schooling Offices was part of the *general* decentralization of the Czech public administration, and as such was *externally imposed* on the education sector. Decentralization has never been high on the *educational* agenda. Similarly, it has not been directly associated with the efficiency issue. Rather it has been seen as a value per se, an expression that schools should be governed at the most immediate (or local) level.

An emphasis on competition is another key feature of NPM. In education, this mostly means competing for funds and students. In principle, there are three types of arguments supporting school choice (Musset 2012): 1) through market mechanisms it will remedy inefficiencies in the system; 2) parents have a right to choose; 3) it is a way of making education systems more equitable. In the Czech Republic students are initially assigned to basic schools according to their residence (catchment area), and the founding body (municipality) is obliged to provide enough places for its residents. However, parents can apply for schools outside their catchment area, and often do so. Because funding follows students, there is a strong incentive for the schools to accept as many applications as they can accommodate. With the exception of suburban areas around big cities, schools usually have a lot of spaces. Thus especially in towns and cities parents have many choices. According to PISA 2012 85 per cent of Czech students attend schools whose principals reported competition for students in the same area, compared to the OECD average of 76 per cent (OECD 2013b: 386, own calculations). Obviously, in villages and small towns there is usually only one basic school, so the choice of school is limited because of this practical reason. However, in general the choice of schools is wide enough and this established policy is rarely challenged. Hence, the second argument for parental free choice is by far the most dominant in the Czech discourse as an expression of the parental *right* to choose a school according to their way of life and values, not as a way to improve schools' performance and effectiveness.

Together with school choice, private schools were introduced immediately after 1989. Their proportion is, however, not substantial, which is common to some other Central European countries (Slovak Republic, Poland). Again, private schools were not introduced as a way of increasing efficiency and performance in the system but as a way of democratizing and widening the spectrum of education programmes. It was believed that these schools would 'form an innovation sector and will introduce a new curriculum, new subjects, new teaching styles etc. and will help to diffuse these innovations into the whole system' (OECD 1996). The innovation role, rather than the 'cost-effectiveness' one, is also seen in the fact that private schools can be publicly subsidized with basic subsidies equivalent to between 50 and 80 per cent of those received by basic schools, depending on a range of criteria including inspections by the Czech School Inspectorate (Santiago *et al.* 2012: 16).

138 Arnošt Veselý, Jan Kohoutek and Stanislav Štech

Another core value associated with NPM is frugality (feature 7 in 9.1): cutting costs and doing more for less (Hood 1991). Again, frugality has never been a major concern in the Czech education debate. Even the right-wing governments have admitted that the education sector is underfinanced, especially in terms of teachers' salaries. This view has been supported by OECD data which has repeatedly showed that in international comparisons the system is in general very effective: the Czech students usually perform about the international average, while the public investment has always been substantially under the average (OECD 2014d). As a result, efficiency has never been an issue. The discourse has been led by the question of how to *increase* the budget, and not how to cut it. The decline in PISA results was one of the major arguments for increasing the public funds in education, instead of calling for greater efficiency in resource use. The schools have never been blamed for being cost-ineffective.

NPM can be present not only in rhetoric and policies, but also – and perhaps most importantly – in everyday school *practices*. NPM includes the introduction of private sector practices into the public sector, such as performance-related pay or firing on the basis of underperformance. It is very difficult to evaluate the presence of such NPM ideas, since there is very little research on this topic. However, given the legal and financial constraints, it is clear that there is little space for merit-based pay and similar practices. Indeed, the difference between the minimum and maximum teachers' salaries is less than 30 per cent in the Czech Republic which is one of the lowest in the OECD. This stands in contrast to some other Central European countries, namely Poland and Hungary, where teachers' maximal salaries are at least double their starting salaries (OECD 2014d: 458).

As for the *management* styles of principals and officials, again there is very little research evidence. However, much can be inferred from the context in which they work. There is a strong tradition of legal accountability in the Czech Republic, and a tendency to regulate as many aspects of school life by law and other binding norms as possible. Consequently, external school evaluation by the Czech School Inspectorate is predominantly an assessment of how the legal requirements are met, or how the School Education Programme adheres to the Framework Education Programmes. It focuses upon compliance with legislation rather than the promotion of school improvement (Santiago *et al.* 2012). Despite the growing rhetoric about the need for 'leadership', principals have quite limited space for it and are far from 'free to manage' as NPM presupposes. This is because they have a number of competing obligations, while their discretionary power is rather limited in practice because of legal and financial constraints. It is therefore hard to speak of Czech school principals as *managers* in the NPM sense.

To sum up, Czech education embodies several important policies and governance arrangements that are in strong congruence with NPM *ideas*. Some of these have been there since the early 1990s; some of them have been introduced only recently. Yet, as we have seen, they have not been legitimized by NPM *rhetoric*. Neoliberal ideas stressing market mechanisms and individual responsibility and downplaying the role of the state have certainly been strongly present in Czech society after 1989. However, they have entered the education sector rather indirectly, incoherently and with a time lag. They have also been accompanied by quite different ideas on how to practically implement them, subject to inherited practices (path dependencies). Therefore, as in other post-Communist countries, the Czech education system is a mixture of components based upon ideas of various origins (Sztompka 1996: 120), with some of them bearing *only ideational* resemblance to NPM-driven *managerialism*.

Conclusions

As we have seen, Czech education after 1989 has not been intentionally guided by NPM values or principles. Some basic ideas have even been at odds with NPM. Even now few Czech educational policymakers and other stakeholders are familiar with the concept and meanings of NPM. In this respect, NPM in the Czech Republic has always been travelling on side roads. Nonetheless, this does not mean that the basic ideas of NPM have not been unintentionally adopted by policymakers, the media and public stakeholders as required norms coming from international bodies and developed countries. During the last decade several principles of NPM have strongly entered into education, most importantly decentralization, pressure for results as well as attempts at standardization. This development is, however, not a result of carefully planned policy based upon adoption of a coherent NPM ideology but rather the consequence of a mix of different – and often conflicting – ideas and also previous policies with aims and rationales different from NPM. The application of NPM to Czech education thus attests to yet another paradoxical case in which it is often quite difficult to judge to what extent changes such as decentralization have been brought about by NPM ideas (though indirectly and in a 'different guise'), or whether they would have been realized even without NPM ideology.

Although NPM arrived in Czech education from a side road rather than a main road, it seems to be on the rise, at least in terms of some recently implemented measures. This is also because different 'side roads' sometimes are heading in the same direction. For instance, newly established regions call for more standardization of the curriculum as well as the introduction of standardized testing at the end of basic school. At the same time, as described above, decentralization has led to the abolition of the District Educational Centres' network which in effect has undermined teachers' professionalism.

As we have seen, many NPM ideas have been heavily opposed by supporters of professional autonomy and student-centred learning. NPM as a whole has been to a large extent discredited. However, we should be aware of Hammersley's (2001) claim that the neoliberal mode of governance makes use of subtle techniques of so-called rhetorical violence. Who could possibly oppose efficiency, creativity, autonomy or flexibility? Only the foolish would. The rhetorical effect of NPM terms is such that any critical opposition is discredited at the outset. Thus we are presently at a junction and it is unclear whether NPM will create a new highway or return to the side roads. Given the country's anti-NPM communist heritage and two recent decades of paradoxical experience with NPM ideology, we do not think it likely that NPM will predominate in the future even in terms of ideas. However, even conceptually disregarded policies are often enacted and implemented. It is therefore possible that the educational sector in the Czech Republic will see the realization of some of the NPM principles in other than an NPM guise.

10

ELEMENTS OF NEW PUBLIC MANAGEMENT IN THE CONTEXT OF THE HUNGARIAN EDUCATION SYSTEM, 1990–2010

Anna Imre and Ágnes Fazekas

Introduction

Hood and Peters (2004) distinguish periods in the history of New Public Management (NPM) in the countries in which features of it first appeared. The experiences of other countries may be even more varied than those of Hungary: NPM did not appear at the same time or in the same way, with the same elements, in public policymaking, and experiences have also been different (Hood and Peters 2004; Pollitt *et al.* 2007). The defining ideas of NPM – for example, modernisation, efficiency, emphasis on performance as a guiding principle in organisations, change in the role of the state – can be found in most European countries, but beyond the general principles there are also many differences, for example with regard to autonomy for schools, marketization, competition between schools and consumer orientation, and these differences are even more pronounced when we take implementation into account. In Hungary, as in the other central and eastern European countries, some of the central ideas and tools of NPM were and are present but in a less coherent way, embedded in different contexts. The experience of Hungary provides a different, specific example of NPM.

The Hungarian education system and NPM

With regard to changes in the Hungarian education system, it is important to know that the system which developed and functioned in Hungary from the mid-nineteenth to the mid-twentieth century was based on the German model. After World War II, Hungary was one of the socialist countries whose social policy followed the Soviet model, with a strongly centralized administration.

After the regime changed the governance of the Hungarian education system showed many similarities with, but also several differences from, those of other

142 Anna Imre and Ágnes Fazekas

central and eastern European countries (CEEC) (Balázs and Halász 2000; Nagy 1999). In his discussion of public management, Tamás M. Horváth (2005) argues that in CEEC countries government policymaking typically lacks the concept of public management, although the content and implementation of the reforms following regime change contained numerous elements borrowed from the practice of more developed countries, including elements of NPM. The transition started from a socialist planned economy to a market economy also covered the performance of public duties, and in this area several elements of NPM had a large impact on how the conditions developed. These included privatization in the public sector, the strengthening of market logic in public service provision and its marketization as well. A complete transformation in the role of the public sector did not appear in public management terminology because the transformation appeared as part of a deeper and more comprehensive change of the system in the post-socialist countries. The changes in the societies of these countries were of a depth that far exceeded the measure by which the Western countries departed from their traditional practices. As a result, the orientation of NPM in government reforms was much weaker in the post-socialist countries than in Western countries. Some popular themes and sub-areas can be seen (e.g. deregulation, contractualization, quality assurance), but these were not significant in number or in depth of application, and the whole was less coherent than in the more developed countries (Horváth 2005).

Comparing Hungary with the developed (and particularly the English-speaking) countries, its experience shows a different pattern. Following regime change there was significant demand to accelerate the process of modernisation, to catch up with the Western countries and adopt associated tools and solutions. Many ideas and tools linked to NPM appeared in the Hungarian education system as elements of modernization or tools of problem solving, but this cannot be described as a system or policy framework for New Public Management. In Table 10.1 we give a short overview of the key terms of NPM in the Hungarian context based on the 4 Ms in the Introduction, where the key categories of NPM all appear in educational policy in Hungary but due to the lack of coherent framework they could not be fully institutionalized and they remained partly ambiguous. With regard to *managers* there was an emphasis on empowerment based on management principles and an expectation of professionalization. Although training possibilities for school leaders have been widened, their attitude has changed much more slowly. According to the *managing* aspect, the tools of quality management including data necessary for performance accountability appeared but outcome regulation and incentives and sanctions were not to be linked to it. With aspects of *management*, the emphasis was on autonomy and competition. The idea behind this was that greater autonomy promotes better performance through professional development and competition with other schools, but since capacity building and professional skills were not yet strong enough, the emphasis was put more on competition in itself, than on professional work. Due to the lack of a systemic approach, framework and the relative weakness of NPM elements and their application, we cannot speak as yet of *managerialism*. Due to the lack of a systemic approach the NPM elements which emerged after the change of the regime could not be institutionalized in the education system and after a gradual and incoherent emergence of NPM elements, a decline in the use of them could be observed. After 2010 a sharp change gave way to different, more centralized policy principles and tools.

After the application of NPM elements having been contextualized in previous pages, the study focuses on three comprehensive issues: the maintenance of schools (including effectiveness), the efficiency of the system, and EU developments. Our analysis is based on a study of the literature and on interviews with a small number of experts and decision makers. In analysing the longer term macro-processes in the education system, the regular analytic reports on the education system appearing every three or four years and Jelentés a *magyar* közoktatásról [Report on the Hungarian Education System] research reports and papers published by the few researchers dealing with this subject[1] were used.

TABLE 10.1 NPM in Hungary

Factors	Ideas	Tools and practices
Managers	Manager-type leaders having autonomy and professional expertise; open to consumer demand; invigorate the functioning of the organisation	Growing choice of leadership training programmes. Making completion of management training compulsory for second and subsequent leadership appointment
Managing	Quality assurance built on consumer demand Institutional evaluation and planning based on facts Individual elements of accountability; possibility of incentives and sanctions	Introduction of institutional quality assurance. Promoting use of market services through competition. Availability, usability and publication of performance data (OKM measures) Taking account of results in the assessment of teachers; bonuses for teachers who perform well. Obligation to develop an improvement plan for underperforming schools
Management	Decentralised governing framework and broad institutional autonomy Greater freedom promotes better performance, partly in itself and partly through competition with other schools	Institutional freedom (eg. curriculum, HR management) to develop a local curriculum taking account of the requirements of the national curriculum and to appoint teachers Significant latitude for institutions in the area of pupil enrolment. Free choice of schools for parents. Promotion of competition through funding linked to pupil numbers

144 Anna Imre and Ágnes Fazekas

Two decades of the Hungarian education system

We surveyed the history of Hungarian education administration from the change of regime. We divided this period into two parts: before and after the turn of the millennium. In the first decade three different governments were in power, and a new decentralized framework was developed for the administration of public education. Following the emergence of new problems, education administrators sought ways and means to solve them in a decentralized administrative framework and to increase efficiency and effectiveness. In the second decade, international influence increased: this decade was above all marked by accession to the European Union and was a period of new opportunities and old challenges. The emphasis was on efficiency and inequality of opportunity, though questions remained about some functions of the education system. The end of this second period is marked by the election of a new government in 2010, which opened a completely new chapter in the story of education in Hungary.

The first decade: 1990–2002

The new administrative framework for public education developed in the first decade after regime change. Several elements of the decentralized administrative framework which emerged as a result of a period of intensive legislative activity

TABLE 10.2 Two decades of the Hungarian education system and NPM

Year	Regulations, programmes	Changes	Governments
1990–1993	Local Government Act Public Education Act	Decentralisation, school autonomy	Hungarian Democratic Forum (1990–1994)
1995–1998	National Core Curriculum and local curricula	Two-level content regulation	Hungarian Socialist Party- Free Democrats (1994–1998)
1999–2000	Comenius 2000	Quality questions; quality assurance made mandatory	FIDESZ (1998–2002)
2001	National Assessment of Basic Competencies	Elements of an accountability system	
2003–2009	Amendments to the Public Education Act	Equity and efficiency questions	Hungarian Socialist Party- Free Democrats (2002–2010)
2004	Accession to European Union	Launch of HEFOP, TÁMOP programmes	
2010–	Public Education Act	Recentralisation, continuation of TÁMOP programme	FIDESZ (2010–2014, 2014–)

coincided with elements of administrative reform which could be observed in the developed countries, particularly decentralization and the application of market principles to many aspects of the system. The emerging non-state sector remained very small in the first decade, and was made up mainly of church schools opened as a result of legislation providing for the return of church property.

One of the most important transformation processes that led to reshaping the education system was the reform of government and public administration structures, the creation of the new local government system and local administration. After many decades in an extremely centralized administrative framework, primary and secondary education institutions became the property of politically independent local authorities, bringing the whole public education sector into a new sphere of influence. Under the Local Government Act, previously state-owned schools were now owned and operated by more than two thousand on average fairly small local authorities (Halász, no date). Thus a public education system came into being in Hungary which was remarkably decentralized even in global comparisons (OECD Education at a Glance 2008). The demands of society, previously restricted to a minor role, now played an important part among the forces shaping the new framework of public education.

Regime change in education was affirmed by three new laws adopted by parliament in 1993 on public education, training, and higher education. The legislation gave far-reaching autonomy to both institutions and parents. Legislation in the early 1990s providing for the return of expropriated schools to the churches contributed to the establishment of non-state schools in church or other private ownership. At the same time, legislation on public employment, gave all those working in the education sector the status of public employee (Halász no date).

Alongside the transformation processes new actors emerged, among them international organizations, in order to support the transition process and help build a market economy (e.g. World Bank, European Community). These international influences were felt primarily in the areas of VET and higher education and less directly in primary and secondary education. Professional training and external developments funded by the World Bank were required to apply and proceed with NPM-linked management processes. The first EU programme office (Tempus Public Foundation) was set up in 1996 to manage similar programmes. The implementation of the Tempus programme contributed to the creation of an institution with a significant radiating force, which transmitted NPM project management tools through their activities from the early 1990s.[2]

Maintenance of schools: local and institutional autonomies

The system of education created in the early 1990s gave broad autonomy within a decentralized administrative framework to the various actors, which could be run efficiently with indirect government tools, and in which

146 Anna Imre and Ágnes Fazekas

agreement, the development of balance and cooperation between the actors (or a learning process leading to it) was important. In the new administrative structure, many small local authorities with the same rights and duties as bigger ones made decisions on the most fundamental issues in education. The economic crisis which emerged between 1994 and 1996 highlighted the limitations of the new decentralized administration. A fundamental issue within the given framework was the employment and payment of the large teaching body inherited from the socialist regime. The employment and payment of teachers was decided at institutional level with the approval of the maintainer, but it had to be aligned with the framework set up at central level in relation to working hours and public employee status and pay scales. The crisis was exacerbated by a demographic trough of declining pupil numbers, but the local authorities and education institutions failed to adapt to this new situation. Central government tried to force the local authorities to make more rational use of their resources and make savings by increasing teachers' contact hours, but this was not successful. A small number of institutions were closed and some teachers were laid off, but far fewer than was to be expected (Halász and Lannert 1997). The problem highlighted the fact that local authorities had become administrative entities following their own interests rather than the expectations of central government.

One of the fundamental tools to create independence for schools was the development of local curricula. In the 1990s, efforts were concentrated on a two-level curriculum system geared to decentralized administration. Capacity building started in relation to content regulation, with a series of training courses for school heads and teachers. A system of training for school heads was developed, marking a demand for professionalization of the leadership role, which carried wide-ranging personal responsibility[3]. From 1997, continuing professional development became compulsory for teachers (120 hours over seven years). An in-service training system based on demand principles was developed on a market basis, and internal developments inspired by international patterns enabled the application of some NPM tools.

Within a few years, institutional autonomy, which had been blended into the concept of 'freedom' (Berényi 2014), resulted, in practice, in unexpected effects as well as the desired ones. In a few years it became clear that the system which had developed lacked transparency and was difficult to govern. From the middle of the decade there was increasing demand for checks and balances, and for evaluation. Other problems with the new arrangements also emerged towards the end of the decade. A combination of institutional autonomy, freedom of choice, normative financing, and declining pupil numbers led – as in England – to the application of market logic and therefore intense competition between institutions. Social demands, previously kept within tight limits, were now very strongly articulated, first and foremost for entry to institutions and programmes which gave pupils a competitive advantage in terms of entry to higher education. In response to parental demand, education institutions set up varied programmes and made great efforts to offer what parents wanted, and six and eight-year secondary schools were opened. The primary role of school heads became making their school attractive and meeting consumer demand. As a result of selection processes which began in the mid-1990s, major differences in attainment and opportunity between schools and groups of pupils intensified.

Efficiency tools: quality assurance

From the mid-1990s it became clear that the lack of an evaluation system was a problem. After the winding up of the central inspectorate in 1985, the Hungarian education system had no ability to evaluate its work. The Public Education Act placed a duty on school maintainers from 1996 to evaluate their schools but the local authorities were only gradually able to meet these expectations: a 1999 research study showed that 29 per cent of them had not carried out any form of evaluation. Of the evaluations carried out in the first years, 60 per cent were purely economic and only 27 per cent extended to professional aspects (Halász and Lannert 2000). From 1999, education policy promoted and supported the use of expert services for evaluation and organized competitions for the provision of these services. Following the change of government in 1998, creating and developing local conditions for inspection, evaluation and quality assurance became a priority in education policy. Initiatives in this period include the appearance of quality assurance systems and the development of the Public Education Quality Development Programme. In the background, these attempted to solve the problem of providing a necessary counterbalance to the freedoms of decentralized administration. The iconic programme of that period was the Comenius 2000 programme, extending to a quarter of all schools and built on the Total Quality Management model: this represented the appearance of a real NPM tool in Hungary. The programme was initiated by Hungarian experts. It introduced a basically soft version of quality assurance, based on self-assessment and development, to the bidding institutions.[4] At the same time, other quality models (e.g. ISO) also gained ground and from the mid-1990s there were frequent conferences on quality issues. An education advisory market began to develop, partly as a result of funding for training courses being allocated to schools and the development of a system of accreditation.

The Comenius programme contributed to the spread of some management techniques (e.g. assessment of consumer demand, institutional self-evaluation). Another effect of the programme was to promote a change in outlook and the spread of quality assurance terminology, thereby introducing market terminology to education practice (Berényi 2014). Although NPM, complete with its ideological elements, typically did not appear as a subject of conversation or debate in professional discourse in Hungary, its terminology (e.g. services, service providers, supply and demand, consumers) entered the professional

148 Anna Imre and Ágnes Fazekas

language and was widely used even without the underlying theoretical framework. The development of partnerships between organizations has been described as one of the main effects of the programme, though it is emphasized that the effect of this did not reach classroom level (Györgyi and Török 2002).

The second decade: 2002–2010

The second decade was marked by attempts to remedy previous problems and deficiencies as well as by efforts, prompted by PISA results, to improve effectiveness and introduce a system of measurement and evaluation, and not least by initiatives to deal with inequality of opportunity. Following Hungary's accession to the EU in 2004, international – particularly EU – influences became more intensive and had an increasingly significant effect on the aims of Hungarian education policy such as development of competence-based programmes, reducing inequality of opportunity and to providing lifelong learning, which priorities received significant EU support. By the middle of the decade, parallel with accession to the EU, development programmes started (e.g. integration programmes, competence-based programmes) that made issues of development policies particularly important. The struggle for efficiency continued, with issues relating to how a fragmented school network and administrative system could be sustained (e.g. by promoting partnerships). (Halász and Lannert 2006).

Efficency tools: measurement and external evaluation

The issue of efficiency remained on the agenda, but was augmented with issues of competence development and remedying inequality of opportunity. Policy aims in the second decade were set in an international context as a result of PISA assessments and EU aims. The first PISA results at the beginning of the decade took Hungarian experts and decision-makers by surprise, and contributed to issues of quality and efficiency remaining on the agenda, and to the development of the National Assessment of Basic Competencies. The development of a Hungarian assessment system was made acceptable to both major political parties by the opportunities and greater legitimacy of decision-making based on facts and data (Lawn and Grek 2012). The initiative also had significant precedents (e.g. IEA measures) and actively supported by Hungarian experts.

The National Assessment of Basic Competencies (OKM) is an annual assessment system measuring the competence in mathematics and reading comprehension of all pupils in years six, eight and ten. Assessment started in 2001 with a limited number of pupils and was extended to all pupils in the relevant year groups in 2008. The declared aim of the assessment was not accountability but development of competence, in other words the promotion of a culture of evaluation and analysis in schools. Later, the issue of accountability emerged, and a few elements to enable this were cautiously added to the OKM by an amendment to the 2006 Education Act, which specified that underperforming schools were to produce an action plan publishing their test results, and the test results were to be taken into account in the evaluation of teachers within the school's quality assurance programme. However, due to the weakness of education policy intentions in this area, data from the OKM did not in fact become elements of accountability, nor was a central set of standards developed. Despite this, OKM data are increasingly used in education institutions (e.g. for planning and target setting).

In the second decade, amendments to the legislation ensured that evaluation at institutional and maintainer level became standard practice. The 2003 amendment specified that both school maintainer local authorities and institutions had to prepare their own quality management programmes. With the spread of evaluation of schools by maintainers, NPM tools also began to spread: evaluation techniques, use of data and indicators, use of expert services made available on a market basis. A significant proportion (68 per cent) of these school evaluations was carried out on behalf of maintainers by profit-oriented companies and independent experts using techniques and indicators for the evaluation of attainment (Halász and Lannert 2003). In order to appoint assessment expert, local authorities were able to use central funding. This opportunity was taken up primarily by larger towns and cities, some of which also developed systems for regular local evaluations. Even with funding available, evaluation was not universal: according to a survey in 2007, 85–90 per cent of local authorities evaluated their schools and 17.5 per cent also had their own assessments. Eighty per cent of local authorities took account of assessment data in professional evaluation, and 80–85 per cent also made use of OKM results in their evaluation (Sinka 2009). From 2006 the requirement to evaluate teachers, taking account of assessment data, formed part of the institution's quality assurance framework. Teacher evaluation was limited by the fact that universal criteria were not formulated, and legislation relating to public employees also meant that it was not possible either to apply strong sanctions or to give incentives amounting to more than a very modest bonus. Elements of evaluation gradually appeared in the education system but were not combined into a system. In these processes it was mainly Hungarian experts who played an active part, some of them becoming actors in the service provision market. Quality assurance requirements and the availability of schools' own OKM data strengthened the management role of school heads. A process of capacity-building and professionalisation of school heads began, linked to the 2003 amendment to the Education Act, which made appointment to a second headship conditional on completion of a two-year professional training course. Although NPM-linked management tools gradually appeared in institutional practice (e.g. market competition, quality assurance, use of data), a significant proportion of Hungarian school heads did not become true management-oriented leaders,[5] hampered by the lack of central government communication reinforcing the presence of NPM tools, and by some of the earlier patterns remaining in place.

150 Anna Imre and Ágnes Fazekas

Another problem was the relative lack of tools: both the public employee status of teachers and the limited possibility to reward quality work meant that school leaders' options in terms of human resources were limited. On the other hand, teachers were not exploited to the same extent as in the developed countries (Bottery 1996), due partly to their public employee status and partly to the lack of accountability tools.

Maintenance of schools: partnerships and integration

In the decade after 2000 the struggle to rationalise and improve efficiency continued. The creation of sub-regions from 2004 served the aim of improving efficiency in school maintenance, and there was increasingly intensive promotion of partnerships. Despite financial incentives, there was no significant increase in the number of local authorities willing to become partners in sub-regions. (Balázs and Kovács 2012). By the second half of the decade school closures and amalgamations became increasingly common in smaller settlements due to funding difficulties, and transfers of schools by local authorities to non-state bodies also became common (Balázs *et al.* 2011). These processes implied that it was not possible to stabilize the local government system for the long term in the new millennium.

At the end of the decade the prime minister instigated a round table discussion by experts, whose proposals included setting up a system of accountability. Other unresolved problems (e.g. development of the lower intermediate level of administration, dealing with inequality of opportunity, and the importance of teacher training) also received increased emphasis[6] (Neumann 2010). A smaller proportion of the proposals were implemented in the subsequent period.

The effect of EU developments[7]

As a result of international development plans implemented in Hungary, the effects of a management approach based on performance and efficiency were increasingly felt. The main motivation for the widespread use of NPM tools was access to EU funds, and the main context of the process was Europeanization. After Hungary's accession in 2004, the associated management tools also became part of the planning, coordination and evaluation of locally managed developments, because the extent of Hungary's required contribution to EU-funded projects exhausted the resources it could have used to develop the sector. The more important interventions implemented in Hungarian public education after 2004 were achieved with the support of the EU, which placed particular emphasis on managing for results and accountability (Halász, 2010; Fazekas and Halász, 2014).

The government aims mentioned above – reducing inequality of opportunity and the propagation of lifelong learning – provide the two main directions for the content of EU-funded interventions affecting classroom processes to this

Hungary **151**

day. In the planning, implementation and evaluation of these programmes, NPM tools reached actors at macro, meso and micro levels. The number of institutions participating in these programmes reached a critical mass in all teaching subsystems: one third of public education institutions participated in these development programmes (Fazekas 2015).

A risk of using NPM techniques is that in an environment unprepared for their limitations, they can easily generate negative effects. The use of these tools, including evaluation systems, requires significant HR capacities which research suggests were not available in most of the responsible organizations. Effective management was hampered by the fact that the actors did not know the principles behind the implementation of developments, and project management training only rarely focused on the development of higher-level strategic thinking. This was due not only to lack of knowledge of implementation and evaluation but also to lack of commitment: in many cases the actors did not take real responsibility for implementing the programmes in a way that could generate real social changes. In addition, the fact that the implementation of developments was measured through indicators often diverted the actors' attention to measurable elements and away from phenomena to which the measures did not extend: for example, highlighting the number of cooperation contracts instead of the spread of good practice (Ex ante 2006; Magyar Köztársaság 2007; Emberi 2014).

The main problem in the education system was that project management logic had to be applied in organizations which did not work on a project basis, so that two different systems of organizational logic had to be reconciled to each other. Problems were caused by the fact that new leaders connecting to project management emerged, who were often different as people in leadership positions within the institutions. Thus project managers allocated tasks, resources and decision-making rights to subordinates on a contractual basis, even though according to the operating regulations of the institutions they did not have the power to do so. This new situation required a higher level of cooperation within institutions, together with new working methods more typical of matrix organizations. The emergence of parallel powers often generated conflict within institutions, usually because the institutions participating in the projects did not adapt their structures to the needs of the project processes.

The tools of commercial management reached public education institutions through the implementation of the competition system, support contracts, central monitoring systems, and undertakings affecting organizational function. In order to reinforce the content directions in schools, from 2008 a nationwide network of schools was built up to trade in 'good practice', seeking to stimulate schools with the tool of supply and demand.[8] The provision of a support system for curriculum developments (resources for teachers, study aids, online contents, training courses, networks of mentors) was done by newly created non-profit public agencies working to market rules. Though a management outlook and partnership-centred, service provider functioning presented a significant challenge to many schools, research has shown that the vast majority

152 Anna Imre and Ágnes Fazekas

of schools which adopted the EU programmes are working more effectively as a result than they were previously. In a national survey (Fazekas 2015), almost 600 heads and teachers were interviewed at schools where interventions affecting the curriculum had taken place in the previous ten years, and 82 per cent of heads and 76 per cent of teachers thought their school was working much more effectively as a result of the programmes.

A new era (2010–): recentralisation

The new decade began with a change of government, with the conservative party gaining power. This was followed by a radical transformation of education, with the result that after a period of 20 years, schools were returned to state control. The previous decentralising approaches were shelved; government communications turned away from the consumer-oriented approach typical of NPM. The transformation of the education system was enshrined in new legislation (e.g. on professional training and higher education). One of the basic principles of the 2011 Education Act is that public education is to be interpreted as a public service whose 'overall framework and guarantees are provided by the state'.[9]

Decision-makers hoped that recentralisation would simultaneously solve the problems of efficiency, effectiveness and inequality of opportunity. Institutional autonomy was replaced with professional autonomy for teachers, and other tools available to institutions were restricted. New government tools gained prominence: centralized school maintenance was set up with a central office and devolved regional offices. In keeping with this trend, schools are no longer independent legal entities and no longer have their own budgets, so that the concept of trade in good practice mentioned above could not continue in its original form. Teachers became state employees, and there has been a move towards regarding them as belonging to a single public service corpus rather than as employees. In terms of corporate organization, teachers are in a profession in which a hierarchical system of levels has been defined. In addition, in new government tools efforts to restrict market mechanisms can be observed (e.g. introduction of state provision of textbooks, reduced support for private schools).

However, management of corporate function has not completely excluded the use of NPM tools. The post-2010 system has preserved those NPM elements which concentrate on efficient administration (e.g. handling large databases), not on promoting market operation (contracts, competition).

Based on the experiences of the first few years, problems relating to centralized maintenance of institutions gradually surfaced, and the possibility of lower intermediate-level decentralisation emerged as a possible solution. With regard to effectiveness and evaluation, instead of using soft tools the government has placed emphasis on centralized tools: a single centralized inspection system has been developed, of which institution-level self-evaluation forms part. The issue of remedying inequality of opportunity has again been put aside.

Despite the changes which occurred after 2010, NPM tools (project management, benchmarking, indicators, evaluations, contracts, outsourcing) are still used in EU-financed development programmes requiring management on attainment principles. As in previous years, in the post-2010 period central ideas have been brought into EU developments. Thus the introduction of the career model for teachers is being implemented with EU finance, with the result that it has moved out of the legislative regulation framework to become a project managed by agencies, supported by research and tested with pilot programmes.

The most important actors in this new period are the government's professional bureaucrats, and local experts brought in with EU finance. A significant number of school heads have been replaced, and the role of international organizations has declined compared to the preceding period. The restriction of foreign influence can be seen in intergovernmental links, though less in the case of the EU due to strong integration and the need for funding.

Summary

The demand for modernising the Hungarian education system while keeping distance from the previous regime led to a decentralised system. In time, this radical solution itself became a difficult problem for which no satisfactory solution could be found in two decades, and laid down a defining framework for numerous other initiatives for change.

It is largely in this context that NPM in Hungary can be interpreted. NPM was not 'introduced'. Some elements of it did appear in practice in Hungary, as in other countries, primarily linked to efforts to improve efficiency and to EU developments, but they did not become a system, we cannot speak of managerialism. There were barriers against it both at the central and the local levels. At central level, partly due to lack of consensus and conflicts of interest, and remaining of old public management elements, it had no significant effect. At local and institutional level, efforts to improve school leadership also encountered barriers – in the case of many school leaders, the attitudes of the former period remained.

Despite this, elements of NPM appeared in managing practice, supported by experts and external influence in fragmented form and as problem solving tools in the new decentralized administrative environment. However, this was not underlined by NPM principles and aims, which only appeared in professional discourse. Experts urged the introduction of comprehensive NPM solutions, but most of these proposals did not reach the macro level or could not replace the remaining old management structures. Thus the application of NPM principles and solutions was typically sporadic and was successful primarily in larger towns and cities with local and institutional autonomy.

Some elements and tools of NPM entered the education system, but their effects were often uneven, contradictory and weak. Indicators appeared in the second half of the 1990s but they were not widely used and did not become

154 Anna Imre and Ágnes Fazekas

dominant in policy or institutional decision-making. External and internal assessment did become standard practice, but were not linked to any serious consequences. Other elements had lesser, or even counterproductive effects on the Hungarian education system. The maintenance of excessive decentralisation led to serious problems of efficiency. The introduction of market logic to the education system led to persistent problems with the consequent competition between schools and growing tendency to select and segregate. EU-funded developments contain several NPM tools; it is these elements of NPM that have survived in a transformed post-2012 framework which is developing on different principles.

It must be added that numerous external factors have contributed to the difficult circumstances of the education system: structures which preserved the values of the socialist period, frequent changes of government with consequent sharp changes in education policy, and not least the economic crisis at the end of the studied period. However, there are hints of even deeper causes. Despite the change of regime in Hungary, numerous elements of 'path dependence' can be observed: earlier attitudes were preserved in many respects, such as a mentality accustomed to central direction, and the conflicting interests of individuals or groups, which worked against cooperation, were able to surface more easily and intensify in a decentralized environment.

Notes

1 Gábor Halász, the Hungarian researcher who has worked most in this area, interprets the changes in government and administration systems as a response to the increasing complexity of social subsystems, which may allow the maintenance of checks over these social subsystems. In his opinion, the situation which has developed in the Hungarian public education system allows great complexity, which also involves increased risk. The creation of the necessary tools to handle this situation requires a process of intensive development, and their use assumes a social learning process (Halász 2002).
2 See www.tka.hu/
3 There was only slow change in school leadership in the early 1990s: only one third became head teachers after regime change; another third were already head teachers before, others were deputy heads before. Another important characteristic was their strong loyalty to their teaching staff: if cuts had to be made, they preferred to confront the maintainer rather than have internal conflict (Halász and Lannert 1997).
4 The defining logic of the assessment was to strengthen the teaching community and work within the autonomy of schools, not to monitor teaching activity.
5 Research data show that in the views of school leaders the most strongly represented is the rational model typical of the former system; the proportion of leaders thinking in terms of an open systems model is much weaker but increasing (Baráth 1998). Another analysis shows that Hungarian school leaders regard the ability to cooperate as the most important leadership quality (Halász and Lannert 2006).
6 The round table's proposals are for the use of scientifically established tools to remedy the severest problems of the system: the extent of inequality of opportunity, the lack of a system of accountability, the fragmented structure of education administration, and the deficiencies of teaching quality and training.

Hungary **155**

7 This section builds partly on verbal information provided by Gábor Halász.
8 The idea was that schools could offer their good practice for sale, and those which were successful in the market could earn significant profits, which they could invest in new developments. Schools made 'advertisements' for their good practices in a set format, and could publish these on an online marketplace. A competition involving several thousand schools and nurseries produced the website, and the competition also included funding for institutions to purchase the good practices.
9 See www.net.jogtar.hu/jr/gen/hjegy_doc.cgi?docid=A1100190.TV

11

NEW HEAD TEACHER ROLES FOLLOWING THE DECENTRALIZATION OF ROMANIAN EDUCATION

Ana-Cristina Popescu

Introduction

In this chapter I am focusing on exploring New Public Management (NPM) in public education in post-Communist Romania. In Romania, the decentralization of education is part of the wider programme of NPM aimed at the restructuring of the state and public administration (Popescu 2010). After the fall of communism (in December 1989) the transition to a more democratic society has been largely influenced by preparations for European Union accession, which happened in 2007. In addition, the financial contribution of international institutions to Romanian education began in the 1990s. For example, the World Bank and the Organization for Economic Cooperation and Development contributed from the 1990s to the 2000s. Through the loan terms from these international bodies, the Romanian Government committed itself to a certain set of reforms and policies. Similar reforms were expected of Romania by the EU (in the late 1990s and early 2000s) as a precondition for accession, one of which was decentralization. Then, in the late 2000s, due to the economic crisis, the International Monetary Fund as a lender to the Romanian state with very strict repayment schedules and conditions also became an important player impacting upon policy in Romania. Thus, NPM and the decentralization of education adopted by the Romanian government find their origins in western models and are, effectively, externally imposed (Popescu 2013). After borrowing the decentralization policy from western democracies, the process was then implemented in a former totalitarian country. Whilst the 'how' NPM is being implemented in Romania is more complex, the 'why' it is happening is actually quite simple – external influences.

I begin by exploring the ways in which NPM has permeated education in post-Communist public education in Romania. I go on to illustrate some of the visible aspects of NPM in Romanian education, including decentralization and school-based management. I emphasize how the roles of Romanian head teachers have changed in recent years. In addition, I comment on the impact that the Communist legacy has on head teachers in terms of strong politicization of the education system (Popescu 2013). Then I position NPM reforms in education internationally and the background to Romania's political history in order to show why these reforms happened in Romania in the section before last. This is followed by reflections in the last section of the chapter.

NPM reforms in Romanian education

The 1990s marked an important shift from communism to the beginnings of a more democratic, neo-liberal state in Romania. Whilst communism was characterized by a strong tradition of centralism of all services, the 1990s witnessed the beginning of a redirection towards the modernization of the state. This meant the creation of 'private' entities, through the introduction of a neoliberal agenda: competition and markets, managers and managerialism.

School based management is an important feature, whereby schools are now funded through a formula based on student numbers (though this does vary in practice), and schools operate as businesses where an Administrative Board hires and fires staff. Head teachers are positioned as managers, and aspire to take on chief executive roles, though qualified teacher status remains a requirement for appointment. As managers, heads are taking on business language, with some trained about management by foreign trainers and consultants. Head teachers had to learn how to write and use business plans, review performance, and hire/fire personnel. Such managing by head teachers is increasingly complex, with a focus on all school matters such as budgets, personnel (educational and administration), admissions, marketing, and working with the community and local authority. Juxtaposed with this decentralization, is the continued central control of the curriculum, though the idea and reality of state provision is increasingly under pressure as more and more private educational institutions are being accredited by the national Ministry of Education, and so marketization is generating local competition. While management and managing have developed rapidly as features of the school system, there is little evidence of managerialism. This is because of the legacy of the Communist state, where political allegiance (or every boss has a boss within a hierarchy) matters, and so head teachers are more likely to be removed because of political rather than data driven performance reasons. Importantly, while personnel management has been decentralized, staffing is still controlled centrally through accreditation and tenure, rather than performance.

Governance in Romania is in the process of shifting from a hierarchical state model to what I call 'politicised decentralisation' in all areas, not just in education. In this form of decentralization, some responsibility (especially financial) is being transferred from national level to local authorities and, in education, further to the

158 Ana-Cristina Popescu

level of schools. Yet, at the same time, it is still largely a centralized system. It is important to point out that in Romania, whilst eight administrative regions were set up in the post-Communist period (in line with EU guidance), these regions do not operate like the federal regions of Germany (Bavaria, Schleswig Holstein etc.) or Spain (Catalonia or the Basque Country etc.), or the national governments within the UK (Northern Ireland and Scotland etc.), for example. There are no regional elections, regional taxes or even regional government authorities as such – regions exist largely in name only. Due to the number of political parties and frequent changes in coalition government, political instability is rife. More importantly for public education, the ministers of education and many of their subordinates (national and county inspectors) are political appointments, which can change with each change in government.

Thus, in Romanian public education, the NPM agenda as outlined as the 4 Ms in the introductory chapter is a hybrid of neoliberalism and Communist legacies. On the one hand, decentralization, quasi-markets and school-based management were introduced into public education on the recommendation of international donors. The word 'privatization' started being used from the early 1990s, and was seen as negative as it impacted on the stability of employment and working conditions. Indeed, the endurance of Communist practices made it difficult for professionals to adapt to new professional responsibilities and accountability frameworks. In this context, the roles and responsibilities of national policymakers, county school inspectors and head teachers have been reconceptualized. Of all these stakeholders, the findings from my study show that head teachers noted the most dramatic changes in accountability frameworks, professional responsibilities and relationships with different stakeholders such as inspectors, local authorities, as well as parents and students as consumers of education (Popescu 2013). In the section below I will focus on school based management and head teachers in more detail as this represents the core of this chapter.

The effects of school based management on head teachers in Romania

Traditionally (including in Communist times), Romanian head teachers' main role was to implement education policies on behalf of the state, local councils or County School Inspectorates. When the initial steps of NPM and decentralization in education were made (1998–2002) their titles changed from 'School Directors' to 'Managers', but their responsibilities were largely unchanged. However, legislation is now in place that places far greater responsibility on head teachers as 'Managers'. Local authorities have delegated certain financial powers to schools that can now manage their own budgets. This form of decentralization was termed School-Based Management. It can be described as shifting the power to the school unit in terms of managing human (firing and hiring teaching staff) and financial resources. This implies changes in school governance arrangements resulting in increased roles for heads and school boards.

In the period 2009–2013, I conducted research looking at the effects of decentralization on head teacher roles in Romania (Popescu 2013). The responses of head teachers to decentralization in general and School-Based Management in particular, varied. The findings of this study were divided into six themes: new professional responsibilities (executive versus administrative roles, the school board composition and role including heads' appointments and remuneration), juggling multiple activities and accountability systems, professional identity, budgets, market forces and competition, and politicization. A brief summary of the key points is developed below.

Heads are adopting the Chief Executive role and are in charge of budgets. An emphasis is now placed on the managerial side of their role:

> I think that the head now needs to be…a Manager, not a Director; s/he has to know how to plan her/his activities; to have business knowledge, to think about efficiency … work within the allocated budget so as to ensure all the resources that their teacher colleagues need.
>
> (Tony, head)

However, the lack of clarity in legislation made it difficult for heads to understand how to become managers or what roles they should personally assume.

Heads face multiple new roles and accountability systems both within and outside of the school. These include local authorities and parents with a decreased role of County School Inspectorates:

> We are in a relation of subordination to the School Inspectorate for instructional issues and school curriculum. Each and everybody has their own role in the new maze and I think that collaboration between all these bodies is welcome.
>
> (Laura, head)

There is probably a lack of awareness of the new level of accountability represented by the local authorities: 'I've never seen this as subordination, but more like collaboration because I am only subordinate to the Mayor from a financial management point of view.' (Diane, Head). Whilst most of the heads have an excellent relationship with local authorities, not all of them are in favour:

> This idea of subordination to the local authorities is quite daunting in my opinion; … I find it perfectly normal for a head to be checked and audited by someone else, but that person should not be from the local community, but from the County School Inspectorate … the Town Hall that does not know exactly what it is that I am doing in my school.
>
> (Anna, head)

Romanian Heads still see themselves both as teachers and head teachers, not least because of their instability in post: 'Headship is a fleeting stage in one's career ... you go back to teaching ... this is what you were trained to do' (Daniel, Head). They fear they might lose their identity as subject leaders if they do not teach anymore. This finding has not been encountered elsewhere in the international literature, largely because in other countries, once heads become heads, this becomes (and remains) their profession until retirement or the adoption of a new career trajectory. Romanian heads feel that the workload and bureaucracy is increasing. Heads are concerned that they are now spending less time with their families. Nevertheless, with their families' support, they manage to juggle their professional and personal responsibilities.

The budget or financial manager role is, perhaps, the most important change to Romanian Heads' roles and largely welcomed by Heads interviewed:

> In decentralisation, heads will be confronted with another challenge: to become entrepreneurs. As has always been the case, heads are teachers ... In my view, it is mandatory for prospective heads to be trained in educational and financial management.
>
> (Paul, policymaker)

They have found it most challenging, because of the lack of training (and the cultural background of an administrative role within a Communist, hierarchical state). Head teachers, however, relish some of the funding choices it enables them to make. Due to the financial crisis, however, financial delegation came to a halt in 2011. In spite of an agreed standard cost per student for the year 2011 (Government Decision 1395/2010), in practice schools did not receive the necessary funds because they were not available any more. Or, if they were, any excess was transferred to other schools that could not afford to pay teachers' salaries (for example, due to a small number of students).

The introduction of NPM reforms through School-Based Management saw the emergence of a quasi-market, though competition is developing the relationships with other heads are not yet as competitive as in other countries. Daniel's school is in the top 5 in the city in terms of number of students – of sixty schools in total: 'competition for students is a real challenge ... a school's reputation is really important here' (Daniel). Moreover, heads say competition is beneficial to education:

> It is natural to have competition between institutions and organisations in any field of life. This is beneficial to education because it leads to an increase in the quality of delivery in school.
>
> (Peter, head)

Many schools were closed or amalgamated, and those heads who survived began to operate their schools as businesses, competing for students and finding new avenues for generating revenues: 'Over the weekend, we've let some of our spaces to universities. We used this money to celebrate our School's Day with students, parents, teachers, local authorities and inspectors' (Diane, Head).

The School Board is now one third teachers (including the head), one third parents and one third representatives of the Local Authority. Whilst schools now have more financial powers, the inclusion of Local Authorities on the school board politicizes key decisions at school level. As teachers and the head now represent a minority on the board (and the head is no longer the Chair), this does also mean that some heads believe they have less power than before. Some also disagree with this level of outside 'interference' in education:

> Heads will … experience pressures from the Mayor or other political appointees with regard to whom to hire in their schools. This is the biggest challenge heads will have to face. This will happen especially in large, urban, renowned schools. Heads will be struggling to hire the best teachers professionally instead of the ones *recommended* (original emphasis) politically.
>
> (Paul, policymaker)

Appointments of heads and staff are to be performed by the School Board (2011 Education Act) although this has not yet happened in practice. School Boards and the appointment of heads are covered in more detail in the first vignette below.

Hence while markets are developing, the data show how politicization is a key theme in the findings. This is covered in a little more detail in the second vignette below, as it is a key feature of the Romanian context:

> People did not apply for a position in headship if they didn't have the support of a political party or another or one important person or another. It might have been the Mayor or the General County School Inspector, or both. The resilient ones would succeed.
>
> (John, policymaker)

Dan is one such example. He was a head in three different periods; 'I was appointed head due to a favourable conjecture' (Daniel, head). Whenever the interviewees mention 'favourable conjecture' it is implicit that, in fact, they refer to being proposed for the position by their political party.

Examination of these changes will now take place through two vignettes.

First vignette: School boards and the appointment of head teachers in practice

In their new NPM endeavours head teachers are helped by the Administrative Boards. In line with the 2011 Education Act (updated and amended several times), the membership of the Board is now a tripartite system (teachers-parents-local authorities) in which the local community and parents represent two thirds. This is an important development in the role of civil society in education (as compared to the previous Education Act in 1995) and a complete novelty in Romania. Parents have now come to play an important role in school life for the first time. However, the parents' and local authorities' gain is often the teachers' and head teachers' loss, at least in terms of power. Whilst head teachers have more control over budgets, they have less control of the Administrative Board. In recent years, both before and after the adoption of the 2011 Education Act, the composition of the board was a site of discord between various ministers of education, parliament, teacher unions, etc. Previously representing 50 per cent of the board apart from the head in the 1995 Act and various versions of the new Act, teachers are now in the minority.

The provisions of the 2011 Act regarding the Administrative Board and extended role of heads and governors have been applied as from the 2011–2012 school year. Head teachers now ensure the executive leadership of the school (according to Art. 97 in the 2011 Act) and manage school budgets. Together with the Board, heads are responsible for the selection of both teaching and non-teaching personnel, even though they are not the Presidents of the Board any more, as used to be the case before the 2011 Act. All of these changes have had notable effects on head teachers:

> I don't have a problem with the principle of the new Board, i.e. including more parents and representatives of the local community on the Board. This is one thing that all former ministers from the past seven years have agreed upon. My problem though is that in the new Board, ... teachers are in the minority. I cannot agree with taking the decision-making from the school and giving it to the local community and parents.
>
> (Paul, policymaker)

According to the legislation all heads are supported by between one and three deputies (depending on the number of students in school) and a number of subject leaders. In spite of delegating some tasks on a daily basis, Romanian heads tend to retain control at most levels. Apart from being a cultural post-Communist issue, this is also the case because head teachers and Administrative Boards are formally accountable for the running of the school.

The legal framework for the appointment of head teachers and deputy heads is represented by the 2011 Education Act (Art. 246, paragraph 3; Art. 257, paragraph 1) and the secondary legislation. The methodology for heads' appointment was long awaited. Prior to the new Education Act in 2011, head teacher selection and appointment process was centralized. According to national legislation and guidelines that were previously in use, County School Inspectorates were responsible for organizing the open competition for heads and deputy heads. This was a two-stage selection process. In the first stage, prospective eligible candidates applied for a position in headship and took a written examination. In the application file, they included proof of experience, qualifications and a four-year management plan. The candidates for headship had to score at least 70 per cent in order to proceed to the interview stage. In the second stage, the candidates for headship went to the County School Inspectorate for an interview. The aim of the interview was to establish whether the prospective heads had thorough knowledge of legislation in education as well as having a good medium-term institutional development plan for the school.

Since 2011, heads are meant to be appointed by the School Administrative Board following national guidelines (Art. 257 paragraph 2/2011 Education Act). The Administrative Body also holds responsibility for leadership development and training. It is now the case that the new heads should be Members of the National Body of Experts in Educational Management. Interestingly, the National Body of Experts in Educational Management was founded after the adoption of the 2011 Act and it is still not fully functional in 2015. At the time of writing this chapter, the selection of heads continues to be done by County School Inspectorates (as per the previous Act) despite legislation saying Administrative Boards would perform this function. Moreover, despite the selection criteria legislated, as mentioned earlier, head teachers are often removed from their position on political grounds, if the government or coalition in power changes. This raises issues about accountability at the macro and meso levels. In addition, these are clear examples of discrepancies between what is legislated and how it is implemented.

Second Vignette: the Communist legacies: head teachers and politicization

In Communist Romania, it was common practice for head teachers to be members of the Romanian Communist Party. With the emergence of more parties on the political scene after the fall of communism, heads can now choose to be members of a political party or not and if so, to which political party. In theory this is a normal democratic development and should work well. In practice, Romanian head teachers have to choose carefully their political allegiances as choosing the wrong (or no) party can cost them their headship. Even before decentralization, it would be typical for Ministers, Directors, County School Inspectors and also head teachers to be changed when a new national government was appointed.

Even when aligned to the party in power locally and/or nationally, there was no guarantee that head teachers would complete their headship. Unfortunately for schools, the impact is real as head teachers are often replaced with each of the changes in government. The fluidity of the political situation means that heads are also changing frequently, despite being appointed for four years. While most European heads are in post for at least eight years (with heads in England and Wales in post for ten years on average, according to Howson, 2005), only the most resilient heads in Romania stay in post for such a long time period.

My study showed that some heads do manage to stay in their post for as much as twenty or thirty years. However, these represent the exception rather than the rule and their resilience will often have been achieved by juggling memberships of political parties. Other heads do not manage to keep their post for more than one year. Another group consists of heads that are on their second or third headship and who have had several breaks in between, stepping back to a teacher role and then back to head teachers a few years later. All this comes at a cost. Being forced to step out midway through their headship causes serious problems for Romanian heads. These range from emotional problems, to material and employment ones. In the long term, this affects their rather fragile identity as heads. It also helps to explain why so many of them see themselves as both teachers and head teachers, since they often alternate to and fro between the two roles in the course of their career. In effect, the instability of the political system in Romania has implications for the other two levels in the Romanian education system as follows.

At macro level, the multiple changes in government mean the momentum for devising, adopting and implementing NPM reforms is lost. A policy needs time to be implemented. In Romania, normally, a government should be in power for at least four years until new elections are held. Four years is not enough for policy implementation, but it is a good start for the implementation process. However, if during those four years, the members of the cabinet change more frequently, sometimes even a few times per year (there were three different cabinets in 2012 alone, and seven ministers of education in the period 2008–2013), the chances of success of any policy are seriously reduced. So, by the time new people are appointed, get used to their new responsibilities, are brought up to date with policies, precious implementation time is lost. Soon thereafter, there might be a new change of government or minister and the process starts all over again.

At meso level, county school inspectors are the ones creating the link between the macro and micro levels. Changes at the top also mean changes for county school inspectors who are political appointments. In consequence, the messages (legislation, directives, etc.) sent from the top downwards lack consistency and coherence.

In summary, the Romanian experience of even the most basic aspects of NPM has been a challenging one. Whilst some progress has been made towards school-based management and managers this is still far less advanced than in some western countries which have been refining this for decades. Managerialism, for example, has been prevented through the enduring Communist legacy of politicization.

General context of NPM reforms in post-Communist Romania

A former totalitarian regime for over four decades, Romania has made constant efforts to move towards a democratic system since the fall of communism in December 1989. In Romania, as well as in other Central and Eastern Europe Countries (CEECs), the transition from communism to capitalism meant a thorough restructuring of the state, in many cases with the aid of supranational structures such as the European Union or international western institutions such as the World Bank. In Romania, by suggesting policies, the international bodies encouraged a 'westernisation' of the former Communist states' transition. In effect, international institutions' aid is usually accompanied by certain conditions (i.e. in Romania, financial aid is dependent on the implementation of the policy of decentralization). With little or no prior experience in state restructuring and policy design, and blindly looking to benefit from the experience and or funds of the western institutions, former Communist countries (including Romania) can fall into the trap of transferring or borrowing policies that might not be suitable for them (Ozga and Jones 2006; Barzanò 2007).

Policy design and implementation are contextual. They depend on a country's values, aspirations, history, socio-political and cultural backgrounds. Whilst it is important to look at the policies adopted by other states, simple policy transfer from elsewhere is not always the best solution. The aim of foreign policy analysis is to enable a better understanding of one's own national context (Gordon and Pierce 1993).

In order for the same policies to work everywhere, homogeneity is needed on two different fronts: one refers to western states in which policies originate and the second one refers to all the former Communist states (CEECs) to which policies are transferred. Unfortunately, homogeneity does not exist on either front here. All western countries have their own unique legislation, market principles, cultures and a different combination of centralization and decentralization, public and private sectors. In addition, all former Communist states in Europe are also heterogeneous. There is a great diversity of ethnicities, languages spoken, histories and starting points or degrees of centralization as well as different types of Communist regimes. Whilst, for example, the Romanian regime under Ceausescu was oppressive, the former Yugoslav regime under Tito was characterized through both keeping good relationships with other Communist countries and developing relationships with the West. There are some CEECs which share a few common features and indeed, they have been categorized into four types by Cerych (1997). However, even within his four categories each and every country within these groups is still remarkably heterogeneous and displays its own national character, culture and values.

As a consequence of this lack of homogeneity, any policy borrowing into Romania should be performed with care. This country is quite different from western states (and also many CEECs). Even if intelligently 'borrowed', the

166 Ana-Cristina Popescu

transition process from an ex-Communist to a westernised state takes time. Birzea (1994) considers that any former Communist state experiences not one, but three interdependent transitions with separate aims and timelines. These are political transition (five years), economic transition (ten years) and cultural transition (twenty-five years). I present an analysis of Romania's experience of transition from a Communist state to a more democratic state through these three lenses and present them below, from the one with fastest pace on the time continuum to the one with the slowest.

Political transition can be achieved in approximately 5 years

The greatest shifts noted in Romania immediately after the fall of communism were political – 'moving from a totalitarian to a democratic government' (Eurydice 2009: 9). On the national political scene, one of the first steps undertaken in the transition from Communism to the establishment of a more democratic society was the restoration of the so-called 'historical political parties': the National Liberal Party, and the National Peasant Christian Democrat Party. These were the most prominent political parties in pre-Communist Romania and had been silenced during communism. Subsequently, approximately two hundred new political parties appeared in the early 1990s (Keil 2006; Eurydice 2009).

With respect to external policy, after the overthrow of the Communist regime which caused four decades of isolation from the West, the Romanian Government's main priority was to join the supranational structures. In 2004, Romania joined NATO and following the Copenhagen Council of June 1993, Romania was invited to start the process of joining the European Union (EU). Preparations for EU accession took over a decade and entailed major reforms in all sectors, a special emphasis being put on reforming public services – including education.

With regard to education, in the first instance, political transition translated into the removal of Communist ideology from the curriculum. Due to the slow pace of reforms, Romania and its southern neighbour Bulgaria were the last of the Central and Eastern Europe countries (CEECs) to join the enlarged European Union in January 2007 (Keil, 2006) that now consisted of twenty-seven member states.

Economic transition can reach its aims in about 10 years

Economic transition depends on the level of centralization and degree of collectivization (the appropriation of the lands by the Communist state in order to be administered centrally) prior to transition. For example, countries in the former Soviet Union under Stalin and Romania under Ceausescu reached a high level of collectivization.

In Romania in the 1990s, notable economic changes emerged by moving from a planned economy to the beginnings of a market economy (Eurydice

2009). The main aims of reforms were to reduce the role of the State and to introduce private initiative into public life through structural reforms (Birzea 1996, 1997; Marga 1998, 1999, 2000; Eurydice 2009; Popescu 2010). This was a particularly challenging endeavour both for the post-Communist governments, and for the population in the first decade after the fall of communism. The collapse of industry and the privatization of state-owned enterprises led to tens of thousands of redundancies, a decrease in the GDP and an economic crisis.

Cultural transition is the most complex of the three and can take up to 25 years to be completed

Cultural transition involves major changes of 'lifestyle, values, attitudes, skills, and social relationships' (Birzea and Fartusnic 2003: 71). The resistance of the first post-Communist governments to western ideology led to delays in democratization (Linz and Stepan 1996) and marketization (Pop 2006). In addition, the instability caused by the large number of political parties allowed for the strong politicization of Communist times to continue in post-Communist Romania and was a key-factor in Romania's slow and challenging transition. This political instability also translated into frequent changes of ministers of education and other top-level civil servants. The endurance of Communist practices and other cultural factors are the most important causes in the delays in the implementation of educational reform in Romania.

The reasons for the introduction of NPM reforms in Romanian education

Over the last three decades, globalization led to the growing influence of supra-state/organizational structures (such as the European Union and the World Bank) on individual states in policymaking and implementation. These international organizations' firm belief in neoliberalism and New Public Management reforms as the way forward in public services meant that 'policy migration' between nation states was adopted internationally. In the 1980s New Public Management came to the forefront of public policy agendas in western Anglophone states (such as Australia, New Zealand, the United Kingdom, and the United States of America) and other western countries (such as Italy). A decade after the initiation of NPM reforms in these countries, a NPM policy transfer in former Communist countries in central and eastern Europe followed, as well as in developing countries in Africa and South America. The reasons, forms and degrees of NPM adopted depended on socio-cultural, political and economic contexts of implementation across the different countries. It is beyond the scope of this chapter to elaborate on the forms of NPM implemented from state to state. However, in many cases, the adoption and implementation of New Public Management reforms was directly linked to membership of

168 Ana-Cristina Popescu

supranational bodies, which often required new governance arrangements such as a shift from centralization to the decentralization of public services.

The issue of why a state decides to transfer power downwards has been the subject of long debates. Several authors have argued that the reason the state is shifting responsibilities to regional or local level is to bring decision making closer to the point of consumption of services. There is some debate as to whether this is the main reason or not and also whether it is happening intentionally. It may be instead, for example, that central government is losing control or does not want to be responsible for (local) public services any more (Pierre and Peters 2000; Newman 2001; Bell and Hindmoor 2009; Newman and Clarke 2009). There are a number of competing and complex themes associated here, such as the value of local autonomy, empowerment of those delivering local services, empowerment of the local public administration, parents and students as 'consumers' of education, the efficiency of a decentralized system, whether NPM reforms actually improves public services (e.g. student performance), decentralization's effect on equality of opportunity and so forth.

Conclusion

Romania, a former Communist country, adopted some New Public Management reforms in public administration from the 1990s. This was done at the suggestion of external institutions such as the World Bank, the International Monetary Fund, and the European Union etc. The introduction of New Public Management in Romania occurred at a time of deep cultural, social, economical and political change. Importantly, before the fall of communism, there was not a private sector in Romania, hence everything was nationalized and belonged to the Communist Party. Therefore, the birth of the private sector meant the introduction of the market values and practices, managers and managerialism.

In education, lying at the core of this chapter, NPM reforms were characterized by decentralization, quasi-markets and School Based Management. I analysed the effects of these reforms in education through a major study of head teachers' experience of school based management in Romania (Popescu 2013). Here, I will summarise why the Romanian situation is different and what this means for public education. Specifically for post-decentralization head teachers, their role changed tremendously over the past twenty years. They are now school managers that overview both the instructional and the financial aspects of education, at the same time competing for students in the marketplace. Currently, Romanian head teachers have more power to decide over finances, compared to their predecessors, the school directors, only responsible for the instructional side of things. However, current heads still lack the power to decide over most of the staff they are working with, i.e. educational staff is still selected based on national exams, teacher tenure, etc. This is no different to their Communist predecessors. Currently, this lack of full responsibility over the human resources part of their role leaves heads frustrated. They were promised full control over the reins of their schools once with the introduction of decentralization, School Based Management and quasi-markets and this is not happening as promised. In the long run, if heads are unable to choose their own teachers but at the same time have to raise standards, this will potentially have an impact on the quality of public education delivered. This, in turn, could lead to many schools being closed as a direct result of the educational marketplace.

What is particularly different in twenty-first century Romania is the level of politicization of education (and other public services) at both national and local levels. School Based Management has led to real empowerment at local and school level, especially in terms of finances. This empowerment, however, comes with a few conditions for the actors involved, not least membership (preferably) of the respective national or local party in power. The politicization of education impacts deeply on the entire public education system, with ministers, inspectors and head teachers changing repeatedly in a short period of time. In the short term, this means a high level of uncertainty amongst professionals and potentially low head retention, lots of tensions and frictions between the different levels of authority (schools, local authorities, and national government). In the long run, this brings about inconsistency in reform implementation, thus a delayed response to reforms (whether positive, or negative). Consequently, despite change happening, it happens at a much slower pace than in other countries as the three types of transition identified by Birzea (1994): political, economic and cultural are still ongoing.

Conclusion

12

NPM AND THE DYNAMICS OF EDUCATION POLICY AND PRACTICE IN EUROPE

Helen M. Gunter, Emiliano Grimaldi, David Hall and Roberto Serpieri

Introduction

The research reported within this collection is concerned with education policy as an example of public policy, and by this we mean, 'the actions and positions taken by the state, which consists of a range of institutions that share the essential characteristics of authority and collectivity' (Rizvi and Lingard 2010: 4). Consequently, education policy as a political matter is descriptively nested within a context but is also normative through how values, ideas and activities focus on what should be done, and instrumental through how this can be achieved and compliance secured. Our contribution through these accounts demonstrates that the field needs to do some serious thinking about knowledge claims, not least that as the nation state continues to change, this impacts on policy processes and outcomes (Rizvi and Lingard 2010), and this influences how the field of education policy plans, conducts and debates research and practice. Specifically, public policy does not come out of nowhere, and research that is politically and sociologically informed needs to investigate and provide accounts of the relationship between boundaries, ideas and actions. In this concluding chapter, we present an overview of the key patterns, but we do more than this as we consider the implication of our analysis for how the field conducts itself as a field and the knowledge claims that are made through locating within the social sciences. In doing so we confront the current debates focused on constructing a cosmopolitan sociology of education policy, and we make the case for the deployment of robust insights and conceptual tools from political studies.

New Public Management in education in Europe

Our reported research shows that NPM as radical and planned reforms of education within European states has been and continues to be significant. The aggregated outcomes of the analysis across the chapters support Hood's (1989) summary statement about a particular approach to good government:

> Much of the thrust of NPM has been a form of 'Taylorism with computers' applied to public services and has been built on standard corporate management assumptions, notably that no organization can function effectively unless all its operations are overseen by 'managers', that management is a defined and portable skill which can be abstracted from any particular context, and that there are a set of general conditions which lead to corporate 'excellence'.
>
> (ibid. 350)

By deploying our frameworks (see Chapter 1) to read our co-author's descriptions of the features of NPM within each nation state we can recognize some key features of the 4Ms:

- *Managers:* there is evidence (e.g. Catalonia, England, Finland, Norway, Sweden) of a shift from professional notions and practices towards work, roles and identities as *managers*. For example, in Romania head teachers have taken on a chief executive role regarding budget control and management, though this is often in tension with educational identities, and is taking place without training. In other countries such training is happening (e.g. England, Hungary, Finland), though in Italy the intervention is through evaluation systems and the demands these make on school principals. In Norway the manager identity is developing at school and municipal levels, where fieldwork shows how this happens through changes in practice. In other accounts, such as the Czech Republic, France and Hungary, such manager identities are under developed where previous political legacies endure. England is ahead of the game in regard to non-educational experts entering and delivering management tasks and processes.
- *Managing:* there is evidence of interventions into organizational processes towards an evidenced technology of delivery as *managing*. For example, the accounts describe the introduction of management by objectives (Sweden); data production and performance (England, Hungary); evaluation and auditing (Catalonia, Italy); testing and assessment (Czech Republic, Norway); and the growth in output controls and the minimizing of risk (England, Norway). Incentivization through performance systems (rewards and sanctions) is emerging in Norway but not evident in Finland, and in other states such as the Czech Republic and Hungary there are movements towards parent choice but no merit payment system. Legacies remain strong,

NPM and education policy and practice in Europe **175**

and while there are some developments in France, the strong bureaucratic system and culture remains.

- *Management*: there is evidence of interventions designed to break up state monopolies of provision through site-based *management* and with new providers, where the school as an organization is increasingly focused on *management* efficiency and effectiveness. There are major differences in regard to choice strategies, where in Catalonia there is autonomy regarding school finances, organization and pedagogy, in France there are no markets but there have been experiments with school choice. The accounts show evidence of varied emphasis on decentralization (Czech Republic, Romania), through turning schools into businesses (England, Sweden); parental choice (Sweden, Hungary, Czech); and schools outside of local democratic governance such as free schools (England, Sweden). However, in Norway and Italy, while managers and forms of managing are developing, the importance of common school remains strong.
- *Managerialism*: there is some evidence of direct interventions to change power relationships with line management and technical accountability systems as a form of *managerialism*. For example, in England there are a range of policies that have structured the work of the head teacher as performance leader, who is accountable for the production of data and the quality judgements regarding contracts and the continuation of the school. This seems to be the most evident in England, and this stands out in comparison to the other countries, where this is either not a feature or just glimpses can be seen through a 'pick and mix' approach to reforms (e.g. the Czech Republic, Hungary). The historical legacies of political culture and the continued vitality of bureaucracy are provided as reasons for this, not least in France where the Napoleonic tradition is the starting point for how reform is conceptualized. Even in nation states where major rifts have taken place such as the transition from dictatorial periods in Catalonia and Italy, and the Communist systems in the Czech Republic, Hungary and Romania, the legacy of bureaucracy is strong and is often in tension with supranational organizations (EU, OECD, World Bank) that can act as NPM colonizers.

While such patterns of convergence and divergence across the ten states are visible, we do need to recognize the endurance of administrative traditions, as Pierre (2011) has argued NPM plays differently where it is based on 'public law' or 'Rechsstaat' (ibid. 673) as in Germany, France, and Scandinavia, compared with 'public interest' (ibid. 673) systems as in the US and the UK. Hence 'although the broad aims of producing more efficient, effective and responsive public services may have been widely shared, the mixtures of strategies, priorities, styles and methods adopted by different governments have varied very widely indeed' (Pollitt 2000: 184). There is a general agreement that this is because 'public management reform is first of all a national matter' (De Vries and Nemec

176 Gunter, Grimaldi, Hall and Serpieri

2013: p10) and so how NPM is constructed, read, interpreted, and engaged with is varied, where reforms overlay, intervene and do not necessarily replace what has gone before, and can be repealed. While research shows that NPM is not the product of one type of political system (Aoki 2015), we would concur with Pollitt (2000) who argues that the 'heartlands have never really extended beyond Australasia, North America and the UK', and even though some 'methods may have been selectively borrowed by other countries – especially the Dutch and the Nordics – these countries have never unconditionally accepted (NPM's) authority' (ibid. 196).

Consequently we give attention to what Aoki (2015) calls 'NPM-ness' (ibid. 166), or the shift from intentions to contextual practices:

- *The location of NPM activity*: Hood (1990) argues that there are 'radically different orientations on who exactly is to do the 'managing'' (ibid. 208). The complexities lie in whether central and local politicians/officials do the managing and/or whether they hand over this role to others. For example, in Romania there is the interplay between the national political system of ministers managing change, local inspectors overseeing change, and head teachers delivering change. While Pollitt and Dan (2011) make the point that the leadership and management of change is seen as vital, the situation is so complex that other factors in addition to NPM make a difference, not least whether the reforms are recognized as legitimate in relation to the claims that are made. Indeed, the account of Catalonia shows how politicians on both the right and left have different purposes and arguments regarding NPM purposes and proposed gains.
- *The oversight of NPM activity*: Hood (1990) argues that there are different 'procedures for appointing chief executives and monitoring their progress' (ibid. 209) where activity can be moved to departments or to units. In England there is evidence of both centralized oversight through the Department of Education in London, and the use of arm's length bodies to engage in delivery control. However, in other states the over-layering of NPM onto strong public state systems means that such 'oversight' is not installed or may slip (e.g. France, Norway), or is mixed and subject to political change (e.g. Catalonia); and in post-Communist states the legacy of entrenched political cultures impacts on practice (e.g. Hungary, Romania).
- *Working conditions*: Hood (1990) argues that 'there are marked differences in the extent of the shift in conditions of employment in the public service' (ibid. 209) such as the length of contracts and who the legal employer is. In this sense the existence of the centralized systems (e.g. France), the regional and municipal systems (e.g. Catalonia, Norway) and school based systems (e.g. England, Sweden) means that depending upon where NPM interventions take place the likely outcomes will be varied, and where direct rejection may be more prevalent in centralized than in deregulated systems. An illustration is through the varied adoption of performance related pay

NPM and education policy and practice in Europe **177**

(PRP) and incentivization policies, which are evident in England and Catalonia. Indeed Pollitt and Dan (2011) show how PRP is related to local conditions, not least that it does not fit with patronage or where there is no bonus culture (e.g. Italy).

It seems that researchers need to take into account that 'countries have not *started* from the same point, either in terms of the make-up of their public sectors or in terms of the way they think about the role and character of the state' (Pollitt 2000: 185, original emphasis). Indeed, our ten chapters show that NPM reforms in education are located in particular historical contexts within the nation state, whether that is extreme economic dislocation (e.g. England) or economic success (e.g. Norway); major political ruptures (e.g. Czech Republic, Hungary, Romania), demands for more autonomy within a state (e.g. Catalonia) and political instability (e.g. Italy). What needs to be taken into account is that public administration varies as an idea and as a practice from state to state, where different traditions and legacies (see Chapter 1 regarding Liberal, Social Democratic, Napoleonic, post-Communist; see also Windzio *et al.* 2005 for other cluster approaches). Consequently, NPM's promotion of competition and markets has to be considered alongside the 'variation in extent and style of privatization' (Hood 1990: 209) in European education 'systems' where, for example, school autonomy allows 'for profit' education in Sweden but not in Italy (see Simons *et al.* 2013).

Certain intellectual resources have more traction in different political cultures, where England is more receptive to pragmatic change than is France where it is not clear if NPM exists in education (though it does in the health service). Legal and constitutional arrangements can mean that 'governments have not all possessed the same *capacities* to implement reforms' (Pollitt 2000: 185, original emphasis), where change in a Federal system can take more time than a unitary one (see Klitgaard 2008 on school vouchers in the US compared to Sweden). Our co-authors are therefore able to show how England can be regarded as a laboratory for NPM, whereas by contrast Finland's approach is described as 'NPM light' because it is seen as a PISA success story and Norway is a 'reluctant adopter' because the impact of PISA generated a discourse about quality. Some show, such as Catalonia, how change is uneven and contradictory over time, while others show, such as the Czech Republic, how aspects have been adopted not because there is ideological commitment but because politicians have 'heard it through the grapevine'. It seems that reforms may look to be the same, may be enacted by governments of the Left and Right, and may use same language, but NPM may not be the outcome of the same motivations (Hood 1995).

178 Gunter, Grimaldi, Hall and Serpieri

The state we are in

Our main contribution through the accounts of NPM within national systems is to give recognition to the endurance of the nation state, and our task here is to consider what this means for the field of critical education policy studies.

It is the case that 'within' state analysis is a core feature of the field (e.g. Derouet and Normand 2011; Grek and Ozga 2010; Grimaldi and Serpieri 2013; Hall *et al.* 2015; Møller and Skedsmo 2013; Ozga 2009; Ozga *et al.* 2009; Paletta 2012; Rautalin and Alasuutari 2009; Verger and Curran 2014), where the contribution is to engage in contextualized policy production. It is also the case that the field has sought to move 'beyond' state borders, and examine the relationships between territory, borders and policy ideas. At a time of international networking, globalized neoliberalization of trade and exchange, with corporate elites in private foundations and consultancy businesses (see Ball 2012; Gunter *et al.* 2016; Gunter and Mills 2016; Saltman 2010; Spring 2012), the field is concerned to examine and conceptualize the relationship between policy changes and the 'bigger picture' processes (Ozga 1990). For example, Ozga and Lingard (2007) take on globalizing trends through the adoption of '*vernacular globalization*' where they argue that 'there is change and reconfiguration in global, national and local interrelationships, but mediated by local and national history and politics' (ibid. 72). Hence what takes place is more than 'external' demands, but instead the context in which change is taking place is 'an active element in the framing of education policy and politics' (ibid. 79). These insights suggest that globalization impacts are 'largely indirect' (Dale 2007: 62) or through a process of 'recontextualization' (Nordin 2014: 143), and can be understood in terms of what Ozga and Jones (2006: 1) identify as 'travelling' and 'embedded' policy, where they are argue that 'while policy choices may be narrowing, national and local assumptions and practices remain significant and mediate or translate global policy in distinctive ways' (ibid. 3).

Understanding what is increasingly being labelled as 'transnational policy flows' (see Nordin and Sundberg 2014) is being pursued in a range of ways, not least through examining what it means to be in receipt of NPM ideas and activities that travel between states, national and international elites, international and transnational organizations and networks. These policy flows are institutionalized through processes of agenda setting, peer reviewing of policies, comparative statistics, and increasingly what Alexiadou (2014) presents 'policy learning' as a 'particular mode of control of the direction, nature and content of the desired reforms, while at the same time there are appeals to its political neutrality and operational effectiveness' (ibid. 123). This can operate at a number of levels, from direct borrowing through to confirmation that the strategy being pursued locally makes sense. The relationship between learning and examining the institutionalization of NPM ideas and activities within supranational organizations such as the European Union and the OECD is through the identification of what Brenner (2004) calls 'state rescaling'.

The EU is characterized as a 'new transnational state' (Lawn and Grek 2012: 9), where the Lisbon Agenda is seen as important through how 'a set of implications and responsibilities for education were elaborated, with the proviso that they could only be met at the level of the Union, not that of individual Member States' (Dale 2009a: 31). For example, Lange and Alexiadou (2010) examine the development of education policy through the open method of coordination (OMC), aiming to reform European education systems through frameworks of common objectives, exchange of information, and building of knowledge about policy priorities. Additionally, Rizvi and Lingard (2010) show how there has been 'pressure to decentralize' from OECD, UNESCO and APEC (ibid. 121), and what seems to be emerging is variously a European education policy field (Lawn and Grek 2012), and a global education policy field regarding the OECD, the impact of PISA, and the annual publication of educational indicators in *Education at a Glance* (Rizvi and Lingard 2010: 124). The production of 'governing by numbers' (Ozga *et al.* 2009: 16) or 'a 'scientization' of education governance, where it is increasingly assumed that it is only knowledge (and in particular, statistical knowledge) that can reveal problems and shape solutions' (Grek and Ozga 2010: 272), means that not only is the emphasis upon the design of knowledge through statistics and ICT, but also upon the construction of 'calculable worlds' that indicators shape and promote (Gorur 2014: 578). Such worlds can be individual, organizational, and, sub-, national, and supra- national states, where there are sites through which the person through to the organization can be compared; and where Taylor and Henry (2007) argue that within the OECD there can be a clear national identity but also 'a sense of commonality among the like-minded' (ibid. 111). But the OECD is more than this, through 'acting as an international mediator of knowledge – an independent policy actor – rather than, simply, a comparative forum' (ibid. 111).

The field has tended to adopt 'governance' as an umbrella term for conceptualizing such forms of governing, or the shift from public institutions towards networks of interests. This approach is located in two main trends: first, the identification of experts who associate and exchange knowledge outside of national institutions, where Grek *et al.* (2009) identify '…the existence of networks through which data may flow, and through the capacity of technologies (software, data sharing systems, statistical techniques, statistical and analytical bureau) to connect individual student performance to the national and transnational indicators of performance' (ibid. 7), and second, the identification of networked activity outside of formal institutional places through mapping policy spaces:

> which is being shaped by constant interaction between small groups of linked professionals, managers and experts. This space does not have a constitutional position, a legislative legality, a fixed place of work or a regulated civic or business mission. Yet it is being formed between state

and EU offices, between agencies and subcontractors, between academics and policy managers, between experts and officials, and between voluntary and public sector workers. It is a growing culture, which exists in the interstices of formal operations, in the immaterial world. It is shaped by the opportunities and fears of globalization.

(Lawn and Lingard 2002: 292)

The emergence of a 'European education policy space' as a focus of analysis has been charted by Lawn and Grek (2012: 9), where they argue that 'it does not seek harmonization or a globalized uniformity' but rather 'it is built on the same soft governing approach – it cajoles, persuades and enables – but it is powered by data and standards…' (ibid. 153).

This inter-relationship between the person 'on the ground' who engages in vernacular cross border policies is replete within our ten examples, as is how policy developments on a different scale to the nation state is important in regard to rendezvous knowledge exchanges. While this project trajectory within critical education policy studies is helpful to the field, we would want to identify that the contribution of sociological knowledge as an intellectual resource needs troubling through accessing analysis from political studies. The relationship between knowledge production and powerful interests, and how this is evident on a different scale to the nation state is an important tranche of research and analysis. The productive use of conceptual tools of space and place from geography is adding to the richness of agenda setting (e.g. Seddon 2014). Importantly, such intellectual resources have enabled the field to shift beyond the descriptive where the interplay of sociological, geographical, political and historical conceptual tools have enabled the realities of practice to be made transparent (e.g. Ball *et al.* 2011; Maguire *et al.* 2014) inter-related with broader globalizing policy trends as structuring power structures (Bourdieu 1992). However, the endurance of legacies within our ten stories, whilst recognizing the importance of national mediation (Hall *et al.* 2016) show that Ozga *et al.*'s (2009) assessment that the nation state mediates rather than originates is premature. Correspondingly our contribution is to show how government and governmentality as forms of governing are important contributions from political studies.

Implications for research and practice

Our reading of current education policy research and analysis indicates a tendency to focus away from the nation state towards supranational entities such as the EU, where policy flows are carried and influenced by policy actors to, within and from supranational 'organizations' such as the OECD. The argument is made that the state remains but is doing things differently, where there is a need to give recognition to how change has impacted. Without this shift the researcher could be guilty of what Dale (2009b) identifies as 'methodological statism' (ibid. 124) where: 'the state is the source and means of all governing

NPM and education policy and practice in Europe **181**

activity, which, though it is typically taken for granted, is essentially contingent', and 'is the idea that it is the state that (necessarily) governs 'its' society, with an assumed unity between territory, society and political organisation' (ibid. 124). The shift required is outlined by Robertson (2006) who argues that:

> by developing a critical spatial analytic, we can see more clearly how the social relations of space and scale are not pre-given but the outcome of political projects and struggles. It is thus possible to imagine and create a different assemblage of social relations in new spaces of engagement with a different geometry of power, set of knowledges and politics of representation.
>
> (Robertson 2006: 313)

We would agree that this is integral to our analysis, and in the research reported in this book our co-authors have shown how NPM, as one of a range of transnational educational policy flows, has worked through the nation state interplayed with supranational organizations. However, we are mindful that NPM is about espoused good governance at state level, and hence while outside and cross border policy processes are important to chart and examine, a key anchor point that needs more recognition is the sovereign state, government and governmentality.

The current shift in thinking in the field towards 'out-of-state' analysis is located concerns within the field about 'methodological nationalism' (see Dale and Robertson 2009; Lawn and Grek 2012; Seddon 2014). Beck (2006) identifies this as a 'territorial prison theory of identity, society and politics' (ibid. 7) where:

> the result was a system of nation-states and corresponding national sociologies that define their specific societies in terms of concepts associated with the nation-state. For the national outlook, the nation-state creates and controls the "container" of society, and thereby at the same time prescribes the limits of "sociology".
>
> (Beck 2006: 2)

In summarising the approach prior to critiquing it (see below) Chernilo (2006) characterizes Beck's arguments as being about 'self-centred narcissism of the national outlook and the dull incomprehension with which it infects thought and action' (ibid. 2). Beck (2006) responds to such limited sociology through making the case for a 'cosmopolitan turn in social and political theory' (Beck and Grande 2010: 410). This requires 'the cosmopolitan outlook' (Beck 2006: 2) where 'we can grasp the social and political realities in which we live and act' (ibid. 2), and where 'national borders and differences are dissolving and must be renegotiated in accordance with the logic of a "politics of politics"' (ibid. 2). Such an outlook is impacting on the sociological researchers within policy studies, where globalization in regard to trade, and supranational organizations

182 Gunter, Grimaldi, Hall and Serpieri

in regard to the World Bank and Amnesty International are recognized, but how cosmopolitanism is different because it changes what people think and do through 'a sense of boundarylessness' (Beck 2006: 3), it is both a challenge and an agenda of possibilities, 'it is simultaneously a sceptical, disillusioned, self-critical outlook' (ibid. 3). But Beck (2006) is concerned with what he calls 'banal cosmopolitanism' (ibid. 19) where you may eat outside of a traditional national menu but you do so under your own flag. Hence as researchers there may be attention to the international and global but without a shift in outlook the data remains trapped in boundaries that have been shattered by capital, the media, and population movements.

This is challenging to critical education policy researchers, not least that much data that is produced officially is through national institutions and agencies, funding for projects may determine a nationally located sample, and participation in out-of-state meetings and organizations is legitimated through appointment to a national and legally controlled organization. For example, we are conscious that within the field of school leadership the nation state as a 'container' is prevalent (see Bush 2014), and even though there are plans to move beyond this, the case is made by Clarke and Wildy (2009) that what they call the 'Europeanization' of research is fragile (ibid. 358). We would agree that there is a need to think outside and beyond borders, and that there is a need to examine the relationship between knowledge production, social science disciplines, and territory. But our contribution in this volume shows that political studies as a resource needs to be engaged with in order to develop researcher orientation, perspective and contributions. Let us say some more about this.

The challenge that exists is that the state is seen as in play but it is also something of a nuisance because of that; the continued primacy of the state limits beyond state claims, and requires such claims to be linked back to the state. As such the drive to create a new trajectory within the field or even a new field is held back, and there is a danger of developing 'an allegedly autonomous research programme that bullies previous social sciences and declares them obsolete' (Chernilo 2006: 11). We would like to make a contribution that recommends that before this new direction within the field has traction as a discourse and practice there is a need to seriously visit the concept of the state.

Chernilo (2006) argues that in order to create the arguments regarding 'methodological nationalism' there is a need to script the nation state as 'the organizing principle of modernity' (ibid. 6), with a tendency to see the nation state as an 'it' or stable and solid in order to show how supranational organizations and transnational policy flows render 'it' to be doing some things differently or even possibly fractured and en route to extinction: 'the nation-state is a fetish when it is conceptualized as the self-sufficient, solid and well-integrated representation of the modern society – when it is thought of as *the natural organizing principle of modernity*' (ibid. 14). Therefore there is a need to recognize that 'the nation-state has been *historically opaque, sociologically uncertain, and normatively ambivalent*' (ibid. 15).

NPM and education policy and practice in Europe **183**

In this sense, and following Chernilo (2006), *historical opacity* is located in how the state is a product of and produces the modern, and so in our accounts we can see how recent or past ruptures both generate new directions but also draw on historical legacies. *Sociological* resources can only be helpful if they can enable the field to recognize that the state must and does create an image and rhetoric of stability, particularly through the endurance of public institutions of government within a legitimate constitutional framework (otherwise it is deemed to be a failed state), not least because control and authority are integral to purposes. However, as our co-authors have shown 'the nation-state is in a state of permanent crisis that threatens to divide the nation and weaken the state. The nation-state is an unfinished project that paradoxically presents itself as an already established form of socio-political organization' (ibid. 16).

Normatively, researchers are being called to work differently, where the main issue that needs confronting is how the nation-state is located within the contextual tensions of self-determination and a globalizing world, and so there is a need for 'nationalism and cosmopolitanism... to be reconstructed as co-original and in co-evolution, rather than two opposing forces...' (ibid. 16). Our analyses within and across ten nation states shows potential regarding this, not least because as Chernilo (2006) points out there is a need to get underneath the illusion that logic and history are automatically linked. Logically the case is made that sociology has constructed a link between society and the nation state, and historically the case is made that the nation state is the prime location of identity formation and development. Chernilo (2006) argues that the two are linked but they need not be, and this is the problem with the analysis: 'Beck is missing a theory of the nation state beyond methodological nationalism' (ibid. 13), and so he 'reintroduces a *methodologically nationalistic conceptualization of the nation-state* in spite of itself' (ibid. 13).

For education policy researchers there is a need to go beyond a recognition that the state matters, with a move to examining out-of-state activities. Indeed Ball's (2012: 7) debates within political science are helpful here: 'it is important that we do not underestimate the powers of the state but also important that we do not in abstract overestimate them or treat the state as an undifferentiated whole'. This matters because our co-authors have shown in detail how the reading, interpretation, selection and introduction of NPM ideas and strategies within national education systems are about creating the illusion of solidity and stability rather than a product of a modern state, and how in doing so further instabilities can be created that require new forms of NPM, or post NPM to be engaged with. Engagement with supranational organizations is directly related to this, and how interests that are located within and external to national borders use, refine, reject NPM in regard to political, economic and social advantage within and outside of public institutions.

The analysis regarding the conceptualization of government, governance and networks within political studies matters for the field (see Ball 2009; Goodwin 2009), not only through the identification of connections but also the way

184 Gunter, Grimaldi, Hall and Serpieri

power is constructed and deployed to build and deny influence. In this sense recognition needs to be given to state institutions that 'create constraints and opportunities for those involved in policy-making' (Béland 2005: 3). Davies' (2011) contribution is important, not least the claim that hierarchy remains in place, even though networks were meant to eradicate it. Analysis of the entryism into public institutions by corporate elites is also significant, not only in terms of how they work within/outside and for/against the nation state (see Spring 2012), but also because NPM is less a feature of supranational organizations than how it is aligned with property rights, or how claims are made that the 'private ownership of the assets of an organization results in superior profitability and effectiveness' how this is done within 'a self-referential framework in which its principles are assumed to be self-evidently good, even when they might conflict with other equally important goals' (Rizvi and Lingard 2010: 89).

What does this mean for research and practice? Accounts by our authors and our analysis of how the field is moving forward regarding education policy studies in Europe is suggesting that the contribution of sociological analysis that also draws on other disciplinary tools is a productive one, but we need a more sophisticated conceptualization of the state than the one that has produced claims about methodological nationalism. What seems to be emerging is what Appadurai (2013) identifies as elite cosmopolitanism (with the potential of Eurocentric elite cosmopolitanism), particularly since as a community we might end up denouncing each other and forgetting in whose interests our publicly funded research is being done. Following Ball (2008b), there is a need to trouble the 'optics of power' (ibid. 651) regarding how agency and structure are interplayed in civil society within family, schools and communities, and how in doing this there is a moral question: 'critical researchers, apparently safely ensconced in the moral high ground, nonetheless make a livelihood trading in the artefacts of misery and broken dreams of practitioners' (Ball 1997: 258). This leads us to challenge elite forms of boundary maintenance and crossing, and give recognition to what Appadurai (2013) in studying Mumbai calls 'cosmopolitanism from below' where the emphasis is on recognising the existence and political vitality of the local, not as a restriction on thinking and analysis, but 'driven by the exigencies of exclusion rather than by the privileges (and ennui) of inclusion' (ibid. 198). Work from the global South remains vitally important to how the state and public institutions present themselves in scoping and enacting reforms, combined with how on going challenges interact and are challenged through political processes, civil society and education, not least the analysis from Porte Alegre (see Gandin and Apple 2003; Jones 2013; Robertson 2006).

Our ten accounts show that what is and is not NPM, and why, is a political policy complex of nation state governmental and constitutionally structured institutions, histories, geographies and economics as well as sociologies, that create agendas and have such agendas shaped by globalising and cross border trafficking in ideas and policy strategies. The challenge for the field is to give recognition to not only sociological resources, but also a range of social science tools that can be used to describe and explain the structure and exercise of power. This enables boundary drawing, sovereignty, institutionalism and constitutionalism to be interplayed with scalar politics, not least how activism and inclusion/exclusion are manifest.

REFERENCES

AcadeMedia (2014) *Annual report (Årsredovisning). Räkenskapsåret 2013-07-01–2014-06-30 för AcadeMedia AB.* Available online at www.academedia.se/content/uploads/2014/12/AcadeMedia-AB-140630.pdf (accessed 4 May 2015).

Ahola, S. and Mesikämmen, J. (2003) Finnish higher education policy and the ongoing Bologna process, *Higher Education In Europe*, 28 (2), 217–227.

Ahonen, P. (2011) Markkinaohjaus: Kehkeytyminen, muodot, sudenkuopat ja kehittäminen. In Hyyryläinen, E. and Viinamäki, O-P. (eds) *Julkinen hallinto ja julkinen johtaminen. Juhlakirja professori Ari Salmisen 60-vuotispäivän kunniaksi.* Vaasa: Vaasan Yliopisto, 132–145.

Ahonen, S. (2014) A school for all in Finland. In Blossing, U., Imsen, G. and Moos, L. (eds) *The Nordic Education Model: 'A School For All'.* Dordrecht: Springer.

Alexiadou, N. (2013) Privatising public education across Europe: Shifting boundaries and the politics of (re)claiming schools, *Education Inquiry*, 4 (3), 413–422.

Alexiadou, N. (2014) Policy learning and Europeanisation in Education: the governance of a field and the transfer of knowledge. In Nordin, A. and Sundberg, D. (eds) *Transnational Policy Flows in European Education*, Oxford: Symposium Books, 123–140.

Alexiadou, N. and Van de Bunt-Kokhuis, S. (2013) Policy space and the governance of education: transnational influences on institutions and identities in the Netherlands and the UK, *Comparative Education*, 49 (3), 344–360.

Anderson, G. and Cohen, M. I. (2015) Redesigning the identities of teachers and leaders: A framework for studying new professionalism and educator resistance, *Education Policy Analysis Archives*, 23 (85), 1–25.

Antikainen, A. (2006) In search of the Nordic model in education, *Scandinavian Journal of Educational Research*, 50 (3), 229–243.

Aoki, N. (2015) Institutionalization of New Public Management. The case of Singapore's education system, *Public Management Review*, 17 (2), 165–186.

Appadurai, A. (2013) *The Future as Cultural Fact*, London: Verso.

Apple, M. W. (2001) *Educating The 'Right' Way: Markets, Standards, God, and Inequality*, New York: Routledge.

References   **187**

Armstrong, P. (2015) School business management in English state schools. In Wright J. D. (ed) *International Encyclopaedia of the Social and Behavioural Sciences* 2nd Edition, Oxford: Elsevier.

Bache, I. (2003) Governing through governance: education policy control under New labour, *Political Studies*, 51 (2), 300–314.

Balázs, É. and Halász, G. (eds) (2000) *Oktatás és decentralizáció Közép-Európában. [Education and Decentralisation in Central Europe]*, Budapest: Okker Kiadó.

Balázs, É., Kocsis, M. and Vágó, I. (eds) (2011) *Jelentés a magyar közoktatásról. [Report on the Hungarian Public Education System]*, Budapest: Oktatáskutató és Fejlesztő Intézet.

Balázs, É. and Kovács, K. (eds) (2012) *Több célú küzdelem. [Multifunctional Struggle]*, Budapest: Oktatáskutató és Fejlesztő Intézet.

Ball, S. J. (1997) Policy Sociology and Critical Research: a personal review of recent education policy and policy research, *British Educational Research Journal*, 23 (3), 257–274.

Ball, S. J. (1998) Big policies/small world: an introduction to international perspectives in education policy, *Comparative Education*, 34 (2), 119–130.

Ball, S. J. (1999) Labour, learning and the economy: a 'policy sociology' perspective, *Cambridge Journal of Education*, 29 (2), 195–206.

Ball, S. J. (2003) The teacher's soul and the terrors of performativity, *Journal of Education Policy*, 18 (2), 215–228.

Ball, S. J. (2008a) *The Education Debate*, Bristol: Polity Press.

Ball, S. J. (2008b) Some sociologies of education: a history of problems and places, and segments and gazes, *The Sociological Review*, 56 (4), 650–669.

Ball, S. J. (2009) Beyond networks? A brief response to 'which networks matter in education governance', *Political Studies*, 57 (3), 688–691.

Ball, S. J. (2012) *Global Education Inc: New Policy Networks and the Neoliberal Imaginary*, Abingdon: Routledge.

Ball, S. J. and Junemann, C. (2012) *Networks, New Governance and Education*, Bristol: Policy Press.

Ball, S. J., Maguire, M. and Braun, A. with Hoskins, K. and Perryman, J. (2012) *How Schools Do Policy. Policy Enactments in Secondary Schools,* Abingdon: Routledge.

Ball, S. J., Maguire, M., Braun, A. and Hoskins, K. (2011) Policy actors: doing policy work in schools, *Discourse: Studies in the Cultural Politics of Education*, 32 (4), 625–639.

Ball, S. J. and Youdell, D. (2008) *Hidden Privatization in Public Education*, Brussels: Education International.

Baráth, T. (1998) A közoktatás hatékonysága. Vezetői értelmezések és modellek. [The efficiency of public education. interpretations and models of leaders]. In Balázs, É. (ed) *Iskolavezetők a 90-es években [School Leaders in the 90s]*, Budapest: Okker Kiadó.

Barber, M. (2007) *Instruction to Deliver. Tony Blair, Public Services and the Challenge of Achieving Targets*, London: Politico's.

Barrère, A. (2006) *Sociologie des chefs d'établissement: les managers de la République.* Paris, Presses Universitaires de France.

Barrère, A. (2014) Un management bien tempéré: l'expérience des chefs d'établissement de l'enseignement secondaire français, *Education et Sociétés*, 32 (2), 21–34.

Barzanò, G. (2007) *Headship and accountability in three European countries: England, Italy and Portugal*, PhD thesis, Institute of Education, University of London.

Barzanò, G. and Grimaldi, E. (2013) Discourses of merit. The hot potato of teachers' evaluation in Italy, *Journal of Education Policy*, 28 (6), 767–791.

Beck, U. (2004) *Der kosmopolitische Blick*, Frankfurt am Main: Suhrkamp.

Beck, U. (2006) *Cosmopolitan Vision*, Cambridge: Polity.

188 References

Beck, U. and Grande, E. (2010) Varieties of second modernity: the cosmopolitan turn in social and political theory and research, *The British Journal of Sociology*, 61 (3), 409–443.

Beckett, F., and Hencke, D. (2009) *Marching to the Fault Line: The Miners' Strike and the Battle for Industrial Britain*, London: Constable.

Béland, D. (2005) Ideas and social policy: an institutionalist perspective, *Social Policy and Administration*, 39 (1), 1–18.

Bell, S. and Hindmoor, A. (2009) *Rethinking Governance: the Centrality of the State in Modern Society*, Cambridge: Cambridge University Press.

Bellè, N. and Ongaro, E. (2014) NPM administrative reforms and public service motivation: improving the dialogue between research agendas, *International Review of Administrative Sciences*, 80 (2), 382–400.

Benadusi, L. and Consoli, F. (eds) (2004) *La governance della scuola*, Bologna: Il Mulino.

Benito, R. and González, I. (2007) *Processos de segregació escolar a Catalunya*, Barcelona: Fundació Jaume Bofill.

Berényi, E. (2014) *Az autonómia kormányzása – a rendszerváltástól 2010-ig eltelt időszak közoktatáspolitikáinak diszkurzív elemzése*. [*The Administration of Autonomy: Discursive Analysis of The Period from Regime Change to 2010*], unpublished PhD thesis, Eotvos Lorand University, Budapest.

Berlinguer, L. (2001) *La Nuova Scuola*, Bari: Laterza.

Bertozzi, F. and Graziano, P. (2004) Italy's adaptation under external pressures: whose influence? In Armingeon, K. and Beyeler, M. (eds) *The Oecd and European Welfare States*, Cheltenham: Edward Elgar Publishing, 169–182.

Bevir, M., Rhodes, R. A. W. and Weller, P. (2003) Traditions of governance: interpreting the changing role of the public sector, *Public Administration*, 81 (1), 1–17.

Biesta, G. (2004) Against learning: reclaiming a language for education in an age of learning, *Nordisk Pedagogik*, 24 (1), 70–83.

Biosca, C. (2009) La comunitat educativa es posiciona davant la LEC, *Activitat Parlamentària*, 19, 20–24.

Birzea, C. (1994) *Educational Policies of the Countries in Transition*, Strasbourg: The Council of Europe.

Birzea, C. (1996) Educational reform and power struggles in Romania, *European Journal of Education*, 31 (1), 97–108.

Birzea, C. (1997) The dilemmas of the reform of Romanian education: therapy, the infusion of innovation, or cultural decommunisation? *Higher Education in Europe*, 23 (3), 235–247.

Birzea, C. and Fartusnic, C. (2003) Reforming the Romanian system of education: the agenda ahead. In Polyzoi, E., Fullan, M. and Anchan, J. P. (eds) *Change Forces in Post-Communist Eastern Europe*, London and New York: RoutledgeFalmer, 74–93.

Blomqvist, P. (2004) The choice revolution: privatization of Swedish welfare services in the 1990s, *Social Policy and Administration*, 38 (2), 139–155.

Bobbitt, P. (2002) *The Shield of Achilles*, London: Penguin.

Bonal, X. and Tarabini, A. (2013) The role of PISA in shaping hegemonic educational discourses, policies and practices: the case of Spain, *Research in Comparative and International Education*, 8 (3), 335–341.

Bottery, M. (1996) The challenge to professionals from the NPM: implications for the teaching profession, *Oxford Review of Education*, 22 (2), 179–197.

Bourdieu, P. (1992) *The Logic of Practice*. Cambridge: Polity Press.

Brenner, N. (2004) *New State Spaces: Urban Governance and the Rescaling of Statehood*, Oxford: Oxford University Press.

Bunar, N. (2011) Multicultural urban schools in Sweden and their communities: social predicaments, the power of stigma, and relational dilemmas, *Urban Education*, 46 (2), 141–164.

Bush, T. (2014) Special themed issue on school leadership in Europe, *Educational Management Administration and Leadership*, 42 (4), 3–174.

Caldwell, B. and Spinks, J. M. (1988) *The Self-Managing School*, Lewes: The Falmer Press.

Cashin, S. (2014) *Place not race: A new vision of opportunity in America*, New York: Beacon Press.

Cerych, L. (1997) Educational reforms in central and eastern Europe: processes and outcomes, *European Journal of Education*, 32 (1), 75–96.

Červenka, S. (1993) *Učit se. Učit se? UČIT SE! Aneb angažované učení v praxi [To learn. To learn? To LEARN! Engaged TeachingLearning in Practice]*, Prague: Agentura Strom.

Chalupová, E. (2002) *Být v profesi: prestiž učitelské profese zvnějšku a zevnitř [Being Inside the Profession: Prestige of the Teaching Profession from the Point of View of Insiders and Outsiders]*, Prague: Univerzita Karlova.

Chernilo, D. (2006) Social theory's methodological nationalism, myth and reality, *European Journal of Social Theory*, 9 (1), 5–22.

Chitty, C. (1992) The privatization of education. In Brown, P. and Lauder, H. (eds) *Education for Economic Survival: From Fordism to Post-Fordism*, London: FalmerPress.

Christensen, T. and Lægreid, P. (2007) Introduction – theoretical approach and research questions. In Christensen, T. and Lægreid, P. (eds) *Transcending New Public Management: The Transformation of Public Sector Reforms*, Aldershot: Ashgate, 1–16.

Christensen, T. and Lægreid, P. (2011a) Complexity and hybrid public administration–theoretical and empirical challenges, *Public Organization Review*, 11 (4), 407–423.

Christensen, T. and Lægreid, P. (2011b) Beyond NPM? Some development features. In Christensen, T. and Lægreid, P. (eds) *The Ashgate Research Companion to New Public Management*. Farnham: Ashgate, 391–403.

Christensen, T. and Lægreid, P. (2011c) Democracy and administrative policy: contrasting elements of new public management (NPM) and post-NPM, *European Political Science Review*, 3 (1), 125–146.

Chubb, J. E. and Moe, T. M. (1990) *Politics, Markets and America's Schools*, Washington, D.C.: The Brookings Institution.

Clarke, J. and Newman, J. (1997) *The Managerial State, Power, Politics and Ideology in the Remaking of Social Welfare*, London: Sage.

Clarke, J., Cochrane, A. and McLaughlin, E. (1994) Introduction: why management matters. In Clarke, J., Cochrane, A. and McLaughlin, E. (eds) *Managing Social Policy*, London: Sage, 1–12.

Clarke, J., Gewirtz, S. and McLaughlin, E. (2000) Reinventing the welfare state. In Clarke, J., Gewirtz, S. and McLaughlin, E. (eds) *New Managerialism, New Welfare?* London: Sage, 1–26.

Clarke, S. and Wildy, H. (2009) The Europeanisation of educational leadership: much ado about nothing? *European Educational Research Journal*, 8 (3), 352–358.

Clayton, T. (1998) Beyond mystification: reconnecting world-system theory for comparative education, *Comparative Education Review*, 42 (4), 479–496.

Colyvas, J. A. and Jonsson, S. (2011) Ubiquity and legitimacy: disentangling diffusion and institutionalization, *Sociological Theory*, 29 (1), 27–53.

Council of the European Union (2014) *Council Recommendation on Sweden's 2014 national reform programme and delivering a Council opinion on Sweden's convergence programme*. SWD(2014)428, final. Brussels.

190 References

Courtney, S. J. and Gunter, H. M. (2016) Privatising leadership in education in England. In Waite, D. and Bogotch, I. (eds) *The International Handbook of Educational Leadership*. Hoboken, NJ: Wiley-Blackwell Publishers. In press.

Courtney, S. J. (2016) Mapping school types in England, *Oxford Review of Education*, 41 (6). In press.

Crozier, M. (1986) *Etat moderne, Etat modeste. Stratégies pour un autre changement*, Paris: Fayard.

Cytermann, J. R. (2006) L'architecture de la loi organique relative aux lois de finances (LOLF) dans les domaines de l'éducation et de la recherche: choix politiques ou choix techniques? *Revue française d'administration publique*, 1, 85–93.

Dale, R. (2006) From comparison to translation: extending the research imagination? *Globalisation, Societies and Education*, 4 (2), 179–192.

Dale, R. (2007) Specifying globalization effects on national policy: a focus on mechanisms. In Lingard, B. and Ozga, J. (eds) *The RoutledgeFalmer Reader in Education Policy and Politics*, London: Routledge, 48–64.

Dale, R. (2009a) Contexts, constraints and resources in the development of European education space and European education policy. In Dale, R. and Robertson, S. (eds) *Globalisation and Europeanisation in Education*, Oxford: Symposium Books, 23–43.

Dale, R. (2009b) Studying globalisation and Europeanisation in education: Lisbon, the open method of coordination and beyond. In Dale, R. and Robertson, S. (eds) *Globalisation and Europeanisation in Education*, Oxford: Symposium Books, 121–140.

Dale, R. and Robertson, S. (eds) (2009) *Globalisation and Europeanisation in Education*, Oxford: Symposium Books.

Dan, S. and Pollitt, C. (2014) NPM can work: an optimistic review of the impact of New Public Management reforms in central and eastern Europe, *Public Management Review*, 17 (9), 1305–1332.

Daun, H. and Siminou, P. (2008) Decentralization and market mechanisms in education – examples from six European countries, *Education and Society*, 26 (3), 20–31.

Davies J. S. (2011) *Challenging Governance Theory: From Networks to Hegemony*, Bristol: Policy Press.

De Vries, M. and Nemec, J. (2013) Public sector reform: an overview of recent literature and research on NPM and alternative paths, *International Journal of Public Sector Management*, 26 (1), 4–16.

Dean, M. (2010) *Governmentality: Power and Rule in Modern Society* (second edn), London: Sage.

Derouet, J. L. (1992) École *et Justice. De l'égalité des chances aux compromis locaux?* Paris: Métailié.

Derouet, J. L. and Derouet-Besson, M. C. (2008) *Repenser la justice dans l'éducation et la formation*, Genève: Peter Lang.

Derouet, J.L. and Normand, R., (2011) Caesars and rubicon: the hesitations of French policymakers in identifying a third way in education and training, *Journal of Educational Administration and History*, 43 (2), 141–163.

Devine, T. M. (2006) The break-up of Britain? Scotland and the end of empire: the Prothero lecture, *Transactions of the Royal Historical Society (Sixth Series)*, 16, 163–180.

Du Gay, P. (ed) (2005) *The Values of Bureaucracy*. Oxford: Oxford University Press.

Du Gay, P. (2008) Without affection or enthusiasm. Problems of involvement and attachment in responsive public management, *Organization*, 15 (3), 335–353.

Dunleavy, P., Margetts, H., Bastow, S. and Tinkler, J. (2006) New Public Management is dead – long live digital-era governance, *Journal of Public Administration Research and Theory*, 16 (3), 467–494.

References 191

Edwards, L. (2009) Testing the discourse of declining policy capacity: rail policy and the department of transport, *Australian Journal of Public Administration*, 68 (3), 288–302.

Emberi Erőforrások Minisztériuma [Ministry of Human Resources] (2014) *Emberi Erőforrás Fejlesztési Operatív Program EFOP [Human Resource Development Programme]*, 2014–2020, Budapest.

Engel, L. C. (2008) Breaking the centre–periphery mould: exploring globalisation and educational governance in Catalonia, *Globalisation, Societies and Education*, 6 (3), 265–279.

English, R. and Kenny, M. (2001) Public intellectuals and the question of British decline. *British Journal of Politics and International Relations*, 3 (3), 259–283.

Erixon Arreman, I. and Holm, A. S. (2011) Privatization of public education? The emergence of independent upper secondary schools in Sweden, *Journal of Education Policy*, 26 (2), 225–243.

European Council (2013) Council conclusions on investing in education and training – a response to 'Rethinking education: investing in skills for better socio-economic outcomes' and the '2013 annual growth survey', *Official Journal of the European Union*, (2013/C 64/06).

Eurydice (2007) *School Autonomy in Europe, Policies and Measures*, Brussels: European Commission.

Eurydice (2009) *Organisation of the Education System in Romania 2008/2009*, Brussels: European Commission.

Eurydice (2010) *Organisation of the Education System in the Czech Republic 2009/2010*, Brussels: European Commission.

Evetts, J. (2009) New professionalism and New Public Management: changes, continuities and consequences, *Comparative Sociology*, 8 (2), 247–266.

Ex-ante Tanácsadó-Consulting Iroda (2006) *Humánerőforrás-Fejlesztési Operatív Program időközi értékelés. Indikátorok elemzése* – Zárótanulmány 2005 *[Ex-ante Evaluation of Human Resource Development Operative Programmes. Analysis of Indicators* – Final report], *Budapest: Ministry of Employment and Labour.*

Fazekas, Á. (2015) A közoktatás-fejlesztési beavatkozások hatásmechanizmusai – jelentés az empirikus adatfelvételről [Impact Mechanisms of Development Interventions on Public Education – Research Report], *Budapest: ELTE PPK Felsőoktatás-menedzsment Intézeti Központ. Manuscript.*

Fazekas , Á. and Halász, G. (2014): Az uniós finanszírozású kurrikulumfejlesztési programok implementálása. [Implementation of EU-financed Curriculum Development Programmes] ELTE PPK Felsőoktatás-menedzsment Intézeti Központ. Manuscript. Available online at www.impala.elte.hu/2013/12/27/iv-szintezistanulmany/ (accessed: 30 Nov 2014).

Fejes, A. and Nicoll, K. (eds) (2015) *Foucault and the Politics of Confession in Education*, London: Routledge.

Fellman, S., Hjerppe, R. and Hjerppe, R. (2010) Does a strong state create a welfare state? The case of Finland. Paper presented at APEBH 2010 Asia-Pacific Economic and Business History Conference, 17–19 February 2010, Victoria University of Wellington, New Zealand.

Ferlie, E. and Geraghty, J. (2005) Professionals in public service organisations: implications for public sector reforming. In Ferlie, E., Lynn, L. Jr. and Pollitt, C. (eds) *The Oxford Handbook of Public Management*, Oxford: Oxford University Press, 422–425.

Fernández-Polanco, V. (2007) El futuro incierto de la enseñanza pública, *A Parte Rei. Revista de Filosofía*, 50, 1–2.

192 References

Ferrera, M. (ed) (2005) *Welfare State Reform in Southern Europe*, London: Routledge.

Ferrera, M. (2013) Liberal neo-welfarism: new perspectives for the European social model, *OSE Opinion Paper* [online], 14, 1–12. Available online at www.ose.be/files/publication/OSEPaperSeries/Ferrera_2013_OpinionPaper14_Liberal_neowelferism.pdf

Feřtek, T. (2014) *Státní přijímačky (ne) jsou jako státní maturita* [State entrance exams are (not) like secondary school leaving exams]. Available online at www.eduin.cz/clanky/lidove-noviny-statni-prijimacky-nejsou-jako-statni-maturita/ (accessed 30 April 2014).

Figlio, D. and Ladd, H. (2010) The economics of school accountability. In Brewer, D. and McEwan, P. (eds) *Economics of education*, San Diego, CA: Elsevier, 351–356.

Finland, Ministry of Education and Culture (2012) *Education and Research 2011–2016: A Development Plan*, Helsinki. Available online at www.minedu.fi/export/sites/default/OPM/Julkaisut/2012/liitteet/okm03.pdf (accessed 3 May 2015).

Finland, Tilastokeskus, (2014) *Oppilaitosten määrä väheni edelleen, peruskouluja 67 edellisvuotta vähemmän*, Helsinki. Available online at www.tilastokeskus.fi/til/kjarj/2013/kjarj_2013_20140213_tie_001_fi.html (accessed 3 May 2015).

Flinders, M. and Wood, M. (2014) Depoliticisation, governance and the state, *Policy & Politics*, 42 (2), 135–149.

Foucault, M. (1977) *Language, counter-memory, practice: selected essays and interviews*. In Bouchard, D.F. (ed). New York: Cornell University Press.

Fraser, N. (2013) *Qu'est ce que la justice sociale? Reconnaissance et redistribution*, Paris: La Découverte.

Fredriksson, U., Holzer, T., McCluskey-Cavin, H. and Taube, K. (2009) Strengths and weaknesses in the Swedish and Swiss education systems: a comparative analysis based on PISA data, *European Educational Research Journal*, 8 (1), 54–68.

Friedman, M. (1962) *Capitalism and Freedom*, Chicago, IL: University of Chicago Press.

Frontini, S. (2009) Global influences and national peculiarities in education and training: the Finnish case. In Holmarsdottir, H. and O'Dowd, M. (eds) *Nordic voices: Teaching and Researching Comparative and International Education in the Nordic countries*, Rotterdam: Sense Publisher.

Fryer, R. (2011) *Teacher Incentives and Student Achievement: Evidence from New York City Public Schools*, Cambridge, MA: National Bureau of Economic Research.

Gallego, R. (2003) Public management policymaking in Spain, 1982–1996: policy entrepreneurship and (in)opportunity windows, *Journal of International Public Management*, 6 (3), 283–307.

Gamble, A. (1981) *Britain in Decline*, London: Macmillan Press.

Gamble, A. (1988) Privatisation, Thatcherism, and the British State, *Journal of Law and Society*, 16 (1), 1–20.

Gandin, L. A. and Apple, M.W. (2003) Educating the state, democratising knowledge: the citizen school project in Porto Alegre, Brazil. In Apple, M. W., Aasen, P., Cho, M. K., Gandin, L. A., Oliver, A., Sung, Y. K., Tavares, H. and Wong, T. H. (eds) *The State and the Politics of Knowledge*, New York: Routledge, 193–219.

Garcia-Alegre, E. and Del Campo-Canals, M. (2012) ¿La corresponsabilidad es una estrategia de éxito? *Revista de Educación*, Número extraordinario, 220–248.

García-Sánchez, I. M. (2007) La nueva gestión pública: evolución y tendencias, *Presupuesto y Gasto Público*, 47, 37–64.

Gleeson, D. and Husbands, C. (ed) (2001) *The Performing School. Managing Learning and Teaching in a Performance Culture*, London: RoutledgeFalmer.

Goodwin, M. (2009) Which networks matter in education governance? A reply to Ball's 'new philanthropy, new networks and new governance in education', *Political Studies*, 57 (3), 680–687.

Gordon, L. and Pierce, D. (1993) Why compare? A response to Stephen Lawton, *Journal of Education Policy*, 8 (2), 175–181.

Gorostiaga, J. and Ferreira, A. (2012) Discourses and policies on education quality in Argentina, 1990–2010, *Research in Comparative and International Education,* 7 (3), 364–375.

Gorur, R. (2014) Producing calculable worlds: education at a glance, *Discourse: Studies in the Cultural Politics of Education*, 36 (4), 578–595.

Gray, R. (2010) Is accounting for sustainability actually accounting for sustainability… and how would we know? An exploration of narratives of organisations and the planet. *Accounting, Organizations and Society*, 35 (1), 47–62.

Green-Pedersen, C. (2002) NPM reforms of the Danish and Swedish welfare states: the role of different social democratic responses, *Governance*, 15 (2), 271–294.

Green, H., McGinnity, A., Meltzer, H., Ford, T. and Goodman, R. (2005) *Mental Health of Children and Young People in Great Britain 2004*, London: Palgrave.

Greger, D. and Kifer, E. (2012) Lost in translation: ever-changing and competing purposes for national examinations in the Czech Republic, *Journal of Pedagogy*, 3 (1), 43–81.

Greger, D. and Walterová, E. (2007) In pursuit of educational change: transformation of education in the Czech Republic, *Orbis Scholae*, 1 (2), 11–44.

Greger, D. (2011) Dvacet let českého školství optikou teorií změny vzdělávání v post-socialistických zemích [Twenty years of Czech education through the lenses of educational change in post-socialist countries], *Orbis Scholae*, 5 (1), 9–22.

Grek, S. and Ozga, J. (2010) Reinventing public education: the new role of knowledge in education policy making, *Public Policy and Administration*, 25 (3), 271–288.

Grek, S., Lawn, M., Lingard, B., Ozga, J., Rinne, R., Segerholm, C. and Simola, H. (2009) National policy brokering and the construction of the European education space in England, Sweden, Finland and Scotland, *Comparative Education*, 45 (1), 5–21.

Grimaldi, E. (2011) Governance and heterarchy in education. Enacting networks for schools innovation, *Italian Journal of Sociology of Education*, 8 (2), 114–150.

Grimaldi, E. (2012) Analysing policy in the context(s) of practice: a theoretical puzzle, *Journal of Education Policy*, 27 (4), 445–465.

Grimaldi E. and Serpieri, R. (2010) The reforming trajectory of the Italian educational system. Site-based management and decentralization as a challenge for democratic discourse, *Journal of Educational Administration and History*, 42 (1), 75–95.

Grimaldi, E. and Serpieri, R. (2013) Jigsawing education evaluation. Pieces from the Italian New Public Management puzzle, *Journal of Educational Administration and History*. 45 (4), 306–335.

Grimaldi, E. and Serpieri, R. (2014) Italian education beyond hierarchy: governance, evaluation and headship, *Educational Management, Administration and Leadership*, 42 (4), 119–138.

Grugel, J. and Riggirozzi, M. (2007) The return of the state in Argentina, *International Affairs, 83* (1), 87–107.

Gunter, H. M. (2012) *Leadership and the Reform of Education*, Bristol: Policy Press.

Gunter, H. M. (2014) *Educational Leadership and Hannah Arendt*, London: Routledge.

Gunter, H. M. and Fitzgerald, T. (2013a) New Public Management and the modernization of education systems 1, *Journal of Educational Administration and History*, 45 (3), 213–219.

Gunter, H. M. and Fitzgerald, T. (2013b) New Public Management and the modernisation of education systems 2, *Journal of Educational Administration and History*, 45 (4), 303–305.

194 References

Gunter, H. M. and Forrester, G. (2008) *Knowledge Production in Educational Leadership Project Report*, UK: ESRC.

Gunter, H. M. and Forrester, G. (2009) School leadership and education policy making in England, *Policy Studies*, 30 (5), 495–511.

Gunter, H. M. and Mills, C. (2016) *Consultants and Consultancy: the Case of Education*, Cham, Switzerland: Springer.

Gunter, H. M., Hall, D. and Apple, M. W. (eds) (2016) *Corporate Elites and the Reform of Public Education*, Bristol: Policy Press.

Györgyi, Z. and Török, B. (2002) *A Comenuis 2000 minőségbiztosítási program a résztvevő oktatási intézmények tapasztalatainak tükrében. [The Comenius 2000 Quality Assurance Programme as Reflected in the Experiences of Participating Teaching Institutions]*, Oktatáskutató Intézet, Budapest: IFES.

Hagopian, J. (2014) *More Than a Score: The New Uprising Against High-Stakes Testing.* Chicago, IL: Haymarket Books.

Halász, G. (2002) Az állam szerepének változása a modern közoktatási rendszerek szabályozásában. [The changing role of the state in the regulation of modern public education systems], *Iskolakultúra*, 4, 3–11.

Halász, G. (no date) Az oktatáspolitika két évtizede Magyarországon: 1990–2010 [Two decades of education policy in Hungary: 1990–2010]. Available online at www. halaszg.ofi.hu/download/Policy_kotet.pdf (accessed 30 Nov 2014).

Halász, G. (2010) Az oktatás fejlődése és uniós tagságunk: 2006–2010. [The development of education system and our membership in the European Union], *Educatio*, (Tavasz), 34–53.

Halász, G. and Lannert, J. (eds) (1997) *Jelentés a magyar közoktatásról. [Report on the Hungarian Public Education System]*, Budapest: Országos Közoktatási Intézet.

Halász, G. and Lannert, J. (eds) (2000) *Jelentés a magyar közoktatásról. [Report on the Hungarian Public Education System]*, Budapest: Országos Közoktatási Intézet.

Halász, G. and Lannert, J. (eds) (2003) *Jelentés a magyar közoktatásról. [Report on the Hungarian Public Education System]*, Budapest: Országos Közoktatási Intézet.

Halász, G. and Lannert, J. (eds) (2006) *Jelentés a magyar közoktatásról. [Report on the Hungarian Public Education System]*, Budapest: Országos Közoktatási Intézet.

Hall, D. (2013) Drawing a Veil over managerialism: leadership and the discursive disguise of the New Public Management, *Journal of Educational Administration and History*, 45 (3), 267–282.

Hall, D., Grimaldi, E., Gunter, H., Moller, J., Serpieri, R. and Skedsmo, G. (2015) Educational reform and modernisation in Europe: the role of national contexts in mediating the New Public Management, *European Educational Research Journal.* 14 (5), 487–507.

Hall, D., Gunter, H. M. and Bragg, J. (2011) *End of Award Report: Distributed Leadership and the Social Practices of School Organisation in England*, Economic and Social Research Council, UK.

Hall, D., Gunter, H. M. and Bragg, J. (2013) The strange case of the emergence of distributed leadership in schools in England, *Educational Review*, 65 (4), 467–487.

Hall, D. and McGinity, R. (2015) Conceptualizing teacher professional identity in neo-liberal times: resistance, compliance and reform, *Education Policy Analysis Archives,* 23 (88), 1–17.

Hall, D., Møller, J., Schratz, M. and Serpieri, R. (2016) The diversity of European educational leadership. In Waite, D. and Bogotch, I. (eds) *The International Handbook of Educational Leadership*, Hoboken, NJ: Wiley-Blackwell Publishers.

References **195**

Hammersley, M. (2001) Some questions about evidence-based practice in education. Paper presented at the annual conference of the British Educational Research Association, 13–15 September, Leeds, UK.

Hangartner, J. and Svaton, C. J. (2013) From autonomy to quality management: NPM impacts on school governance in Switzerland, *Journal of Educational Administration and History*, 45 (4), 354–369.

Harvey, D. (2007) *The New Imperialism*, Oxford: Oxford University Press.

Hatcher, R. (2008) Academies and diplomas: two strategies for shaping the future workforce, *Oxford Review of Education*, 34 (6), 665–676.

Henry, M., Lingard, B., Rizvi, F. and Taylor, S. (2001) *The OECD, Globalization, and Education Policy*, Oxford: Pergamon-Elsevier.

Herbst, M., Münich, D., Rivkin, S. and Schiman, J. (2012) *Understanding the divergent trends in PISA test results for Poland and the Czech Republic*. Available online at www.hks.harvard.edu/pepg/PDF/Papers/PEPG12-06_Rivkin.pdf (accessed 16 April 2014).

Herr, K. (2015) Cultivating disruptive subjectivities. Interrupting the new professionalism, *Education Policy Analysis Archives*, 23 (86), 1–22.

Honneth, A. (2000) *La lutte pour la reconnaissance*, Paris: Editions du Cerf.

Hood, C. (1989) Public administration and public policy: intellectual challenges for the 1990s, *Australian Journal of Public Administration*, 48 (4), 346–358.

Hood, C. (1990) De-Sir Humphreyfying the Westminster model of bureaucracy: a new style of governance? *Governance: an International Journal of Policy and Administration*, 3 (2), 205–214.

Hood, C. (1991) A public management for all seasons? *Public administration*, 69 (1), 3–19.

Hood, C. (1995) Contemporary public management: a new global paradigm, *Public Policy and Administration*, 10 (2), 104–117.

Hood, C. and Peters, G. (2004) The middle ageing of New Public Management: into the age of paradox? *Journal of Public Administration Research and Theory*, 14 (3), 267–282.

Horváth, M. T. (2005) *Közmenedzsment [Public Management]*, Budapest: Dialóg Campus Kiadó.

Howson, J. (2005) *The State of the Labour Market for Senior Staff in Schools in England and Wales*. Oxford: Education Data Surveys.

Hoyle, E. and Wallace, M. (2005) *Educational Leadership: Ambiguity, Professionals and Managerialism*, London: Sage.

Hudson, C. (2007) Governing the governance of education: the state strikes back? *European Educational Research Journal*, 6 (3), 266–282.

Husbands, C. (2015) Introduction: Making Sense of the Coalition, *London Review of Education*, 13 (2), 1–3.

Jakku-Sihvonen, R. and Heinonen, S. (2001) *Johdatus koulutuksen uudistavaan arviointikulttuuriin. Arviointi 2*. Helsinki: Yliopistopaino.

Janík, T. (2013) Od reformy kurikula k produktivní kultuře vyučování a učení [From curricular reform towards a productive culture of teaching and learning], *Pedagogická orientace*, 23 (5), 634–663.

Jarl, M., Fredriksson, A. and Persson, S. (2012) NPM in public education: a catalyst for the professionalization of Swedish school principals, *Public Administration*, 90 (2), 429–444.

Jessop, B. (1994) The transition to post-Fordism and the Schumpeterian workfare state. In Burrows, R. and Loader, B. (eds) *Towards a post-Fordist Welfare State?* London: Routledge, 13–37.

Jessop, B. (2002) *The Future of the Capitalist State*, Cambridge: Polity Press.

196 References

Jessop, B. (2010) Cultural political economy and critical political studies, *Critical Policy Studies*, 3 (3–4), 336–356.

Jessop, B. (2014) State and regulation – theoretical perspectives on the European Union and the failure of the Lisbon agenda, *Competition & Change*, 10(2), 141–161.

Johnson, S. (1998) *Who Moved My Cheese?* London: Vermilion.

Jones, K. (ed) (2013) *Education in Europe: the Politics of Austerity*, London: Radical Books.

Kalantzis, M. and Cope, B. (1999) Multicultural education: transforming the mainstream. In May, S. (ed) *Critical Multiculturalism: Rethinking Multicultural and Anti-racist Education*, London: Falmer Press, 245–276.

Karseth, B., Møller, J. and Aasen, P. (2013). Reformtakter – Kunnskapsløftets komposisjon. In: Karseth, B., Møller, J. and Aasen, P. (eds) *Reformtakter: Om fornyelse og stabilitet i grunnopplæringen*. Universitetsforlaget.

Karvi (2014) *Keskustelua arvioinnin tulevaisuudesta Karvin avajaisissa*. Available online at www.karvi.fi/2014/keskustelua-arvioinnin-tulevaisuudesta-karvin-avajaisissa (accessed 15 April 2015).

Kauko, J. and Varjo, J. (2008) Age of indicators: changes in the Finnish education policy agenda, *European Educational Research Journal*, 7 (2), 219–231.

Keil, T. J. (2006) *Romania's Tortured Road Toward Modernity*, Boulder, CO: East European Monographs.

Kemp, P. (2005) *Världsmedborgaren. Politisk och pedagogisk filosofi för det 21 århundradet*. Göteborg: Daidalos.

Kickert, W. (2007) Public management reforms in countries with a Napoleonic state model: France, Italy and Spain. In Pollitt, C., Van Thiel, S. and Homburg, VMF. (eds) *New Public Management in Europe: Adaptation and Alternatives*, Basingstoke: Palgrave Macmillan, 26–51.

Kickert, W. (2011) Distinctiveness of administrative reform in Greece, Italy, Portugal and Spain. Common characteristics of context, administrations and reforms, *Public Administration*, 89 (3), 801–818.

Kiilakoski, T. and Oravakangas, A. (2010) Koulutus tuotantokoneistona? *Kasvatus & Aika*, 4 (1), 7–25.

Kirp, D. (2013) *Improbable Scholars: The Rebirth of a Great American School System and a Strategy for America's Schools*, London: Oxford University Press.

Klitgaard, M. B. (2008) School Vouchers and the new politics of the wefare state, *Governance: An International Journal of Policy, Administration and Institutions*, 21 (4), 479–498.

Knubb-Manninen, G., Niemi, H. and Pietiläinen, V. (eds) (2013) *Kansallinen arviointi kohti tulevaisuutta*, Jyväskylä: Koulutuksen arviointineuvoston julkaisuja 63.

Kooiman, J. and Eliassen, K. A. (1987a) Introduction. In Kooiman, J. and Eliassen, K. A. (eds) *Managing Public Organizations*, London: Sage, 5–16.

Kooiman, J. and Eliassen, K. A. (eds) (1987b) *Managing Public Organizations*, London: Sage.

Kotásek, J. (2005a) Vzdělávací politika a rozvoj školství v České republice po roce 1989: 1. časť. [Education policy and education system development in the Czech Republic after 1989: 1st part], *Technológia vzdelavania*, 13 (3), 7–11.

Kotásek, J. (2005b) Vzdělávací politika a rozvoj školství v České republice po roce 1989: pokračovanie [Education policy and the education system development in Czech Republic after 1989: continued], *Technológia vzdelavania*, 13 (4), 3–6.

Landri, P. (2009) A temporary eclipse of bureaucracy. The circulation of school autonomy in Italy, *Italian Journal of Sociology of Education*, 3 (3), 76–93.

Landri, P. (2014) Governing by standards: the fabrication of austerity in the Italian educational system, *Education Inquiry*, 5 (1), 1–17.

Lane, J. E. (ed) (1987) *Bureaucracy and Public Choice*, London: Sage.

Lange, B. and Alexiadou N. (2010) Policy learning and governance of education policy in the EU, *Journal of Education Policy*, 25 (4), 443–463.

Lawn, M. and Grek, S. (2012) *Europeanizing Education. Governing a New Policy Space*, Oxford: Symposium Books.

Lawn, M. and Lingard, B. (2002) Constructing a European policy space in educational governance: the role of transnational policy actors, *European Educational Research Journal*, 1 (2), 290–307.

LeGrand, J. and Bartlett, W. (1993) *Quasi-markets and Social Policy*, Basingstoke: Macmillan Press.

Lemke, T. (2009) An indigestible meal? Foucault, governmentality and state theory. In Peters, M. A., Besley, A. C., Olssen, M., Maurer, S. and Weber, S. (eds) *Governmentality Studies in Education*, Rotterdam: Sense Publishers, 35–54.

Levacic, R. and Woods, P. (2002) Raising school performance in the league tables (part 1): disentangling the effects of social disadvantage, *British Educational Research Journal*, 28 (2), 207–226.

Linder, S. H. (1999) Coming to terms with the public–private partnership: a grammar of multiple meanings, *American Behavioral Scientist*, 43 (1), 35–51.

Linz, J. J. and Stepan, A. (1996) *Problems of Democratic Transition and Consolidation: Southern Europe, South America, and Post-Communist Europe*, London: The John Hopkins University Press.

Lipman, P. (2011) *The New Political Economy of Urban Education: Neoliberalism, Race, and the Right to the City*, New York: Routledge.

Lubienski, C. and Lubienski, S. T. (2014) *The Public School Advantage: Why Public Schools Outperform Private Schools*, Chicago, IL: The University of Chicago Press.

Lundahl, L. (1997) A common denominator? Swedish employers, trade unions and vocational education in the postwar years, *International Journal of Training and Development*, 1 (2), 91–102.

Lundahl, L. (2002) Sweden: decentralization, deregulation, quasi-markets – and then what? *Journal of Education Policy*, 17 (6), 687–697.

Lundahl, L. (2014) Suede: les marches de l'education, l'autonomie locale et le controle gouvernemental (Sweden: school markets, local autonomy and state control). In Fialaire, J. (ed) *Éducation, Formation, Recherche. Quelle place pour les collectivités territoriales? Droit et Gestion des Collectivités Territoriales*, Paris: Le Moniteur des Travaux Publics, 229–235.

Lundahl, L., Erixon Arreman, I., Holm, A., and Lundström, U. (2013) Educational marketization the Swedish way, *Education Inquiry*, 4 (3), 497–517.

Lundqvist, J. L. (1988) Privatization: towards a concept for comparative policy analysis, *Journal of Public Policy*, 8 (1), 1–19.

Lundström, U. (2012) Teachers' perceptions of individual performance-related pay in practice: a picture of a counterproductive pay system, *Educational Management Administration and Leadership*, 40 (3), 376–391.

Lunt, I. (2008) Ethical issues in professional life. In Cunningham, B. (ed) *Exploring Professionalism*, London: Institute of Education, 73–98.

Lyytinen, H. (2013) Koulutuksen arviointineuvosto muutospyrkimysten ristiaallokossa ensimmäisellä kymmenvuotiskaudellaan. In Knubb-Manninen, G., Niemi, H. and Pietiläinen, V. (eds) *Kansallinen arviointi kohti tulevaisuutta. Koulutuksen arviointineuvoston 10-vuotisjuhlajulkaisu.* Jyväskylä: Koulutuksen arviointineuvoston julkaisuja, 19–36.

Maguire, M., Braun, A. and Ball, S. J. (2014) 'Where you stand depends on where you sit': the social construction of policy enactments in the (English) secondary school, *Discourse: Studies in the Cultural Politics of Education*, 36 (4), 485–499.

198 References

Magyar Köztársaság (2007) Új Magyarország Fejlesztési Terv 2007–2013 (ÚMFT) [New Hungary Development Plan]. Available online at www.palyazat.gov.hu/the_new_hungary_development_plan_ (accessed 06 April 2014).

Mahony, P. and Hextall, I. (2000) *Reconstructing Teaching: Standards, Performance and Accountability*, London: Routledge.

Malm, K. (1999) Finland. In Wachter, B. (ed) *Internationalisation in European Non-university Higher Education*, Bonn: Lemmens.

Maragall, E. (2009) *Com governem l'educació*, Minister of Education conference, Palau de la Generalitat, Barcelona, 21 October 2009.

Maragall, E. and Colomé F. (2013) *Escola Nova, Poble Lliure*, Barcelona: RBA.

Mareš, J. and Beneš, J. (2013) Proměny studia učitelství na pedagogických fakultách v ČR v letech 2000–2012 dané Boloňským procesem [Bologna process-driven changes in teacher education at faculties of education in CR between 2000 and 2012], *Pedagogika*, 63 (4), 427–459.

Marga, A. (1998) *The Reform of Education in 1999*, Bucharest: Alternative.

Marga, A. (1999) Guidelines for the reform of education, *Higher Education in Europe*, 24 (1), 131–139.

Marga, A. (2000) *Education in transition. PHARE Universitas Programme*, Bucharest: Paideia.

Maroy, C. (2009) Convergences and hybridization of educational policies around 'post-bureaucratic' models of regulation, *Compare* 39 (1), 71–84.

Martens, K., Rusconi, A. and Leuze, K. (eds) (2007) *New Arenas of Education Governance: The Impact of International Organizations and Markets on Educational Policy Making*, London: Palgrave Macmillan.

Mausethagen, S. (2013) *Reshaping Teacher Professionalism. An Analysis of How Teachers Construct and Negotiate Professionalism Under Increasing Accountability*, PhD thesis, Oslo and Akershus University College.

McCormick, C. (2013) From post-imperial Britain to post-British imperialism. *Global Discourse*, 31 (1), 100–114.

McGinity, R. (2015) Innovation and autonomy at a time of rapid reform: an English case study, Nordic Journal of Studies in Educational Policy, 1, 62–72.

Meier, D., Kohn, A., Darling-Hammond, L., Sizer, T. and Wood, G. (eds) (2004) *Many Children Left Behind: How the No Child Left Behind Act is Damaging Our Children and Our Schools*, Boston, MA: Beacon Press.

Meyer-Sahling, J. H. (2004) Civil service reform in Post-Communist Europe: the bumpy road to depoliticisation, *West European Politics*, 27 (1), 71–103.

Meyer-Sahling, J. H. (2009) Varieties of legacies: a critical review of legacy explanations of public administration reform in east central Europe, *International Review of Administrative Sciences*, 75 (3), 509–528.

Mikáč, J. (2011) *Případy odvolání ředitelů škol a školských zařízení v letech 2010 a 201* [The cases of dismissed principals in 2010 and 2011], Řízení školy, 8 (10), 8–11.

Ministerio de Educación, Cultura y Deporte (2012), Datos y cifras: Curso escolar 2012–13. Madrid: MECD

Ministry of Education and Culture (2012), Education and Research 2011–2016: A development plan. Available online at www.minedu.fi/export/sites/default/OPM/Julkaisut/2012/liitteet/okm03.pdf (accessed 4 May 2015).

Ministry of Education and Research (2015), Government offices website. Available online at www.government.se/MIUR (2007) *Quaderno Bianco sulla Scuola* [*White Paper on the School*], Rome: Ministero dell'Istruzione, dell'Università e della Ricerca.

Møller, J. (2007) Educational leadership and the new language of learning, *International Journal of Leadership in Education*, 10 (1), 31–49.

Møller, J. and Ottesen, E. (2011) Building leadership capacity: the Norwegian approach. In Townsend, T. and MacBeath, J. (eds) *International Handbook of Leadership for Learning*, Dordrecht: Springer, 619–635.

Møller, J., and Skedsmo, G. (2013) Modernizing education – NPM reform in the Norwegian education system, *Journal of Educational Administration and History*, 45 (4), 336–353.

Montecinos, C., Ahumada, L., Galdames, S., Campos, F. and Leiva, M. (2015) Targets, threats and (dis)trust: the managerial troika for public school principals in Chile, *Education Policy Analysis Archives*, 23 (87), 1–25.

Montin, S. (2006) *Styrnings- och organisationsspåret – teoretiska perspektiv och empiriska illustrationer [The Governance and Organisation Track – Theoretical Perspectives and Empirical Illustrations]*, Örebro: Samhällsvetenskapliga institutionen, Örebro Universitet.

Moos, L. (in press) Neo-liberal governance leads education and educational leadership astray. In: M. Uljens and R. Ylimaki (eds) *Theory of Educational Leadership as Curriculum Work – Towards a Comparative, International Dialogue on Curriculum Theory and Leadership Research*. Dordrecht: Springer-Kluwer.

Muir, H. (2014) Behold, Michael Gove, the Caesar of the schooling system, *The Guardian*, 20 June 2014.

Mungal, A. S. (2015) Hybridized teacher education programs in NYC: a missed opportunity? *Education Policy Analysis Archives, 23* (89), 1–28.

Musset, P. (2012) *School choice and equity: current policies in OECD countries and a literature review*, Paris: OECD Publishing.

NAE (2010) *What influences Educational Achievement in Swedish Schools? A Systematic Review and Summary Analysis*, Stockholm: Skolverket.

Nagy, M. (1999) Közoktatás a politikai rendszerváltás utáni Közép-Európában [Public education after political regime change in central Europe], *Új Pedagógiai szemle*, 11, 45–61.

Nairn, T. (2000) *After Britain: New Labour and the Return of Scotland*, London: Granta Books.

National Board of Education (2015) Report on the definition of the working picture of principals and the renewal of educational requirements [only available in Finnish], *Reports 2013:16*, Helsinki: NBA.

Neave, G. (2012) *The Evaluative State, Institutional Autonomy and Re-engineering Higher Education in Western Europe*, London: Palgrave Macmillan.

Neumann, E. (2010) Az oktatás és gyermekesély kerekasztal: Ki miben tudós. Szakértői tudások találkozója a közpolitika-formálás porondján [Roundtable of education and child prevention: who knows what? Meeting of experts in the arena of public policy formation], *Educatio*, 4, 614–624.

Newman, J. (2001) *Modernising Governance: New Labour, Policy and Society*, London: Sage.

Newman, J. and Clarke, J. (1994) Going about our business? The managerialization of public services. In Clarke, J., Cochrane, A. and McLaughlin, E. (eds) *Managing Social Policy*, London: Sage.

Newman, J. and Clarke, J. (2009) *Publics, Politics and Power: Remaking the Public in Public Services*, London: Sage.

Nilsson Lindström, M. and Beach, D. (2015) Changes in teacher education in Sweden in the neo-liberal education age: toward an occupation in itself or a profession for itself? *Education Inquiry*, 6 (3), 241–258.

200 References

Nordin, A. (2014) Europeanisation in national educational reforms: horizontal and vertical translations. In Nordin, A. and Sundberg, D. (eds) *Transnational Policy Flows in European Education*, Oxford: Symposium Books, 141–157.

Nordin, A. and Sundberg, D. (eds) (2014) *Transnational Policy Flows in European Education*, Oxford: Symposium Books.

Normand, R. (2011) *La mesure de l'école. Une arithmétique politique des inégalités*, Berne: Peter Lang, Presses de l'Ecole Normale Supérieure.

Normand, R. (2012) The doubts and uncertainties of French educators in the face of travelling policies. In Seddon, T. and Levin, J. (eds) *World Yearbook of Education 2013: Educators, Professionalism and Politics: Global Transitions, National Spaces and Professional Projects*, Abington: Routledge, 184–200.

Nuffield Foundation (2013) *Social Trends and Mental Health: Introducing the Main Findings*, London: Nuffield Foundation.

Nuñez, I., Mitchie, G. and Konkol, P. (2015) *Worth Striking For: Why Education Policy is Every Teacher's Concern (Lessons from Chicago)*, New York: Teachers College Press.

OECD (1988–89). *Ekspertvurdering fra OECD. OECD-vurdering av norsk utdanningspolitikk. Kirke-, og undervisningsdepartementet. Kultur- og vitenskapsdepartementet. Organisasjonen for kulturelt og økonomisk samarbeid*, Oslo: Aschehoug.

OECD (1996) *Zprávy o národní politice ve vzdělávání: Česká republika* [News on National Education Policy: Czech Republic], Prague: ÚIV.

OECD (2002) *Education at a Glance,* Paris: OECD Publishing.

OECD (2008) *Education at a Glance,* Paris: OECD Publishing.

OECD (2012a) *Equity and Quality in Education. Supporting Disadvantaged Students and Schools*, Paris: OECD Publishing.

OECD (2012b) *OECD Reviews of Evaluation and Assessment in Education: Czech Republic 2012*, Paris: OECD Publishing.

OECD (2012c) *Education at a Glance 2012: OECD Indicators*, Paris: OECD Publishing.

OECD (2012d) *Education at a Glance: OECD Indicators 2012. Indicator D6: Who Makes Key Decisions in Education Systems?* Available online at www.oecd.org/edu/EAG2012_Annex3_IndicatorD6.pdf (accessed 28 March 2014).

OECD (2013a) *New Insights from TALIS 2013. Teaching and Learning in Primary and Upper Secondary Education*, Paris: OECD Publishing.

OECD (2013b) *PISA 2012 Results: What Makes Schools Successful? Resources, Policies and Practices*, Paris: OECD Publishing.

OECD (2014a) *What Students Know and Can Do: Student Performance in Mathematics, Reading and Science*, Paris: OECD Publishing.

OECD (2014b) *Education at a Glance 2014. Country Note: Sweden*, Paris: OECD Publishing.

OECD (2014c) *Resource, Policies and Practices in Sweden's Schooling System: An In-depth Analysis of PISA 2012 Results*, Paris: OECD Publishing.

OECD (2014d) *Education at a Glance 2014: OECD Indicators*, Paris: OECD Publishing.

Ollikainen, A. (1997) Finland. In Kälvemark, T. and Van der Wende, M. (eds) *National Policies for the Internationalization Of Higher Education in Europe*, Stockholm: NAHE, 73–90.

Ollikainen, A. (2000) European education, European citizenship? *European Education*, 32 (2), 4–21.

Ongaro, E. (2009) *Public Management Reform and Modernization. Trajectories of Administrative Change in Italy, France, Greece, Portugal and Spain*, Cheltenham: Edward Elgar Publishing.

Ongaro, E. and Valotti, G. (2008) Public management reform in Italy: explaining the implementation gap, *International Journal of Public Sector Management*, 21 (2), 174–204.

Osborne, D. and Gaebler, T. (1993) *Reinventing Government*, New York: A Plume Book, Penguin.

Östh, J., Andersson, E. and Malmberg, B (2013) School choice and increasing performance difference: a counterfactual approach, *Urban Studies,* 50 (2), 407–425.

Owens, P. (2009) *Between War and Politics. International Relations and the Thought of Hannah Arendt*, Oxford: Oxford University Press.

Ozga, J. (1990) Policy research and policy theory: a comment on Fitz and Halpin, *Journal of Education Policy*, 5 (4), 359–362.

Ozga, J. (2009) Governing education through data in England: from regulation to self-evaluation, *Journal of Education Policy*, 24 (2), 149–162.

Ozga, J., Dahler-Larsen, P., Segerholm, C. and Simola H. (eds) (2011) *Fabricating Quality in Education: Data and Governance in Europe*, London: Routledge.

Ozga, J. and Jones, R. (2006) Travelling and embedded policy: the case of knowledge transfer, *Journal of Education Policy*. 21 (1), 1–17.

Ozga, J. and Lingard, B. (2007) Globalisation, Education Policy and Politics. In Lingard, B. and Ozga, J. (eds) *The RoutledgeFalmer Reader in Education Policy and Politics*, London: Routledge, 65–82.

Ozga, J., Lingard, B., Croxford, L. and Lawn, M. (2009) *Governing by Numbers: Data and Education Governance in Scotland and England*, ESRC Research Report, RES-00-23-1385. Available online at www.esrc.ac.uk/my-esrc/grants/RES-000-23-1385

Page, E. and Goldsmith, M. (1987) *Central and Local Government Relations: A Comparative Analysis of West European Unitary States*, Beverly Hills, CA: Sage.

Painter M. and Peters, B.G. (2010) Administrative traditions in comparative perspective: families, groups and hybrids. In Painter, M. and Peters, B.G. (eds) *Tradition and Public Administration*, Basingstoke: Palgrave Macmillan.

Paletta, A. (2012) Public governance and school performance, *Public Management Review*, 14 (8), 1125–1151.

Pereyra, M. A., Kotthoff, H. and Cowen R. (eds) (2011) *PISA Under Examination: Changing Knowledge, Changing Tests, and Changing Schools*, Rotterdam: Sense Publishers.

Perryman, J., Ball, S. J., Maguire, M. and Braun, A. (2011) life in the pressure cooker – school league tables and English and mathematics teachers' responses to accountability in a results-driven era, *British Journal of Educational Studies*, 59 (2), 179–195.

Peters, B. G. (2008) The Napoleonic tradition, *International Journal of Public Sector Management*, 21 (2), 118–132.

Peters, T. and Waterman, R. H. (1982) *In Search of Excellence*, London: Profile Books.

Pierre, J. (2011) Stealth economy? Economic theory and the politics of administrative reform, *Administration & Society*, 43 (6), 672–692.

Pierre, J. and Peters, B. G. (2000) *Governance, Politics and the State*, London: Macmillan Press Ltd.

Pollitt, C. (1990) *Managerialism and the Public Services: The Anglo-American Experience*, Oxford: Blackwell.

Pollitt, C. (2000) Is the Emperor in his underwear? *Public Management: an International Journal of Research and Theory*, 2 (2), 181–200.

Pollitt, C. (2007a) New Labour's re-disorganization: hyper-modernism and the costs of reform, a cautionary tale, *Public Management Review*, 9 (4), 529–543.

Pollitt, C., (2007b) Convergence or divergence: what has been happening in Europe? In Pollitt, C., Van Thiel, S. and Homburg, VMF. (eds) *New Public Management in Europe. Adaptation and Alternatives*, Basingstoke: Palgrave Macmillan, 10–25.

Pollitt, C., and Bouckaert, G. (2011) *Public Management Reform*, Oxford: Oxford University Press.

202 References

Pollitt, C. and Dan, S. (2011) *The impact of the New Public Management in Europe: A Meta-analysis*, Brussels: Coordinating for Cohesion in the Public Sector of the Future. Available online at www.cocops.eu/wp-content/uploads/2012/03/WP1_Deliverable1_Meta-analysis_Final.pdf (accessed 3 May 2015)

Pollitt, C., Van Thiel, S. and Homburg, VMF. (eds) (2007) *New Public Management in Europe. Adaptation and Alternatives*, Basingstoke: Palgrave Macmillan.

Ponce, J. and Bedi, A. (2010) The impact of a cash transfer program on cognitive achievement: the 'bono de desarrollo humano' of Ecuador, *Economics of Education Review*, 29 (1), 116–125.

Pop, L. (2006) *Democratising Capitalism? The Political Economy of Post-communist transformations in Romania, 1989–2001*, Manchester: Manchester University Press.

Popescu, A. C. (2010) The decentralisation of the school system in post-communist Romania, *Journal of Educational Administration and History*, 42 (3), 315–336.

Popescu A.C. (2013) *Headteacher and the Decentralisation of Public Education in Post-communist Romania*, PhD Thesis, University of Manchester.

Power, M. (1997) *The Audit Society*, London: Demos.

Power, S. and Whitty, G. (1999) New Labour's education policy: first, second or third way? *Journal of Education Policy*, 14 (5), 535–546.

Prášilová, M. (2008) Řízení základní školy v letech 1990–2007 [Management of primary schools between 1990 and 2007], Olomouc: Univerzita Palackého.

Rautalin, M. and Alasuutari, P. (2009) The uses of the national PISA results by Finnish officials in central government, *Journal of Education Policy* 24 (5), 539–556.

Reay, D. and William, D. (1999) 'I'll be a nothing': structure, agency and the construction of identity through assessment, *British Educational Research Journal*, 25 (3), 343–354.

Regeringskansliet (2014) *Sweden's National Reform Programme 2014. Europe 2020 – the EU's Strategy for Smart, Sustainable and Inclusive Growth*, Government Offices of Sweden.

Rhodes, R. A. W. (1997) *Understanding Governance*, Buckingham: Oxford University Press.

Richardson, R. (2015) British values and British identity, *London Review of Education*, 13 (2), 37–48.

Ridley, F. F. (1996) The New Public Management in Europe: Comparative Perspectives. *Public Policy and Administration*, 11 (1), 16–29.

Ringarp, J. and Rothland, M. (2010) Is the grass always greener? The effect of the PISA results on education debates in Sweden and Germany, *European Educational Research Journal*, 9 (3), 422–430.

Rinne, R., Jauhianinen, A. and Kankaanpää, J. (2014) Surviving in the ruins of the university? Lost autonomy and collapsed dreams in the Finnish transition of university policies, *Nordic Studies in Education, SpecialIissue: Transnationalisation and Nordic Higher Education*, 34 (3), 213–232.

Risse, T. (2000) Let's argue!: Communicative action in world politics, *International Organization*, 54 (1), 1–39.

Rizvi, F. (2007) Postcolonialism and Globalisation in Education, *Cultural Studies – Critical Methodologies*, 7 (3), 256–263.

Rizvi, F. and Lingard, B. (2010) *Globalizing Education Policy*, Abingdon and New York: Routledge.

Robertson, S. L. (2006) Absences and imaginings: the production of knowledge on globalisation and education, *Globalisation, Societies and Education*. 4 (2), 303–318.

References **203**

Robertson, S. L. and Dale, R. (2014) *Toward a 'critical cultural political economy' account of the globalising of education*, paper presented at the CIES Conference, Toronto, 10–15 March 2014.

Romanian Government, (2011) *The 2011 Education Act*, Bucharest.

Rönnberg, L. (2012) Reinstating national school inspections in Sweden: the return of the state, *Nordic Studies in Education*, 32 (2), 69–83.

Rose, N. (1999) *Powers of Freedom: Reframing Political Thought*, Cambridge: Cambridge University Press.

Sahlberg, P. (2011) *Finnish Lessons: What Can the World Learn from Educational Change in Finland?* New York: Teachers College Columbia University.

Sahlberg, P. (2012) Quality and equality in Finnish schools, *School Administrator* 69 (8), 27–30.

Saltman, K. J. (2010) *The Gift of Education*, New York: Palgrave MacMillan.

Sanders, D., Ward, H., Marsh, D. and Fletcher, T. (1987) Government popularity and the Falklands War: a reassessment, *British Journal of Political Science*, 17 (3), 281–313.

Santiago, P., Gilmore, A., Nusche, D. and Sammons, P. (2012) *OECD Reviews of Evaluation and Assessment in Education: Czech Republic 2012*, Paris: OECD Publishing.

Schmidt, V. (2002) Europeanization and the mechanisms of economic policy adjustment, *Journal of European Public Policy*, 9 (6), 894–912.

Schmidt, V. (2006) *Democracy in Europe. The EU and National Polities*, Oxford: Oxford University Press.

Schmidt, V. (2008). Discursive institutionalism: The explanatory power of ideas and discourse, *Annual Review of Political Science*, 11, 303–326.

Scott, J. (2011) Market-driven education reform and the racial politics of advocacy, *Peabody Journal of Education*, 86 (5), 580–599.

Seddon, T. (2014) Renewing sociology of education? Knowledge spaces, situated enactments and sociological practice in a world on the move, *European Educational Research Journal*, 13 (1), 9–25.

Sejersted, F. (2011) *The Age of Social Democracy. Norway and Sweden in the Twentieth Century*, Woodstock, NJ: Princeton University Press.

Serpieri, R. (2009) A 'war' of discourses. The formation of educational headship in Italy, *Italian Journal of Sociology of Education*, 1 (1), 121–142.

Shor, I. (1986) *Culture Wars: School and Society in the Conservative Restoration, 1969–1984*. Boston, MA: Routledge & Kegan Paul.

Siljander, P. (2007) Education and 'Bildung' in modern society. Developmental trends of Finnish educational and sociocultural processes. In Jakku-Sihvonen, R. and Niemi, H. (eds) *Educational Sciences as Societal Contribution*, Frankfurt am Main: Peter Lang, 71–89.

Silvennoinen, H., Seppänen, P., Rinne, R. and Simola, H. (2012) Yhteiskuntaluokat ja kouluvalintapolitiikka ylikansalliselta paikalliselle tasolle ulottuvassa tarkastelussa, *Kasvatus*. 43 (5), 502–518.

Simola, H. (2011) Introduction. In Ozga, J., Dahler-Larsen, P., Segerholm, C. and Simola, H. (eds) *Fabrication Quality in Education: Data and Governance in Europe*, New York: Routledge, 1–8.

Simola, H. (2015) *The Finnish Education Mystery: Historical and Sociological Essays on Schooling in Finland*, London: Routledge.

Simola, H., Rinne, R., Kivirauma, J. (2002) Abdication of the education state or just shifting responsibilities, *Scandinavian Journal of Educational Research*, 46 (3), 247–264.

204 References

Simola, H., Rinne, R., Varjo, J. and Kauko, J. (2013) The paradox of the education race. How to win the ranking game by sailing to headwind, *Journal of Education Policy*, 28 (5), 612–633.

Simola, H., Varjo, J. and Rinne, R. (2012) À contre-courant: dépendance au sentier, convergence et contingence. Vers une meilleure compréhension du modèle finlandais d'assurance-qualité et d'évaluation, *Education et Sociétés*, 28 (2), 35–51.

Simons, M., Lundahl, L. and Serpieri, R. (2013) The governing of education in Europe: commercial actors, partnerships and strategies, *European Educational Research Journal*, 12 (4), 416–424.

Sinka, E. (2009) *Nyilvánosság, helyi elszámoltathatóság és oktatásirányítás [Publicity, local accountability and education administration] (Jedlik pályázat, kézirat)*, Budapest: Oktatáskutató és Fejlesztő intézet.

Skedsmo, G. (2009) *School Governing in Transition? Perspectives, Purposes and Perceptions of Evaluation Policy*, PhD thesis, University of Oslo.

Skedsmo, G. (2011) Formulation and realisation of evaluation policy: Inconsistencies and problematic issues, *Journal of Educational Assessment, Evaluation and Accountability* 23 (1), 5–20.

Skedsmo, G. and Mausethagen, S. (2016) Accountability policies and educational leadership – a Norwegian perspective. In Easley, J. and Tulowitski, P. (eds) *Accountability and EducationalLeadership – Country Perspectives*, London: Routledge, 205–223.

Spilková, V., Janík, T. and Píšová, M. (2014) Co je a co není kariéra učitele, aneb výhrady ke koncepci kariérního system [What is a teacher´s career and what is not: objections to the ministerial conception of teachers' career system], *Komenský: časopis pro učitele základní školy*, 138 (3), 10–14.

Spring, J. (2012) *Education Neworks. Power, Wealth, Cyberspace, and the Digital Mind*, New York: Routledge.

Starr, P. (1988) The meaning of privatization, *Yale Law & Policy Review*, 6 (1), 6–41.

Štech, S. (ed) (1995) *Stát se učitelem [Becoming the teacher]*, Prague: Univerzita Karlova.

Štech, S. (2008) A 'post-egalitarian' society: from statistical to liberal justice, *Orbis Scholae*, 2 (2), 7–17.

Straková, J. (2010) Postoje českých učitelů k hlavním prioritám vzdělávací politiky [Czech teachers' attitudes to the main priorities of educational policy]. In Váňová, R. and Krykorková, H. (eds) *Učitel v současné škole* [The current school teacher], Prague: Univerzita Karlova, 167–175.

Straková, J. (2013) Jak dál s kurikulární reformou [What future for curricular reform?], *Pedagogická orientace*, 23 (5), 734–743.

Straková, J. and Simonová, J., (2013) Assessment in the school systems of the Czech Republic, *Assessment in Education: Principles, Policy & Practice*, 20 (4), 470–490.

Švecová, J. (2000) Privatization of education in the Czech Republic, *International Journal of Educational Development*, 20 (2), 127–133.

Sztompka, P. (1996) Looking back: the year 1989 as a cultural and civilizational break, *Communist and Post-Communist Studies*, 29 (2), 115–129.

Taylor, S. and Henry, M. (2007) Globalization and educational policymaking, a case study. In Lingard, B. and Ozga, J. (eds) *The RoutledgeFalmer Reader in Education Policy and Politics*. London: Routledge, 101–116.

Telhaug, A. O., Mediås, O. A. and Aasen, P. (2004) From collectivism to individualism? Education as nation building in a Scandinavian perspective, *Scandinavian Journal of Educational Research*, 48 (2), 141–158.

Thélot, C. (1993) *L'évaluation du système éducatif: coûts, fonctionnement, résultats*, Paris: Nathan.

References **205**

Thomson, P., Blackmore, J. and Gunter, H.M. (2014) Series Foreword. In: Gunter, H.M. (2014) *Educational Leadership and Hannah Arendt*, Abingdon: Routledge.

Tomlinson, S. (2005) *Education in a post-Welfare Society (second edn)*, New York: Open University Press.

Uljens, M. (2007) The hidden curriculum of PISA – the promotion of neo-liberal policy by educational assessment. In Hopmann, S. T., Brinek, G. and Retzl, M. (eds) *PISA According to PISA. Does PISA Keep What it Promises?* Vienna: LIT-Verlag, 295–304.

Uljens, M. and Nyman, C. (2013) Educational leadership in Finland or building a nation with bildung. In Moos, L. (ed) *Transnational Influences on Values and Practices in Nordic Educational Leadership: Is There a Nordic Model?* Dordrecht: Springer, 31–48.

Uljens and Ylimaki, R. (2015) Towards a discursive and non-affirmative framework for curriculum studies. Didaktic and educational leadership. *Nordic Journal of Studies in Educational Policy.* 1 (3). doi: http://dx.doi.org/10.3402/nstep.v1.30177

Van Zanten, A. and Da Costa, S. (2013) La gestion de la carte scolaire dans la périphérie parisienne. Enjeux, dynamiques et limites de la gouvernance éducative locale, *Education & Formations*, 83, 99–107.

Varjo, J. (2007) *Kilpailukykyvaltion koululainsäädännön rakentuminen: Suomen eduskunta ja 1990-luvun koulutuspoliittinen käänne (Kasvatustieteen laitoksen tutkimuksia 209)*, Helsinki: Helsingin yliopisto.

Varjo, J., Simola, H. and Rinne, R. (2013) Finland's PISA results: an analysis of dynamics in education politics. In Meyer, H-D. and Benavot, A. (eds) *PISA, Power, and Policy: The Emergence of Global Education Governance*, Oxford: Symposium Books.

Verger, A. (2016) The global diffusion of education privatization: unpacking and theorizing policy adoption. In Mundy, K., Green, A., Lingard, B. and Verger, A. (eds) *Handbook of Global Policy and Policy-making in Education*, London: Wiley-Blackwell. In press.

Verger, A. and Curran, M. (2014) New Public Management as a global education policy: its adoption and re-contextualization in a southern European setting, *Critical Studies in Education*, 55 (3), 253–271.

Verheijen, T. (1998) Aims, structure and methodology of the study. In Verheijen, T. and Coombes, D. (eds) *Innovations in Public Management. Perspectives from East and West Europe*, Cheltenham: Edward Elgar Publishing, 3–38.

Veselý, A. (2011) Vzdělávací standardy: správný krok špatným směrem aneb standardy nejsou standardizace [Educational standards: right move in wrong direction as standards are not standardisation], *Učitelské noviny*, 128 (10), 21.

Veselý, A., Pavlovská, V. and Voráč, M. (2012) Celostátní testování žáků v českých denících v letech 1990–2011 [National testing of students in the Czech dailies between 1990 and 2011], *Orbis Scholae*, 6 (3), 99–118.

Vidal, F. (2009) La Llei d'Educació i el sistema educatiu, *Activitat Parlamentària*, 19, 8–19.

Viteritti, A. (2009) A Cinderella or a princess? The Italian school between practices and reforms, *Italian Journal of Sociology of Education*, 3 (3), 10–32.

Vojtěch, J., Trhlíková, J., Skácelová, P., Kleňhová, M., Veselý, A., Vlk, A. and Hiekischová, M. (2011) *Spolupráce odborných škol s jejich sociálními partnery [Technical schools and stakeholders' partnership]*, Prague: NÚOV.

Walford, G. (2006) *Education and the Labour Government: An Evaluation of Two Terms*, London: Routledge.

Wallerstein, I. (1980) *The Modern World System II. Mercantilism and the Consolidation of the European World-Economy 1600–1750*, London: Academic Press.

Weggemans, H. (1987) Personnel and public management. In Kooiman, J. and Eliassen, K. A. (eds) *Managing Public Organizations*, London: Sage, 158–172.

206 References

Weiner, L. (2012) *The Future of Our Schools: Teachers Unions and Social Justice*, Chicago, IL: Haymarket Books.

Weyland, K. (2005) Theories of policy diffusion: lessons from Latin American pension reform, *World Politics*, 57 (2), 262–295.

Whitty, G. (1989) The new right and the national curriculum: state control or market forces? *Journal of Education Policy*, 4 (4), 329–341.

Whitty, G. (2002) *Making Sense of Education Policy*, London: Sage.

Whitty, G. (2008) Changing modes of teacher professionalism: traditional, managerial, collaborative and democratic. In Cunningham, B. (ed) *Exploring Professionalism*, London: Institute of Education, 28–49.

Whitty, G. (2009) Evaluating Blair's legacy, *Oxford Review of Education*, 35 (2), 267–280.

Wiborg, S. (2013) Neo-liberalism and universal state education: the cases of Denmark, Norway and Sweden 1980–2011, *Comparative Education*, 49 (4), 407–423.

Wiliam, D., Bartholomew, H. and Reay, D. (2004) Researching the socio-political dimensions of mathematics education, *Mathematics Education Library*, 35, 43–61.

Windzio, M., Sackmann, R. and Martens, K. (2005) *Types of Governance in Education – A Quantitative Analysis*, TranState Working Papers, No. 025, SFB 597. University of Bremen.

Woods, C. (2014) *Anatomy of a Professionalization Project: The Making of the Modern School Business Manager*, London: Bloomsbury.

Wright, A. (2012) Fantasies of empowerment: mapping neo-liberal discourse in the coalition government's school's policy, *Journal of Education Policy*, 27 (3), 279–294.

Yeatman, A. (1994) *Postmodern Revisionings of the Political*, New York: Routledge.

INDEX

AcadeMedia 75
Accountability: in Catalonia 113, 115;
in Czech Republic 129, 131–2, 138;
in England 22–3, 32; in Finland 40,
44–5, 51; in France 84–5, 88, 90, 95;
in Hungary 142–4, 148–50; in Italy
97, 98–102, 107, 110; as New Public
Management feature 5–10, 13, 175;
in Norway 54–8, 62–5; in Romania
158–9, 163
administrative tradition 14–17, 174–7;
Liberal 15, 24; Napoleonic 15–16,
83–5, 97, 112–13; Post-Communist
16, 127, 130, 141–2, 157; Social-
Democratic 15, 39–42, 53, 66–71
Ahola, S. 46
Ahonen, P. 42
Ahonen, S. 44–5, 47
Alexiadou, N. 66–80, 178–9
Anderson, G. xv–xviii
Antikainen, A. 47
Aoki, N. 176
Appadurai, A. 184
Apple, M.W. xviii, 7, 121, 185
Armstrong, P. 26

Bache, I. 22
Balázs, É. 142, 150
Ball, S. J. 11, 14, 16, 21, 26, 51, 67, 93,
106–7, 109, 178, 180, 183–4
Baráth, T. 154
Barber, M. 29
Barrère, A. 87, 90

Barzanò, G. 108, 165
Beck, U. 4, 40, 181–3
Beckett, F. 27
Béland, D. 184
Bell, S. 168
Bellè, N. 10, 97, 102
Benadusi, L. 103
Benito, R. 114
Berényi, E. 146–7
Berlinguer, L. 106
Bertozzi, F. 100
Bevir, M. 5, 8, 16
Biesta, G. 65
Biosca, C. 120
Birzea, C. 166–7, 169
Blomqvist, P. 70
Bobbitt, P. 5
Bonal, X. 118
Bottery, M. 150
Bourdieu, P. 180
Brenner, N. 178
Bunar, N. 74
Bureaucracy: continued vitality of 11, 84–
5, 89, 94–5, 100, 121–2, 175–6; as New
Public Management paradoxical effect
34, 132, 160; and professionalism 6–7,
15, 101; retreat of 5–6, 33, 42, 99–100,
124, 130; rework of 7–8, 55;
Bush, T. 182

Cashin, S. xvii
Catalonia see accountability,
centralisation, decentralisation,

208 Index

management, managerialism, managers, managing, Napoleonic administrative tradition, neoliberalism, New Public Management, privatization, school autonomy, standardisation
Centralisation: in Catalonia 113; in Czech Republic 127–8, 130–1; in England 22, 24, 27, 30, 33–4; in Finland 44–5, 48; in France 83–5, 91–2; in Hungary 141, 143–4, 146, 152–4; in Italy 98–100, 102–3, 109–10; in Norway, 54–5; as New Public Management feature 10, 15–17, 175–7; in Romania 157–8, 163, 165–6; in Sweden 66, 69–70, 73
Červenka, S. 134
Cerych, L. 127, 165
Chalupová, E. 135
Chernilo, D. 17, 181–3
Chitty, C. 26
Christensen, T. 11, 17, 22, 53
Chubb, J.E. 5
Clarke, J. 5, 7–8, 15, 168
Clarke, S. 182
Clayton, T. 40
Colyvas, J.A. 119
Cosmopolitanism 40, 182–4
Council of the European Union 78, 166
Courtney, S.J. 22, 30, 33
Crozier, M. 86
Curran, M. 111–24, 178
Czech Republic see accountability, centralisation, decentralisation, management, managerialism, managers, managing, neoliberalism, New Public Management, Post-Communist administrative tradition, privatization, school autonomy, standardisation

Dale, R. 17, 115, 178–81
Dan, S. 6, 9–10, 41, 176–7
Daun, H. 72
Davies, J.S. 184
De Vries, M. 175–6
Dean, M. 109
Decentralisation: in Catalonia 113–14, 116–17; in Czech Republic 127–31, 133, 136–7, 139; in England 22; in Finland 42, 44–5, 47; in France 83–4, 86–7, 91–2, 95; in Hungary 143–5, 153–4; in Italy 97–9, 101–3, 109–10; as New Public Management feature 15–16, 175–6, 179; in Norway 53–5;

in Romania 156–9, 160, 165, 168–9; in Sweden 66, 69–72, 74, 79
Derouet, J.L. 14, 83–95, 178
Devine, T.M. 32
Du Gay, P. 5, 24
Dunleavy, P. 10, 22

Edwards, L. 131
Emberi Erőforrások Minisztériuma [Ministry of Human Resources] 151
Engel, L.C. 114, 117
England see accountability, centralisation, decentralisation, management, managerialism, managers, managing, Liberal administrative tradition, New Public Management, privatization, school autonomy, standardisation
English, R. 27
Erixon Arreman, I. 75
European Council 78
Europeanisation 45–8, 89, 127, 150, 182
Eurydice 102, 131, 166–7
Evetts, J. 55, 64

Fazekas, Á. 141–55
Fejes, A. 108, 110
Fellman, S. 52
Ferlie, E. 26
Fernández-Polanco, V. 114
Ferrera, M. 16, 52
Feřtek, T. 134
Figlio, D. 65
Finland see accountability, centralisation, decentralisation, management, managerialism, managers, managing, neoliberalism, New Public Management, privatization, school autonomy, Social-Democratic administrative tradition, standardisation
Flinders, M. 5
Foucault, M. 100
France see accountability, centralisation, decentralisation, management, managerialism, managers, managing, Napoleonic administrative tradition, neoliberalism, New Public Management, privatization, school autonomy, standardisation
Fraser, N. 84
Fredriksson, U. 77
Friedman, M. xv
Frontini, S. 39–52
Fryer, R. 63

Index **209**

Gallego, R. 113
Gamble, A. 24, 27
Gandin, L.A. 184
Garcia-Alegre, E. 116, 118,
García-Sánchez, I.M. 113
Gleeson, D. 90
Goodwin, M. 183
Gordon, L. 165
Gorostiaga, J. xvi
Gorur, R. 179
Gray, R. 9
Green, H. 26
Green-Pedersen, C. 71, 80
Greger, D. 127–8, 133–4
Grek, S. 17, 104, 148, 178–81
Grimaldi, E. 3–17, 96–110, 173–85
Grugel, J. xvi
Gunter, H.M. 3–18, 21–35, 66, 106, 111,
   129, 173–85
Györgyi, Z. 148

Hagopian, J. xviii
Halász, G. 142, 145–50, 154–5
Hall, D. xvi, 3–18, 21–35, 106, 173–85
Hammersley, M. 139
Hangartner, J. 14
Harvey, D. 27, 30
Hatcher, R. 21
Henry, M. 90, 179
Herbst, M. 131
Herr, K. xv-vi
Honneth, A. 84
Hood, C. 3, 5–6, 8–10, 26, 52, 89, 96, 110,
   111, 129, 136, 138, 141, 174, 176–7
Horváth, M.T. 142
Hoyle, E. 45
Hudson, C. 71
Hungary see accountability,
   centralisation, decentralisation,
   management, managerialism,
   managers, managing, neoliberalism,
   New Public Management, Post-
   Communist administrative tradition,
   privatization, school autonomy,
   standardisation
Husbands, C. 21, 90

Imre, A. 141–55
Italy see accountability, centralisation,
   decentralisation, management,
   managerialism, managers, managing,
   Napoleonic administrative tradition,
   neoliberalism, New Public
   Management, privatization, school
   autonomy, standardisation

Jakku-Sihvonen, R. 45
Janík, T. 135
Jarl, M. 72
Jessop, B. 4, 10–11, 17, 51, 112, 115
Johnson, S. xv
Jones, K. 184
Jones, R. 4, 92, 165, 178

Kalantzis, M. 64
Karseth, B. 65
Karvi 49
Kauko, J. 47
Keil, T.J. 166
Kemp, P. 40
Kickert, W. 97, 113
Kiilakoski, T. 46
Kirp, D. xviii
Klitgaard, M.B. 177
Knubb-Manninen, G. 42, 49
Kohoutek, I. 127–40
Kooiman, J. 9, 11
Kotásek, J. 127

Landri, P. 96–110
Lane, J.E. 9
Lange, B. 78, 179,
Lawn, M. 17, 104, 148, 179–81
LeGrand, J. 24
Lemke, T. 4, 17
Levacic, R. 29
Linder, S.H. 123
Linz, J.J. 167
Lipman, P. xvii
Lubienski, C. xviii
Lundahl, L. 41, 66–80
Lundqvist, J.L. 67
Lundström, U. 72
Lunt, I. 106
Lyytinen, H. 49

Maguire, M. 180
Magyar Köztársaság 151
Mahony, P. 90
Malm, K. 46
Management: in Catalonia 112, 114,
   118–20, 122–4; in Czech Republic
   128–9, 134, 138; in England 23–5, 28,
   31; in Finland 40, 44, 51; in France
   84–7, 90, 93–5; in Hungary 142–3,
   153–4; in Italy 96, 98–102, 107, 109;
   as New Public Management feature
   6–8, 12–13, 175–6; in Norway 54,
   57–8, 64–5; in Romania 157–8, 168–9;
   site-based 12–13, 101–2, 109, 175; in
   Sweden 68–9, 75

210 Index

Managerialism: in Catalonia 112, 119–20, 124; in Czech Republic 128, 139; in England 23–5, 28–9, 31, 34; in Finland 40, 43; in France 84; in Hungary 143, 153; in Italy 98–100, 106; as New Public Management feature 6–8, 13, 175; in Norway 54, 62–3; in Romania 157, 164, 168; in Sweden 69, 71

Managers: in Catalonia 112, 122; in Czech Republic 128, 138; in England 23, 25, 28–9, 31, 34–5; in Finland 40, 43; in France 85, 90, 93–4; in Hungary 142–3, 151; in Italy 96, 98, 106, 119; as New Public Management feature 3, 5–7, 9, 12–3, 174–5, 179–80; in Norway 54–5; in Romania 157–9, 164, 168; in Sweden 68–9, 72, 76

Managing: in Catalonia 112; in Czech Republic 128, 136; in England 23, 25, 28, 31; in Finland 40, 43; in France 84; in Hungary 142–3, 150, 153; in Italy 96, 98, 102, 109; as New Public Management feature 3, 6–7, 12–3, 174–6; in Norway 54–8, 62–5; in Romania 157–9; in Sweden 68–9, 72, 75–6, 78

Maragall, E. 118–20, 122–3

Mareš, J. 135

Marga, A. 167

Marketization: in Catalonia 112, 121; in Czech Republic 137, 139; in England 24–6, 33–4; in Finland, 42–4, 47; in France 84–5, 87, 89, 93; in Hungary 141–3, 145, 149–50, 154; in Italy 98, 102–3, 109; in Norway 53, 55–6; and New Public Management xv, 6–7, 9, 11, 13, 175–7; in Romania 157–8, 167, 169; in Sweden 66–7, 73, 79

Maroy, C. 111

Martens, K. 100

Mausethagen, S. 55, 63

McCormick, C. 32

McGinity, R. xvi, 22, 33

Meier, D. 63

Methodological nationalism 4, 17, 180–4

Meyer-Sahling, J.H. 16, 127

Mikáč, J. 132

Møller, J. 14, 53–65, 178

Montecinos, C. xvi, xvii

Montin, S. 67

Moos, L. 41

Muir, H. 31

Mungal, A.S. xvi

Musset, P. 137

NAE 72–74, 76

Nagy, M. 142

Nation state: centrality of 4, 17, 50–1, 173, 175, 177–80; and New Public Management 8–10; theory beyond 40, 178–80

Neave, G. 110

Neoliberalism: in Catalonia 123; in Czech Republic 139; in England 22, 24–5, 29–30, 32, 34; in Finland, 39, 43, 46, 52; in France 90; in Italy 104; in Norway 55; and New Public Management xv-vii, 3, 178; in Romania 157–8, 167; in Sweden 70–1, 79

Neumann, E. 150

New Public Management: in Catalonia 111–24, 176–7; in Czech Republic xvi, xviii,127–40, 177; in education 11–4, 174–7; in England xv-xvi, 13, 21–35, 174–7; in Finland 39–52, 174–7; in France 41, 83–95, 174–7; in general xv, xvii, 4–11, 174–7; in Hungary 138, 141–55, 174–7; in Italy 10, 96–110, 167, 174–7; in Norway 53–65, 174–7; in Romania 156–69, 174–7; in Sweden 13, 41, 43, 66–80, 174–7

Newman, J. 7, 11, 15, 109, 168

Nilsson Lindström, M. 41

Nordin, A. 178

Normand, R. 14, 76, 83–95, 178

Norway see accountability, centralisation, decentralisation, management, managerialism, managers, managing, neoliberalism, New Public Management, privatization, school autonomy, Social-Democratic administrative tradition, standardisation

Nuffield Foundation 26

Nuñez, I. xviii

OECD xv, 4, 8, 33, 39, 53–5, 72, 77–9, 88–9, 100–1, 118, 123, 127, 131, 133, 137–8, 145, 175, 178–80

OECD-PISA: influence of 12, 26, 29, 32–3, 39, 42, 48–9, 52–4, 74, 77–9, 90, 117–18, 122, 127, 131, 136–8, 148, 177–9, shock, 99, 104, 133

Ollikainen, A. 46–7

Ongaro, E. 10, 15–6, 96–7, 101–2, 113

Osborne, D. 5

Östh, J. 76

Owens, P. 30

Ozga, J. 4, 26, 76, 92, 165, 178–9

Page, E. 71
Painter, M. 15, 97
Paletta, A. 178
Pereyra, M.A. 77
Perryman, J. 26
Peters, B.G. 10, 15, 16, 52, 89, 97, 110–11, 141, 168
Peters, T. xv, 8
Pierre, J. 168, 175
PISA see OECD/PISA
Pollitt, C. 6, 9, 10, 14–6, 24, 34, 41, 89, 96, 141, 175–7
Ponce, J. xvi
Pop, L. 167
Popescu, A.C. 156–69
Power, M. 90
Power, S. 21
Prášilová, M. 132
privatization xv, xvii, 3, 5, 9, 177; in Catalonia 114, 120, 123; in Czech Republic 129; in England 30–2, 34–5; in Finland 43, 46, 51; in France 89; in Hungary 142; in Italy 99–100, 109; in Norway 55; in Romania 158, 167; in Sweden 66–7, 73–4, 76, 79–80
professionalism 7, 13, 45, 55, 64, 106, 134, 139

Rautalin, M. 178
Reay, D. 26
re-centralisation see centralisation
Regeringskansliet 79
Rhodes, R.A.W. 4
Richardson, R. 31
Ridley, F.F. 8–10
Ringarp, J. 78
Rinne, R. 48
Risse, T. 115
Rizvi, F. 22, 27, 173, 179, 184
Robertson, S.L. 17, 115, 181, 184
Romania see accountability, centralisation, decentralisation, management, managerialism, managers, managing, neoliberalism, New Public Management, Post-Communist administrative tradition, privatization, school autonomy, standardisation
Rönnberg, L. 76
Rose, N. 33, 109

Sahlberg, P. 45, 51
Saltman, K.J. 178
Sanders, D. 35
Santiago, P. 134, 137–8
Schmidt, V. 40, 45, 51

school autonomy: in Catalonia 111–16, 119–24; in Czech Republic 129–30, 132, 134–5; in England 22–3; in Finland 45, 51; in France 84, 86–9, 94; in Hungary 144–7; in Italy 96–9, 101–5; and New Public Management 12–13, 175, 177; in Norway 55, 65; in Romania 168; in Sweden 66, 68–9, 71–2, 77
Scott, J. Xviii
Seddon, T. 4, 17, 180–1
Sejersted, F. 70
Serpieri, R. 3–18, 96–110, 173–85
Shor, I. 92
Siljander, P. 41
Silvennoinen, H. 47
Simola, H. 45, 47–8, 88
Simons, M. 177
Sinka, E. 149
Skedsmo, G. 14, 53–65, 178
Spilková, V. 136
Spring, J. 178, 184
standardisation: in Catalonia 112, 121; in Czech Republic 128–30, 133, 139; in England 22–3, 25, 28, 30–1; in Finland 47–8; in France 85, 92; in Hungary 149; in Italy 98–9, 104–5, 110; and New Public Management 6, 13, 174, 180; in Norway 64–5; in Romania 160, 169; in Sweden 70, 73, 76
Starr, P. 67
Štech, S. 127–40
Straková, J. 134–5
Švecová, J. 130
Sweden see accountability, centralisation, decentralisation, management, managerialism, managers, managing, neoliberalism, New Public Management, privatization, school autonomy, Social-Democratic administrative tradition, standardisation
Sztompka, P. 139

Taylor, S. 179
Telhaug, A.O. 70
Thélot, C. 90
Thomson, P. 14
Tomlinson, S. 93

Uljens, M. 39–52

Van Zanten, A. 87
Varjo, J. 41, 47–8

212 Index

Verger, A. 111–24, 178
Verheijen, T. 113
Veselý, A. xvi, 127–40
Vidal, F. 114, 118
Viteritti, A. 102
Vojtěch, J. 131

Walford, G. 93
Wallace, M. 45,
Wallerstein, I. 40
Weggemans, H. 11
Weiner, L. xviii

welfarism 15, 27, 32, 39, 52, 55, 96, 103–4, 110
Weyland, K. 115
Whitty, G. 21, 24, 106–7
Wiborg, S. 111
Windzio, M. 177
Wolf, L.A. 39–52
Woods, C. 22, 26, 33
Woods, P. 29
Wright, A. 21

Yeatman, A. 107